# The Red Highway

## By
## Nicolas Rothwell

EasyRead Large

# Copyright Page from the Original Book

Published by Black Inc.,
an imprint of Schwartz Media Pty Ltd
37–39 Langridge Street
Collingwood VIC 3066 Australia
email: enquiries@blackincbooks.com
http://www.blackincbooks.com

The National Library of Australia Cataloguing-in-Publication entry:

Rothwell, Nicolas.

The red highway / Nicolas Rothwell.

2nd ed.

ISBN: 9781863954938 (pbk.)

Rothwell, Nicholas--Travel--Australia, Northern.
Rothwell, Nicholas--Travel--Australia, Central.
Australia, Northern--Description and travel.

919.429

Internal photos: Peter Eve <www.monsoonaustralia.com>
Book design: Thomas Deverall
Printed in Australia by Griffin Press

# TABLE OF CONTENTS

# Praise for The Red Highway

"Few writers can capture the inland as lucidly as Rothwell or with his depth of understanding."—*The Australian*

"Beautiful writing."—*Sydney Morning Herald*

"Rothwell's musings are intelligent, lyrical and melancholic."
—*Overland*

"Rothwell is a caster of spells."—*Australian Book Review*

"[A] marvelous book."—*The Advertiser*

"Masterful."—*Australian Literary Review*

"Nicolas Rothwell makes us see the world anew."
—PICO IYER

Shortlisted for the 2009 *Age* Non-Fiction Book of the Year

# FOR AA

*omnia tu nostrae tempora laetitiae*

# Exile

———

# I

In late June 1956, towards midday, after a swift flight through dry-season skies, the Czech artist Karel Kupka clambered from a prop-plane at Milingimbi airstrip and stepped for the first time into the elusive world of Arnhem Land.

This arrival, which would have life-changing consequences for Kupka, and open a new chapter in Western appreciation of Aboriginal cultures, had been long dreamed of and long planned. Kupka, by then, had already lived in self-imposed exile from his own country for more than a decade. He had made himself into a virtual Frenchman, a Parisian, an aesthetic scholar. He was in pursuit of knowledge, but knowledge of a subtle, momentous kind, almost beyond the reach of words, although he spent weeks on end seeking to pin down the subject of his investigations, and years later, after protracted struggles to reduce his findings to a single statement, he would die with this formula upon his lips. That morning, though, his quest was just beginning, he was full of intuitions and excitement, and the mood is evident in his writings from those days, which are alive with a restrained joy and a sense of impending fulfilment.

Kupka was born in the last year of World War I, in Prague, the capital of the new-formed Czechoslovak

Republic, into a family with strong connections among the intelligentsia. The cubist painter Frantisek Kupka, well known in Central Europe, was a relation of his; his cousin Jiri became a prominent writer during communist times. During his schooldays, Kupka was dispatched by his art-loving father on brief study trips to Paris, where he began painting in his turn and felt the first stirrings of a lifelong interest in prehistoric man. With this background, his pronounced gift for languages and his liberal education, Kupka's path ahead in life seemed smooth, and he was already well into his studies at Charles University when, abruptly, a shadow many of his fellow countrymen had long dreaded fell. The German army invaded and annexed Czechoslovakia; the occupiers shut down the university; there were protests; Kupka took part; they were harshly suppressed. His father was able to find him a mid-level post at Rolnicka, an agricultural insurance firm, where he survived the wartime years, painting, from time to time, small, sentimental landscapes of peasant huts.

It was only late in 1945, well after the liberation of Prague, that Kupka was able to devise a strategy of return to a country that had grown sweeter in his mind with each new year of absence. He enlisted in an Army unit bound for Le Havre, transferred to a post in the Czechoslovak embassy in Paris and started to live a straitened life. He began a doctorate, rather fittingly on aspects of the law of international transport; but most of his time was spent at the Ecole des

Beaux-Arts, where he worked in the studio of the muralist Jean Souverbie.

When Kupka turned to those days, in conversations with visitors in years to come, he passed over the politics of the time, and the communist takeover in Prague, which confirmed him in his choice of adopted home. Instead, he would remember his creative exploits: the watercolours he dashed off in the Place du Tertre for passers-by; the elaborate paintings he exhibited in the yearly salons for young artists; his translation of Fernande Olivier's memoir of her time with Picasso. Some of his early Paris sketches survive: they are executed in pastel, with a tell-tale preference for deep hues of mauve or indigo, and a tendency towards a fragmentation of the visual field, for he had already come under the influence of the Left Bank avant-garde. Among the artists he most admired was André Breton, the master-thinker of the surrealists, and a man keenly receptive to the appeal of tribal art. Often, Kupka would make visits to Breton's studio on the Rue Fontaine, where works from Africa and Oceania were hung alongside paintings from the surrealist circle, and it was under Breton's tutelage that he began haunting the more obscure galleries and museums of Paris, above all the labyrinthine and silent Musée de l'Homme, at that time the centre of French anthropology. Impelled, doubtless, by ideas from these interlocking artistic and academic realms, in the midwinter of 1951 Kupka left the tiny garret he had just bought on the Rue Saint-Sulpice and set off on a journey whose true purpose remains, even now, a touch obscure, although the large-scale collection of artworks was never far from the forefront of his mind.

At Marseille he boarded a flying boat of Trans Oceanic Airways bound for Australia, a continent he had provisionally identified as the best place to find "evidence furnished directly by people whose living conditions and way of life most closely approach those of the first man." But international air travel, in those days, was a slow, haphazard affair: the *Star of Australia* put down for a brief technical stop in Malta. Two days later, during take-off, it crashed and promptly foundered in Valletta Harbour. The passengers and crew escaped and swam to safety. Kupka sat alone on the rocky shore: all he had left was his passport and a sheaf of low-denomination traveller's cheques – and it was hard, for a man of his strikingly imaginative cast of mind, not to feel at once that he had been spared from death for urgent tasks, and also that he had, in some sense, died and been re-born in the stricken aircraft, and that his journey to Australia spelled the beginning of a new and deeper life.

Two months passed before he was able to reach Melbourne and make a set of quick visits to the other capitals of south-east Australia. While there, he met various members of the cultural class, including the painter Carl Plate and the photographer Axel Poignant, who had been strongly affected by a recent journey into Arnhem Land. These men helped refine Kupka's views, and guided him towards the few collections of Aboriginal art then on public display.

He returned to Paris transfixed by the memory of what he had seen: painted shields, rough barks, carved stones, sculpted heads. He had sketched and documented them in detail; he was sure he would be able to "transmit his emotions" on first encountering such works to the museum curators of Western Europe – and so, indeed, it proved. His travels brought him to the city of Basel, where he formed a close connection with the director of the Museum für Völkerkunde, Professor Alfred Bühler. This was the first in a series of professional bonds with father-figures that guided Kupka in his most productive years: the relationship between the two men, which is traced in the museum's records, was one of serene, unbroken trust. It was founded on a broad conception of European culture as their shared patrimony, and on elaborate ideas about creativity and the evolution of art. At that time the Basel Museum possessed only a handful of north-Australian bark paintings, which had been picked up in the field decades before by an intrepid entomologist. Bühler commissioned Kupka to make a journey to Arnhem Land and create there, in concert with the artists of the country, a collection that would catch the spirit of that world.

Such was the mission that had brought Kupka to Milingimbi Island, a place that seems always to hover between the sea and sky. It lies just off the mainland, north-west of the Glyde River mouth; its attendant reefs and sandbars slip away into the Arafura Sea. For centuries it has been a realm of meetings and exchange. Macassan trepang fishers made camp on its shores; Aboriginal clans from all along the coastline gathered there for negotiations; and in the 1920s the Methodist Overseas Mission placed its first regional outpost on the island's eastern edge, close by an established Macassan well – and it was the mission's staff who met Kupka that morning at the airstrip and drove him through the stringy-bark forests, past the swamps and salt-flats, to their little community of mud-brick homes. Nearby, along the shore, beneath tall tamarind trees, the native people kept their camps, segregated by family and by clan affiliations. Visitors of any kind were infrequent then at such remote mission posts; no one had ever seen or heard of an art collector.

Kupka set to work. Within a few weeks he had forged close understandings with two Aboriginal men of high authority, both clan leaders, Djawa and Dawidi. These two became the central artists in his collections, all through his life he referred to them as his brothers – and their association survives in ghostly form today, for on trips out to Milingimbi Island I have often heard young children on the beachfront singing, in the most elegant of Parisian accents, stray snatches of French folk songs or nursery rhymes, imparted to their grandparents decades before by Kupka as part of some elaborate musical exchange.

Djawa, whom Kupka liked to describe as the "chief" or "headman" of Milingimbi, held court beside the boys' nursery, under the giant tamarind: the spot is named Rulku, after the gall bladder of the barramundi, which serves as the totem for the area. Even by the austere standards of the Yolngu tribes of north-east Arnhem Land, Djawa was a grave, impressive figure, much given to explaining the fine points of clan politics, and strongly involved in the domain of the secret-sacred – a realm that seemed ever-present on Milingimbi in those days, so routinely were ceremonies performed beyond the mission compound: initiations and funerals, and rituals for the morning star.

Kupka also spent much time at the next-door camp with Dawidi, who was younger and painted in a style rich with signs and symbols, almost a "painted literature," ideally suited for decoding by the Western eye. These men filled his thoughts: he studied them, he watched them performing their mortuary dances, he took down their every word in his notebooks, and so much of them sank into him that they often seem strangely present in his ramifying, understated prose. There is a lovely, well-known photograph by Kupka, which hints at the bond between him and his subjects: he called it *The Artists' Workshop.* The painters are all sitting cross-legged, bent over, drawing fine lines with tiny brushes on the surfaces of their barks. To one side of the group, a young boy looks up, smiling at the camera; on the other, an old man, his head resting on his hand, his face reflective, gazes up. Sunlight bleaches the background: the blurred leaves at the top of the image look oddly like encroaching, all-consuming tongues of fire.

For much of that dry season, Kupka carried out his interviews at Milingimbi, questioning, collecting, tuning his mind to the thoughts of his informants – and he even made an early stab at capturing those experiences in English, in a brief, emotive piece "by Karel Kupka of Paris," which was printed in a missionary magazine: "I shall always remember vividly my stay at Milingimbi, which was not only the most interesting but also the happiest time I had spent for years." He allows his thoughts to roam across the various challenges before the missions, and the role of ritual, and Christian religion, in Arnhem Land, he even touches on the artistic upsurge underway, before he finds himself retelling the mythological stories he had encountered: creation sagas, apocalyptic, full of deaths and re-animations, the flow of living matter between worlds.

Soon Kupka began making wider forays, crisscrossing the far north, calling in at other missions; he travelled as far afield as Yirrkala, Port Keats and the Tiwi Islands, perfecting his distinctly romantic response to the Australian landscape as he went: "The continent itself belongs to the earth's past. It is a land of strange beauty, so unlike other continents that the visitor sometimes wonders if he has not landed on another planet." Every feature was ambiguous, and Kupka takes a quiet delight in the country's failure to conform with European patterns: "Immense expanses generally end in a perfectly straight horizon. There are few mountains, and those that do exist are usually isolated. The ground is often rocky; the shallow rivers, when not dry, irrigate an apparently sparse vegetation." The animals, too, were anachronistic; they were survivors, for the most part devoid of threatening force, and sometimes engaged in irrational alliances with man. The snakes, for instance, though represented by 150 species, from the most harmless to the deadliest, were "passably discreet," and it even seemed to him that "they had a tacit agreement with their human neighbours, for they tactfully avoid each other."

After the first few of these side trips, a key turned in Kupka's heart. He had pictured himself as an outsider, carrying out profound investigations – investigations which, as he rather tactlessly informed the missionaries, he would not be able to couch in terms simple enough to explain to them. He aspired, initially, to a kind of severe truthfulness; he mistrusted the subjective eye, he was a foe of individual judgment. "The appreciations of an observer would be superfluous, if not actually undesirable," he wrote, in a stern note of reminder to himself. But once he had become more familiar with the far reaches of the Northern Territory, his thoughts about the travels he was making began to shift.

"I refuse to call my journeys 'exploration.' There is a peculiar attraction in the Australian bush, the outback, in spite of its bareness – which in any case is amply offset by the friendliness of its inhabitants, whatever their origins." No longer was he the solitary man of science. "I was warmly received and greatly helped, not only by the Aborigines but also by the white settlers, missionaries and government officials, who took an interest in a lone traveller virtually without baggage." Without the support of the welfare branch of the Territory administration and the backing of the different religious missions, as he well knew, his expeditions would have come to nothing. In a brief note glancing back on his experiences – he published it only years later – Kupka expresses all he longed to find, and all he had been afraid of, in Arnhem Land: "Any fears I may have had of being considered as an intruder were soon forgotten: I was indeed looked on as a friend."

By now his idea of his task was gaining greater definition. He had travelled sufficiently to realise that the north was home to many styles of art. He knew he was the only Western artist, fully alive to the trends and experiments of the modern avant-garde, who had even seen these works. He had just paid his first trip to Croker Island, a slender spine of swamp and stringy-bark that juts out northwards from the Cobourg Peninsula: it holds a number of the region's most potent sacred sites. At Croker's Methodist Mission, Kupka met two artists from the mainland,

Paddy Compass Namatbara and Jimmy Midjawu-Midjawu, who painted sorcery figures: writhing entities with twining hands and deformed bodies, alive with fearful energy. Often the creatures they depicted were Maam spirits, members of a spectral Dreamtime race, dead beings which could become dangerous if not properly appeased – for Namatbara and Midjawu-Midjawu were *marrkitj,* or witchdoctors, and were constantly engaged in acts of healing magic. Their art embodied this hidden field of knowledge, and Kupka was at once drawn to it and troubled by its intensity. He knew that of all the works he had collected, these figures, which teetered on the brink of the grotesque and seemed to inhabit the realm of gargoyles, or creatures from a hallucinogenic dream, would prove the most beautiful to European eyes.

At this point in Kupka's progress, near the end of his first, triumphant collecting season, it seems a simple thing to imagine the thoughts, and plans, and hopes that enticed him on, that led him to believe there was a role for him in northern Australia and in the continued pursuit and explanation of works he saw as mirrors, reflecting from the dawn of time. He told himself that he was searching for the origins of art, its motive forces, the nature of the need that it was striving to fulfil. Such was his overarching idea, but it was also a compulsion: what was original, and pure, and untainted by the mark of Western culture could have redemptive force – could allow him to gaze beyond the veils of the world he knew. For Kupka was in the field at a time when Europe's place as the emblem of beauty was newly overthrown: the continent was shattered, its cities had been bombed and broken; his own homeland was ruled by a collective of bleak dictators. What could be more natural than to turn from this spectacle and put one's trust in an art free from the chains of history and besetting influences: an art that blew straight from the realm of myth to the viewing eye? There was an element in Kupka's personality that welcomed this ill-concealed revolt against his tradition: in place of his own fine pastels and insipid sketches, he would give prominence to works of primal splendour; he would uncover them, and understand them, and – since he was one of those for whom self-effacement is a form of transcendence – he would ensure his own part in their revelation was soon eclipsed. Even as these thoughts unfurled inside him, though, he was also in the grip of an urge that gained a stronger hold on him with every day: it was the collector's disease, that unsleeping impulse to acquire, to classify, to create a microcosm where order and pattern can be shored up against the world. In his trips through Arnhem Land, this was the instinct that came to dominate, and to goad him into spells of frenzied commissioning and buying, as if he expected every day of painting at the missions to be the last. Here was the core of Kupka's attraction to the Aboriginal domain of north Australia, even if he could not yet confess this to himself: like many of his contemporaries, he suspected that it was passing, that it was vanishing before his eyes, and that he was the last man who would see it as it truly was.

All these conflicting beliefs and attitudes can be traced in Kupka's correspondence, and in his memoirs of his first collecting days, which are brief, and vivid, and which paint, for those who seek to follow in his steps, a picture of the artist in the golden moments of his prime – until he seems almost present before the living eye once more, poised, beside some red-dirt airstrip, waiting: tall, and thin, and somewhat out of place.

\*\*\*

As soon as the dry-season months were done and build-up clouds were forming in the sky, Kupka went back to Darwin, where he had a promise to keep. At that time the post-war reconstruction of the city was underway; plans were being drawn up for a new Catholic cathedral to replace the original church, which had been damaged beyond repair in the first Japanese attacks. The resultant building, St Mary's Star of the Sea, stands today on the corner of Smith and Maclachlan streets. Its walls are made from white porcellanite stone, cut from the cliffs of Darwin Harbour; its clean lines and parabolic concrete arches lend it the look of a crouching animal. The architect intended his creation to be neo-gothic, though to many eyes it seems like a species of tropical romanesque, with a distinct air of the military bunker about it, and some members of the local congregation needed years to come to terms with the harshness of its design. Many aspects of the new St Mary's are unusual: it is a war memorial as well as a place of worship; its foundation stone is crystalline metamorphosed rock from the Rum Jungle uranium mine; beneath its floors are little cache burials: blades, spears, muskets, and other emblems of conflict from colonial times. While he was on the Tiwi Islands, Kupka had met Bishop John Patrick O'Loughlin, a man of progressive leanings. The two fell into conversation one night, and the bishop, on learning that Kupka was not only a Catholic, but an artist, made him an unusual proposition. Would he be prepared to paint an Aboriginal Madonna for the new cathedral? This dream had been with Bishop O'Loughlin for many years, ever since his time at the Yule Island mission in Papua, where he had seen how the natives were being encouraged to employ their tribal patterns for ecclesiastical designs. Together with the administrator of the Star of the Sea, Father Frank Flynn, the bishop showed Kupka the cathedral plans and explained what they were hoping for: something, they said, along the lines of the Japanese and Chinese Madonnas that had proved so popular in other missionary outposts of the church.

Kupka accepted at once, and old-timers in Darwin remember his elation in those days, when he was newly back from the bush and full of stories of adventures, and when his grand ideas were taking shape.

He set up a makeshift studio in one of the school-rooms of St Mary's Convent, surrounded himself with his haul of carvings and bark paintings, and plunged himself into the task. For months, he had seen beauty and painted nothing; he had been steeped in a world of worship and magic; his own faith had been subtly remade. Each day, after he had made a beginning, the bishop and Father Flynn would visit the studio and check on his progress; they were particularly touched by the solution the artist had found for the problem of the Madonna's pose. Instead of cradling the Christ-child in her lap, the Madonna is carrying her son on her shoulders, in the fashion of Aboriginal women from the Tiwi Islands and the Daly River, with one of her hands clasping the baby by the ankle, and the other resting gently on his hip. They were also intrigued by the features of the virgin: she had a noticeable air of self-possession about her. They had asked Kupka to present an idealised version of Aboriginal womanhood, blending aspects from different models at the various Catholic missions he had visited. The Madonna's face, though, was clearly delineated, and her character seemed precisely caught as well, much like the Madonnas of certain Renaissance artists, who have the look of a living individual – and there has been speculation about her story in church circles ever since: some think Kupka based her features on a Tiwi woman; others say she has the manner and the bearing of a young mother from Port Keats.

Father Flynn, who prided himself on his sensibility, would often sit with Kupka in the studio, discussing trends in art, and in his memoir, *Northern Gateway,* he gives an account of one of their talks: "For weeks while painting the picture, Kupka was at a loss to find a suitable background for his finished figures. He experimented with a variety of tropical landscapes featuring ghost gums, pandanus palms – but he was not satisfied with any of these. He told me of this difficulty one day when I was in the studio with him after lunch. Around the walls he had hundreds of examples of native art displayed, which he was classifying during the moments when he rested from painting. I cast my eye around these and with a sweep of my hand I said: 'Karel, you have the material for your background right here.'" As Flynn explained it, a combination of clan designs from all across the north would enable the Madonna to represent both the Christian dedication of the native peoples and their "new cultural aspirations as well."

Kupka absorbed this advice, which he had surely expected Flynn to give, and painted in a detailed background of totemic emblems. They shimmered, and lent the painting the gleam of an Eastern icon – and when it was unveiled in the new cathedral, long after Kupka's return to Europe, the work was much admired, and even venerated, for several years. Its prominence, though, has passed. Other Aboriginal artworks are more celebrated today, the missionary focus of the church has dissipated, and a decade ago the Madonna was stolen from the cathedral, by an Aboriginal man, as it happens, who tried to ransom her back to the Darwin diocese; she was returned, a little bruised and damaged, and now she hangs, out of harm's way, high on the east transept wall, where it is hard to see her eyes, or catch the expression on her face.

*** 

Kupka travelled on to Sydney, where he endured a brief celebrity, giving interviews and writing newspaper articles about his explorations. A photographer for the *Daily Telegraph* took his picture during this stay: it is a strictly composed image, almost heraldic in its tone: Kupka is encased in a thick, stiff herringbone tweed jacket; his face is drawn, his eyes are hooded, they look aside, and down, at an incised spearthrower which he is clasping in his hands: it forms a sharp diagonal. Behind him hang rough barks from Beswick and Groote Eylandt, and geometric-patterned  boards from Port Keats. Dominating the scene is a large painting by Midjawu-Midjawu, which shows the thunder spirit, encircled by lightning bolts and grasping a crocodile in one hand. The surface of the bark is oddly accented by faint dabs of mauvish colour; the neck of the spirit-being has been cut off by the photo-frame. Two exhibitions presenting some of the works Kupka had collected on his journeys were organised: at the first, held in the East Sydney Technical College, the opening speech was given by A.P. Elkin, the long-standing professor of anthropology at Sydney University, a former priest and a committed admirer of Darwin's ideas on human origins. Elkin had already written *Aboriginal Men of High Degree,* the slender set of lectures that preserves his name today: it is matchless in its sympathetic account of Aboriginal witchdoctors and magic men, their acts, their beliefs and their moments of access to the supernatural domain.

Pattern, ritual beauty and the quest for hidden insights made a strong appeal to Elkin. A connection was born between Kupka and the professor, who was then already sixty-five years old, and who would serve, for the remaining two decades of his life, as the younger man's protector and confidant, as a consoling presence, an intimate and faithful correspondent – and it is chiefly thanks to this enduring tie that Kupka's advance into the shadows can be tracked at all. That night, Elkin spoke with enthusiasm about Kupka's European imagination and the works he had brought back with him from distant Arnhem Land: how pure they were, in line, and form, and colour: expressions of myth emerging into the present day. The crowd was made up of Kings Cross bohemians, many of whom knew Kupka; but in the gallery, beneath the lights, when his turn came to speak, he seemed a pale, transfigured creature, striking through with his words to some uncharted higher realm. In fact he was spreading before them, in the most tumbled, disordered fashion, the first shards of the quest narrative that was already taking shape inside his head. *Un Art à l'Etat Brut,* which appeared in print in Lausanne only six years later, is a strange production, with its meandering arguments, its retellings of Aboriginal myth, its deployments of theory and its little scenesetting anecdotes. It advances many claims, and yet it has an inert, silent tone, it leaves one with almost nothing; its words feel like the dusty antechamber of a tomb, as if Kupka could not bring himself to disclose the things he knew, or even hint at the lures that drew him on. "The Aborigines of Australia," he declares, "live in a universe of their own, which has yet to reveal many of its secrets" – and this is the tapestry he chooses as the background for his treatise on the birth of art. Why does art exist? How can we know it? It is not merely the expression of our sense of beauty, nor is it a record of lived events. No: "One must see works of art in order to feel them" – and at once Kupka has touched the murky heart of his enterprise: speech, writing and reading are all very well, he argues, in so far as they help towards understanding – "but they cannot be enough in themselves, for it is indispensable to share the emotion of the artist creator, and this experience is too personal to be conveyed by words alone."

Best, in fact, to be an artist, to live the artist's life, to dwell in primal splendour in the depths of Arnhem Land, the world he chronicles in the most dispassionate, objective style over the next nine richly illustrated chapters, before disclosing to his readers that this path to the stars is gone: for even if "today is the golden age for Aboriginal plastic arts," they will not endure much longer, their disappearance is inexorably drawing near. The bark paintings may gain the attention of outsiders, they may even become known around the world; but ahead on this path danger lies, and Kupka is himself the agent of this threat. He is the despoiler coming into the garden: whatever he touches will fade and rot, for in his hands he holds the curses of reward and fame. Kupka drives his words on, he plays to the hilt his own appointed role in this story; he sketches the chain of events that his first arrival in Arnhem Land set inexorably in train. For the prosperity that will follow in his wake is bound to be ephemeral, and, as he writes in his closing pages, "it implies the decline of the art, which, before dying, will become empty decoration, its profound meaning, the basic reason for its existence having disappeared as a result of changes in its creators' life."

Freighted down with such dark conclusions, and guarded by its spare, resistant prose, *Un Art à l'Etat Brut* received only brief attention before it fell into obscurity, as did a later English version, *Dawn of Art,* which Kupka himself translated during a research trip back to north Australia in the following year. The book would have been wholly forgotten were it not for its blazing preface, "Main Première," written for Kupka by André Breton after long talks between the two men.

The composition of this text can be precisely dated: it was sketched out in Breton's studio during the days of the Cuban missile crisis, when the master of surrealism was in renunciatory mood. Breton had never quite shaken off the sense of dread that filled him upon the nuclear bombing of Hiroshima in August 1945; once again, he felt that he was standing on the edge of an abyss, and that "ours is a world in dissolution, shaken by the horror of the passage from one moment to the next." Indeed he was somewhat puzzled that Kupka had actually returned to Paris from Australia. "How is it," he inquired, presciently, "that he has not settled there permanently?" For Australia had a poetic magnetism all its own. Breton's conceptions of the country were a trifle vague: "For ages, children's curiosity has feasted on the unique nature of the land's fauna – marsupials and monotremes – which seems expressly created to strengthen the idea or the illusion of a lost world." But this did not stop him from admiring the barks, or developing a thought about the patterns underlying them in nature – a vertiginous thought, that even today sets the mind free to roam. "Their textures," wrote Breton, "from the tightest to the most supple, correspond so perfectly to the restrained yet very rich range of colours that the immediate pleasure they afford is liable to be confused with that given by shells from that part of the world – cones, volutes, an infinity of shapes. It is as if these paintings borrow the entire panoply of the shells: even the underlying glow of mother-of-pearl is not lacking."

Before returning to Darwin and the north, Kupka, in gratitude, gave Breton one of the most sombre works in his collection, a large bark by Paddy Compass Namatbara, depicting two Maam figures – and for several decades those two spirit beings hung in their contorted splendour, like lonely emissaries at a foreign court, alongside Hopi masks and masterworks of high modernism, on the walls of Breton's studio in the Rue Fontaine.

# II

Midway through the build-up season of 2005, after a year spent in the war zones of the Middle East, I came back to Darwin and set about exploring the city, on the assumption that I would quickly be able to re-acquaint myself with my old surrounds. Each morning, in those first days of my homecoming, I would head off on long walks down the winding pathways of the Esplanade, towards the harbour, the wharves and trawler berths, always varying my route slightly and feeling brief stabs of pain every time I came across some new building or construction site that broke the pattern of my memories – something which happened often, for Darwin in those months was in the grip of a speculative development frenzy without any parallel even in its history of constant annihilations and re-

births. Elevated tropical houses and their untidy, lux-
uriant gardens were being bulldozed on all sides, and
tall, angular structures, with metallic facings and
pastel highlights, rose further skywards in their place
each day, until the old town centre, with cranes and
steel skeletons of half-finished buildings reaching
high above its jumble, resembled, in the dawn's hazy
light, nothing so much as a vast offshore oil platform,
its drilling rigs and superstructure suspended far above
a murky, unmoving ocean.

In the daytime, I found myself staring for hours
on end at this unfamiliar scene, stupefied by the scale
of the transformations taking place. But when evening
came, and the humidity began to fall, it was time for
more extended forays, and I would drive out, windows
wound down so the noises and the smells of the
streets could wash over me. Sometimes these excursions lasted for hours, or all through the night, and
I ended up, hardly knowing how I had got to my
destination, at distant outposts like Gunn Point or
Fogg Dam. More often, though, it was the less glamorous parts of town, which were still largely unchanged, that attracted me: the wide, palm-lined avenues past Casuarina, running beyond the hospital,
or the mazy and ill-kept streets of Moulden, beside
the lagoons and winding swamplands of East Arm. On
trips like these, I was struck repeatedly by the incon-
spicuous signs that pointed out buildings and remains
of significance from World War II, when large numbers
of American and Australian troops were stationed in

the north, and Darwin, almost emptied of its civilian population, served as the front-line base for the Pacific campaign. Many of these structures had already decayed almost to nothing: rough access tracks led out to scrub blocks with no more than a scatter of grey concrete pads breaking the line of the bush. Others, though, had been restored with punctilious attention to detail, and garlanded with elaborate information boards, in an attempt to make them come alive – but the effect was quite different: the sense of time's passage had been stripped from them, they felt like stage sets or counterfeits. More distressing still were the sites that had been wholly reclaimed by the harbour's mangroves, or those that had been built over and were now lying, like ancient archaeological deposits, beneath access roads and recreational fishing ramps. I would come away from explorations to such vanished spots all the more convinced that the North offers us no permanence, nothing to hold on to, that our presence in these parts is only a flicker, a quick disruption within a grander, circling flow of growth and fall.

And it must have been an intuition of this kind, as much as the spectacle of Darwin's heart being razed to rubble and rebuilt again at lightning speed before my eyes, that prompted me one afternoon some days after my return to make a trip out to the military museum, a low-slung building which I had never before visited, despite its prominent position at the very tip of East Point reserve. This peninsula forms the furthest extension of the claw-like outcrop upon which Darwin is somewhat precariously poised, and a tranquil spirit seems to mantle it. The wildlife there is docile and rare creatures abound: fruit doves, rainbow pittas, even stone curlews, those birds of grace, almost always to be seen in solemn poses, immobile, sheltered by the deep shade of mahogany trees. At the centre of the reserve stand the sheds and lean-tos of a riding club: its stable-blocks are full of retired thorough breds, their bodies broken down and pulverised by the rigours of racing on the northern circuit's dusty tracks. Opposite, in the bushland, roam bands of agile wallabies, trusting animals, whose simplicity is sometimes ill-repaid, for every once in a while the butchered carcass of one of their number is found at some old campfire by the park rangers, newspaper headlines condemn the murder, and the Aboriginal long-grassers who drift through the reserve shoulder the blame.

East Point is a place of constant comings and goings, yet I have often been struck by the brevity of the visits the locals make, as if there were some aspect of the reserve that acts to drive them away – and it may be that they are responding to a certain mood from the past that lingers there, a tone of agitation and unrest: for in the days of the Japanese attacks on Darwin, the Point served as the defensive front-line, it was "Port War," its roads were lined with military camps, gun turrets and strong-points stretched along its coastal cliffs, and a boom net to

keep out enemy submarines reached almost six kilometres across the harbour from its furthest-jutting
spit of land.

That afternoon, as I drove out to the museum past
the ruined wartime observation posts, I was alone:
there were no cars moving; no figures headed down
the walking paths. The tide was at its peak; the
fringing mangroves were half-submerged; they edged
off into the waves and gave the impression that the
whole wide floor of the harbour channel was covered
by their thick, leafy carpet and no more than a minor
seismic shift would be needed to expose a soft, green
landscape to human view. This hint of concealed vistas
was only intensified by the shimmer of the heat haze,
and the movement of the cloud formations. Thin,
mist-like streamers were hanging low over the bay,
and between them, as if through the bars of a cage,
a storm front could be made out at a great distance,
almost on the horizon's line: rain veils were tumbling
from its base, only to blur and evaporate before they
struck the ground, while far above, the summit of the
cloud's dark anvil seethed and slowly mounted higher,
hiding the sun, casting a deep, dramatic shadow
across the Point and its surrounding waters.

That sombre sky seemed to be prolonged inside
the museum itself, which was so faintly illuminated
that I needed several minutes to get my bearings. Its
rooms were small and tightly filled with glass cases
devoted to an eclectic range of topics: swords and
their manufacture, the general history of mechanised

warfare, the Australian government's gun buy-back scheme. Only gradually, as I walked back and forth between these little exhibitions, trying to find their thread, did it became clear to me that there was nothing to bind them together: the museum was a dispersed affair, a thing of spaces and gaps, of relations between various components of testimony and evidence. Indeed its chief displays were well concealed in a handful of dispersed bunkers and outhouses, connected by intersecting walkways, and beyond these lay a parkland, almost a belt of rainforest, where a selection of guns, tanks, trucks and fragments of wrecked aircraft had been carefully laid out. After some minutes walking amidst these relics, I found my way into a low-roofed shed of corrugated iron, where a soundtrack, distorted by some malfunction in the speaker system, was playing, but the words being spoken were so faint as to be beyond decipherment: all that could be made out was a distant whisper, much like a soft wind, rising and falling in a constant rhythm.

Upon one wall a selection of laminated photographs had been hung: they depicted scenes from the bombing of Darwin on 19 February 1942: shattered buildings, ships ablaze in the harbour, the twisted wreckage of Stokes Hill wharf, its rails and spars shaped into sinuous patterns by the glinting light. Alongside these photographs, a few printed panels, mottled and discoloured by prolonged exposure to the humid air, gave a brief account of the city's wartime experiences. This narrative, devoid of sentiment and jumping abruptly between points of view, caught, in its staccato style, all the shocking speed of the initial Japanese attack and the scale of the devastation unleashed.

It was still early morning, it began, when the seventeen heavy bombers in the first wave descended upon their target. Below them, the gunners at the main defensive battery in the heart of the city came rushing, some half-clothed, some naked, from their quarters, and took aim, staring into the dazzle of the sky. From above, though, for the pilots, the view was clear: the town was neatly ringed and marked by flashes as their bombers drew slowly nearer, quite untouched by the anti-aircraft fire. Only at the last moment did the defenders, down at ground level, hear a rising, whistling noise, much like the sound effects on a wartime newsreel – and then a dreadful blast, as the first bombs detonated among buildings along the foreshore. Wreckage was thrown in all directions, walls tumbled in: dust and smoke began to rise into the windless air.

In the other panels of this informal narration, arranged seemingly without regard for chronological sequence, so that to read them was to become disoriented in one's turn, the consequences of the raid, which lasted for a mere fifty minutes, were described: the losses of Australian and American aircraft, the destruction of the RAAF station, the casualties, the reduction of the low stone buildings along the waterfront to piles of rubble. Beside the wharf, a passenger ship, the *Neptuna,* which was laden with explosives and depth charges, had been hit and set on fire; flames were also rising from the fuel oil that had spilled out from the hulls of damaged vessels and spread across the surface of the harbour. Men trapped at the end of the burning pier tried to save themselves by diving into the water below, but many of them were killed instantly by the heat of the blazing oil. Not long after the departure of the last Japanese bomber, just as the sound of its engine was fading from the air, the *Neptuna* blew up with an explosion that shook every house in town. The debris was hurled so high that several minutes later chunks of white-hot metal from the ship were still falling to earth. Planks and whole segments of the wooden decking descended on the foreshore and on the town; smaller fragments began raining on the ships still afloat in the outer harbour, many hundreds of yards away. One eyewitness, the correspondent Douglas Lockwood, whose life for years afterwards was dominated by his memory of that day, and his attempts to frame it in narrative, found himself particularly marked by the destruction of the *Neptuna.* He was driving along the Esplanade, attempting to gauge the extent of the damage, when he heard, or felt, the blast: he surmised at once that another wave of attacks had just begun; he stopped and ran for shelter, looking up as he did so: he saw a column of smoke and flames, dwarfing, as he says, all the other smouldering fires from burning ships and buildings that were throwing their shadows across the town, and though he endeavours, all through his reconstruction of the raid, to tell his story through the words and memories of others, his resolve, at this moment, breaks down, he permits himself a snatch of subjectivity: "I will never forget that on top of it all, rolling slowly over and over as though it was a dumb-bell tossed by a giant juggler, there was what I took to be, and now know to have been, *Neptuna's* main mast."

*\*\*\**

I gazed at these images for several minutes with a distanced sadness, feeling myself ever more at one with them, and marvelling at the precise, indifferent breadth of vision time's passage brings. Above all, I was transfixed by a single, blurry photograph of ships in the harbour, taken a short while before the moment of the first attack, showing the decks full of men standing, relaxed or scurrying back and forth with steady purpose, free from the faintest suspicion of what was drawing near. I, though, could see already on the glass surface of the water the fires that would engulf the wharves and slipways, and in place of the sleek warships and supply vessels, berthed or riding at anchor, a line of broken, half-submerged wrecks.

With these pictures still shimmering before my eyes, I made my way through the grounds, down pathways so overgrown they resembled green tunnels, until I came to a metal stairway which led up to one of the pair of gun turrets that formed the heart of East Point's defensive battery. From the firing platform, where a replica of the original nine-inch gun-barrel had been lovingly installed, the view looked out to sea, across green pastures. A few of the thoroughbreds from the riding club were grazing, moving with gentle steps beneath the shade of spreading trees; the cloud banks across the harbour now filled half the sky and had turned a dark grey: their smooth, curved flanks formed an odd rhyme with the weathered concrete of the gun emplacement, a structure that has taken on, with time, a distinctive, hieratic air, much like an altar dedicated to some absent deity.

Many residents of Darwin regard this turret, and its twin which stands close by, as the most striking masterworks of architecture still to be found in northern Australia, though their tale testifies more to the futility than to the effectiveness of foresight and grand plans. During the mid-1930s, in response to regional tensions and the growing military power of Japan, the Australian government decided that the time had come to fortify Darwin, and above all to protect its oil depot. Accordingly, whole barrack buildings were transported across from Thursday Island, in the Torres Strait, and set up anew on East Point. Along the cliffs, command bunkers and observation towers, ammunition magazines and trench networks were prepared, and work began on a pair of large-calibre guns, capable of covering the entirety of Darwin Harbour and its approaches with their fire. The construction, though, advanced slowly, and when the Japanese attack came, the guns were far from finished. Nor, for all their precision, would they have served any purpose had they been complete. They had been intended to resist naval assault and establish a marine exclusion zone – but the Japanese fleet, in February 1942, was 400 kilometres away in the Timor Sea when its fighters swooped down on the gun batteries arrayed along the Darwin shore. The two nine-inch guns, which had cost the Commonwealth, in straitened times, a quarter of a million Australian pounds, were never fired in battle. They remained in lonely splendour on the Point, until they were sold off as scrap metal in 1959, to a Japanese company, Fujita Salvage, which had come to Darwin under contract to remove the sunken ships lying on the floor of the harbour, and, as an afterthought, offered 550 pounds for the pair.

It was already late afternoon when I left the museum enclosure and walked back, past the observation towers, gazing upwards as I went at the silent movement of the clouds. Another car had pulled up alongside mine. It was a red sports coupe – not, for that climate, the most conventional of choices. "GINA B" its personalised numberplate announced – and there, standing alone on the crest of the beachfront, where the low scrub gave out, was the United Nations translator Gina Baldassari, a woman I had met from time to time in the days before my departure, and had always admired, as much for her otherworldly manner as for the brilliance with which she went about her professional tasks. I knew something of her story, which was distinctive even by the standards of Darwin, a place where everyone seems to trail the ill-concealed shadow of their personal narrative. She had been born in Sydney, into a family of Venetian migrants, who moved to the Territory while she was still a child. Very early, her talent for languages had become clear. She outdistanced all her teachers, she lectured at the university, she shone as a bright star of local promise; but she had also discovered an aptitude for interpreting, and above all for simultaneous translation – and that skill became the pathway for her abrupt escape. She left the North without regret, travelled widely, and eventually found a post as an interpreter at the European Parliament in Strasbourg, where she felt both appreciated and fulfilled – though thinking back, she confessed to me with a faint, regretful smile when she first told me the story of this passage of her life, she was quite unable to identify the features of that stilted, provincial milieu which had captivated her, or even to recall in any detail the adventures and liaisons that had consumed the years. And so time passed, without the friends of her youth in Darwin hearing a word of her or her doings, until one day she re-appeared in town, and, as often happens in such cases, her life fell smoothly back into its earlier contours. It soon seemed as if she had never left, and only if one studied her with the utmost care could one even begin to trace in her eyes a note of inward grief or pensiveness.

There she stood, gazing out, and without thinking, as soon as I caught sight of her I called her name and took a few steps in her direction. She wheeled round, a look of anguish on her face – it was the look of someone who had been interrupted in the sweetest of reveries. I began apologising: she placed me in her mind; her expression changed.

"Don't ask!" she said. I could see there were tears running down her cheeks. She wiped them away, then clutched at a thin gold chain around her neck. "Don't say anything! Don't look at me that way. Do I pry into *your* private thoughts?"

"No," I said. "How could you? I was only thinking it's been a long while since we saw each other."

"Did you just come out of that museum?"

"Where else could I have come from?"

"I hate the cult of war and death in this town these days: it's spreading everywhere."

"It is? I'd have to say I've been finding it quite hard to track down any substantial traces of the wartime past."

"Just drive down the Stuart Highway," she said. "What about all those World War II airstrips, which they used in the bombing raids up to New Guinea and the islands – have you taken a look at them recently? They've all been tidied up, and turned into heritage precincts. There's even one where they have full-scale cut-out models of the aircraft that used to land there, parked in a little row beside the information bays, so the tourists can stop and relive the experience. Whenever I go past, I speed up, to avoid seeing them. Surely you understand that reaction?" She paused. "Where have you been, anyway? Are you still living here?"

I told her the story behind my departure, and my return. Our talk wound on, without losing its allusive, slightly sparring edge, until there was a crack of thunder from the cloud front across the bay.

"Perhaps the storm's coming here," I said.

"Don't get your hopes up! You obviously haven't read the latest Weekly Tropical Climate Note."

"The what?"

"Haven't you ever come across the Climate Note? It's the Bible in Darwin: it's the key to everything. Anyone who belongs here checks it regularly. It's put out by the Regional Specialised Meteorological Centre."

I stared at her. She looked pityingly back.

"Listen," she said, after a few well-measured moments of silence, "forget the V-8 Supercars at Hidden Valley. Forget the Darwin Cup. If you're really back here, if you're here to stay, the Climate Note is the one true marker of locality – although there is the Tropical Diagnostic Statement as well, which comes out every month, but that's really only for hardcore climate obsessives, and it's just an expanded version of the Note."

"And what are they about?"

"Oh, monsoons, and other synoptic-scale events: but really they're poetry, more than any-thing else. I know whole blocks of them by heart, because of course the forecast and the pattern doesn't ever change that much." She put on a studious, formal manner and began quoting, in a soft voice: "Early to mid-December saw enhanced tropical convection progress across the area, consistent with a weak Madden-Julian oscillation event, though it failed to culminate in anything more than a weak monsoon trough, which mostly remained north of the marine continent..."

"What's the marine continent?"

"Who knows?" she said, impatiently. "That's not the point."

There was a slight pause, as if we had come through some preliminary stage of re-acquain-tance. Then, hesitantly at first, I began telling her something of my time away: how pictures of the North had been vivid in my thoughts; how I had lived through those days of absence as if I were reporting from a realm of dreams, and could see the world with the still, clear vision dreamers have.

"And now," she said, "back here, things aren't so transparent, friends seem strangers to you, the places you used to know have changed, the light in the sky seems different, your memory's too strong for where you are?"

"That kind of thing."

"The pain of return," she said, in a knowing way. "Would you like me to tell you something about what brought me back, and what keeps me here? It's not the worst of stories."

And she began describing, in a distanced fashion, and in the calmest of voices, the hinge-points of her years away. She painted word portraits of glacial precision; she filled her tale with characters, she caught their styles, and looks, and ways of speaking: a whole realm danced before me: summits, negotiations, encounters across the bridge of language – and even as I realised that she was once more interpreting, compressing, conveying the essence of a drama, she brought her tale to its crescendo. It fell in the days of tense diplomacy before the invasion of Iraq, when a group of generals from the Pentagon had just arrived in Strasbourg, and she was drafted to translate for them – and perhaps it was the case, she said, that the intense repugnance that overcame her at the merest thought of war or conflict influenced her feelings as she steered her guests through the empty corridors of the parliament.

I listened, caught by the telling of the story, and quite unable to say where it might lead.

"On those official visits," she went on, "there was always a tour of the art collection, which, at that time, was mostly made up of pieces borrowed from regional museums. I can still picture the guests in their uniforms beside me, and how hemmed in by them I felt. I led them into the formal reception gallery beside the chamber – that was a part of the building I would never normally have gone near – and at once I came face to face with a painting: a small, rough Aboriginal bark painting. It was just a set of cross-hatched diamonds – nothing more. And yet it seemed to me so...”

“Familiar?” I hazarded.

“No – I mean yes, of course, familiar, but something more. Dear. Beloved. It struck me in the heart – although, like many people who grow up in the North, I'd never taken the slightest real interest in Aboriginal things. It said to me – I'm from your country; I am part of you; and you are part of me. I was very shaken. I hadn't experienced anything like that from a work of art. I went back: I looked at the bark again and tried to make my mind a blank. And then I felt it very clearly: it was acting on me like a rhythm, like a pulse inside my head.”

The next morning, she travelled out to the ethnography museum and made inquiries with the curators there. They told her that her bark came from Milingimbi Island, and that it formed part of a large, ill-researched collection, assembled decades before by Karel Kupka, a Czech exile in northern Arnhem Land.

“Have you ever come across his trail?” she asked.

Kupka was no more than a distant name to me then: I shook my head.

"It might interest you to know about him," she said. "I've always found him a very helpful guide. In fact, I became interested in Kupka's story at once, from the first little things I picked up: what happened to him in Aboriginal Australia, the struggles he faced when he tried to take his collections back with him to Europe; and his experiences in his own country, too – but then, mid-way through his life, he seems to vanish: almost as if he dies inside – and I never came to discover the reason why, although I found him, in his voice, or at least his writings, the most captivating of men."

For some months after this epiphany, without giving much thought to the forces that were active inside her, she immersed herself in a private study of early bark paintings and their collectors. She made trips to Paris and to Basel, and almost succeeded in convincing herself that her destiny lay in compiling a systematic account of the art forms of tropical Australia and their distinctive appeal to Western eyes, or in recording the lives of the first anthropologists in Arnhem Land – and she even began work on both these projects.

"Soon, though," she said, "I understood that I'd been fooling myself. It wasn't only the bark paintings that had been calling to me: it was the country. I was pining away for north Australia, which I'd always thought held nothing for me. There were other things in my life in Europe that weren't working out just then: I booked myself a ticket home. It was one of those interminable flights, when you go through a universe of realisations and regrets: I was dying for it to end. When we began our descent into Darwin, it was already late afternoon, and it was the middle of the burning season: all along the peninsula there were thick black smoke plumes rising: through the aircraft window it looked as if the city had been under fire. The plane came gliding in, and made its turn above the far shoreline. We banked sharply; I gazed down, and picked out the familiar landmarks – the railway bridge, the highway running off into the bush, the power station, all spread out in the haze below – then, as we were levelling out, almost above East Point, my eyes caught something – a swirl, a movement; and now, of course, when I think back, I can tell myself there must have been sand patterns in the water, caught in the current, just beneath the surface – but in that faint light, they looked to me exactly like the crowns of trees – a forest of submerged trees, with their autumnal leaves gleaming, yellow and russet in the sun – and beneath them, staring up from the shadows, I could see a parade of medieval knights in armour, mounted on horseback. They had shields and banners in their hands; their faces were clear, and their eyes were cold."

"And what were they?" I broke in. "An army of fate and death?"

"No, I don't think so. I prefer to think of that moment as some kind of special glimpse of a prophetic world, lying always just out of sight of our own, beyond it, nearby. I've never glimpsed them again; but I feel very close to them, those shining knights. I see them in my mind as my protectors. Whenever things fall out of key in my life, I come out here, to where I imagine I could find them – and somehow it makes me happier simply to be on this shoreline, looking at the storm fronts across the harbour dancing in."

We had come back to our starting point. "Wait for me," she said. "Wait just a second." She darted round to the far side of her car, stretched her hand down beside the passenger seat, then reached over to me. She was holding a book, which she thrust into my hands. "Here: I'd like you to have this. To help you with your return. It helped me: it brought me back. But I've had it long enough. It's time for me to hand it on."

I glanced down. It was an old book: there was dust and moisture beneath its laminated jacket. *Dawn of Art,* announced the title, in white block letters and nothing more, except, in much smaller print, the author's name: "Karel Kupka." I turned it over. On the back cover there was a picture of winding, twisting snakes with staring eyes.

"Why are you giving me this?" I said.

"It's just the luck of the draw," she said. "Sometimes, in our frozen lives, we get something for nothing. Maybe you need it. Maybe giving is its own gift."

"Do you always talk in riddles?"

"Of course."

"I'll return it to you," I said. "I'm sure I'll see you again soon."

"I'm sure you won't! If you really had the hang of Darwin, you'd see the city's like an interlocking set of mazes. You can be in one world all your life and not even know about the other ones lying right next door, within arm's reach. There's no need to give it back. Don't say anything. Just take it. If you read it, and follow where it leads, and listen to its hints and grace-notes, it will reward you – it will repay you well."

She jumped into the car and, with a sudden flow of movements, each of her actions leading smoothly to the next, she reversed, turned, waved over her shoulder and drove off, at speed, past the gun turrets, into the murk of the advancing storm.

*** 

Over the next few days, still playing over inside myself the different stages of this encounter, and what each of us might have divined or known about the other, I edged through the first chapters of *Dawn of Art,* reading slowly, touched by the book's prevailing tone of nostalgia and regret; intrigued, too, by its resistant structure, which seems somehow to lure the reader in, so that to open the book at all is to begin a quest. For Kupka's overarching ideas and theories are pursued fitfully, dropping at times below the textual surface, only to rise up again in almost arbitrary fashion, like some winding desert watercourse. It is in his final sentences, which are dusted with a despairing grandeur, that he at last turns to face his secret subject: he declares that art's simple, noble function, indispensable to man, is to communicate experience directly; and that the trappings of Western existence serve merely to obscure this drive. This is the lesson he extracts from the questing lives of Cézanne and Gauguin, from Picasso and Derain: it is nothing other than the search for purity and immediacy that entices creative artists to make such frequent pilgrimages back to the origins of art, and it is this yearning, too, that has lured Kupka himself into the depths of Arnhem Land: for artists, he announces with a kind of wild dismay, search for every world except the one which is forced on them.

I let Kupka's claims, and all his contradictions, sit with me; they cast their shadow on my thoughts. My curiosity about him and his life began to grow. It stayed in my mind even on long journeys to the Kimberley and the Centre – and one passage above all struck a chord inside me: those few, vivid lines in the envoi, written for Kupka by Breton, in which he speaks of the similarity between bark paintings and the design of shells. That passage was with me weeks later, when I met the scientist Richard Willan, an expert on molluscs and harbour infestations, and something of a celebrity in the research circles of the North. I told him of my childhood fascination with shells and their patterning – and though Richard must have heard of such remembered enthusiasms a thousand times, he agreed to give me a quick tutorial on the marine life of the Top End. I called in at the museum the next day to see him, with an expectation and a sense of looming adventure that seemed to have come straight from the days of childhood. I had tracked him down there with some difficulty and after persistent inquiries, for he was secreted away in his cramped office cubicle – much, I could not help thinking to myself, like a shelled creature – and was sitting behind screens and room dividers, hunched over at a small desk dominated by a binocular microscope. Every available flat surface within his reach was strewn with specimen boxes and piles of technical journals: the shelves were filled with monographs and reference volumes devoted to sea creatures, and almost all of these encyclopedias and field guides were bound in canvas of deep blue, as if to emphasise their provenance from the oceanic depths. We spoke for a while of phyla and phenotypes. Eventually, with an air of gentle patience, Richard offered to show me through a small part of the sample collection, which was housed in the museum's storage vaults. At one point in our passage down the corridors, he waved a hand towards a set of sliding drawers.

"Cone shells," he said, in a beatific voice, as though these two syllables were enough to summon up for him a vision of some underwater paradise. "I have thirty drawers of different species of cone shell here – I could find any one of them for you at any time."

"Aren't they poisonous? I thought a sting from a cone shell was fatal."

"That's right – and I've actually got a purple cone shell here that was used for venom research."

He gestured to me to look more closely at a neat row of the shells: each one had a distinct tracery of lines upon it, much like the links in a suit of chain-mail.

"Pattern in nature!" Richard left a little silence, as if for me to express some philosophical prejudice, before hurrying on. "We understand the basic mechanisms – how, in a chemical sense, these markings come about. But the why! The 'why' questions in biology are the hardest ones to answer. Why should this particular shell have a wavy pattern, and this one a pattern of triangles? As humans, we can only speculate. We think we're superior – but of course we're not ... Surely, though, you're here to ask me about nudibranchs."

"About what?"

"Nudibranchs. I may be the keeper of molluscs and echinoderms, but they're my specialty," said Richard, a touch crestfallen. "Don't you know anything about them? Many people find them quite addictive. They belong among the sea slugs, and without any doubt, in their shapes, and their colouration, and their body forms, they're the most wonderful of all the molluscs. You must have heard of the Spanish Dancer, at least – it's a beautiful creature. It takes its name from its similarity to women dancing the flamenco. They're actually quite easy to see: they can be as much as 600 millimetres long. Perhaps I should give you some background reading material?"

A few days later, I felt myself somewhat better informed about the lovely, savage world of nudibranchs, creatures both short-lived and rare, which, despite their seductive appearance, are little more than mobile poison sacs and devote large parts of their lives to concentrating within their bodies the toxins of nature. Their distribution and their feeding habits remain unclear, though a suspicion of cannibalism hangs over some members of the family, and in one of Richard's more accessible surveys of the field, where he hints at the difficulties faced by underwater photographers in search of nudibranchs, he describes sightings of a predatory species devouring another as "the Holy Grail." The emotional attachments of these elusive molluscs are predictably baroque: loneliness is their pre-ordained fate, so thinly are they distributed through the reef shallows of the southern seas: indeed, marine scientists are amazed that individual nudibranchs, sifting through the perfumed chemical attractants of their watery environment, ever succeed in finding suitable candidates with whom to mate – and it seems very probable that many adults die without once having experienced the entanglements of love. All nudibranchs, though, are hermaphrodites, so on the rare occasions when company comes along, they are well adapted to seize the moment: copulation can last for a few seconds, or as long as a whole day. Both partners leave fertilised, and both soon produce a large spawn mass, shaped much like a coiled watch spring, which yields, within ten days, a freight of tiny larvae quite unsuspecting of the rigours that lie ahead.

Late one afternoon, the details of this fraught life cycle newly committed to memory, I drove out, past the defence communication masts and the Casuarina swamplands, to a rendezvous with Richard near the sand beach at Lee Point, a place where he collected samples often, and where he hoped he might make clearer to me the subtleties and the appeal of the molluscan domain. He was waiting beside an ancient blue hatchback: "No money or valuables inside," proclaimed a stencilled notice on the dashboard – but there was not one passer-by in sight to absorb this helpful piece of information. We strolled along, discussing his role in the eradication of the black-striped mussel from Darwin Harbour, an achievement which he regarded as one of the summits of his professional life; we touched on the charms of side-gilled sea slugs, the cunning adaptations of cowrie shells, and the excellence of the fresh scallop pies that could still be had near Stanley, on the northwest Tasmanian coast.

Then, abruptly, in mid-sentence, Richard's manner changed; we had been walking slowly down the beach, towards the waves.

"We've just reached the zone of bioturbation," he said in a hushed voice, almost whispering into my ear. "We're going to do a vertical transect now." Forward we went, in tandem, Richard waving at the tell-tale traces of activity all around us: there were the sand bubbles thrown up by foraging crabs, there the footprints of Siberian wading birds.

"And look what I've found here!" He was bent over, sieving out a scoop of sand, struggling with his glasses in the hatband of his Akubra. "Do you see? What looks like sterile sand is full of bivalves: full of life. Hundreds, thousands of specimens in each square metre." I peered down obediently beside him, and saw nothing. "Bivalves, of course, are eternal compromises – between the adductor muscle holding the creature together and the ligament causing them to spring apart in death. And here's a murex. How beautiful it is – that single spine is enough to tell me that it's MacGillivray's murex: the notched aperture just there draws in water over the osphradium."

"The what?"

"The osphradium: it's a highly enervated organ that locates the direction of its prey."

"These beautiful things are carnivorous?"

"The murex," said Richard gravely, "is an extreme carnivore. What we see as beauty often tends to be associated with danger. But its beauty hasn't helped this one, in the greater scheme of things. You see that hole in its shell – just above where the liver would have been? It's been drilled – by a moon snail. In fact, you'd rarely find a mollusc shell on the beach that hasn't been drilled like this."

"So I imagine that means you don't care for moon snails very much?"

"Oh, I wouldn't say I anthropomorphise my feelings towards them. You always have to be careful not to be carried away by your own preferences – although if I was being strictly honest, I'd have to admit I would love to have evolved from something like an octopus. But I suppose I can't hide the truth from myself" – this with a little sigh of resignation – "no matter how hard it is to take: it's very clear that there's something much more like a starfish in the distant reaches of our ancestry."

We walked on. I let the crushing scale of this genealogical perspective wash over me, and felt my thoughts drifting, until it occurred to me that I was completely without mooring at that moment, and lost in life, and ever since I came back from my time in the Middle East I had been without a solid thing to hold on to. Richard, meanwhile, would stop, oblivious to these dark intimations, and helpfully point out little finds.

"Here's a sand dollar: *Peronella orbicularis* – after the French naturalist. And here's a lovely thing – it's Hanley's top snail."

"Do you have any special favourites," I asked him, almost unable to bring out the words. "Do you keep special shells, in your private collection?"

"I'm the custodian of a scientific collection. I don't feel any desire to build one of my own. I just have certain shells, very few, at home – shells that have had their walls worn away, that are segmented, and that disclose their architecture."

"Because you like the ruin and destruction?"

"No – the beauty and the order."

Richard spoke on. I felt the stillness that had been invading me take hold. I stared up at the diffused light and the far shore of the harbour, where the green strip of the mangroves and the coastal forests shimmered in the haze. The horizon's line was indistinct: light gathered there, glinted, and fell away – then, as I watched, I began to make out a shadow, moving with great slowness, still half-hidden by the curvature of the earth. It was a vessel, in silhouette. I followed it, transfixed by the gradual, dreamlike quality of its approach: it drew nearer; it took on definition, and in the humid air, where everything seemed linked by a common exhalation, its look became somehow caught up with the stories I had just been listening to. Its sides were black: it had an array of masts, and spars, and funnels, like some floating factory or industrial plant. How sombre it was: how charged with fatality! Was it a new kind of barge, returning from the islands of Arnhem Land, or a laden deep-sea trawler coming in? After a brief interval, rain veils swept back across the outer harbour, hiding the ship from view. I dragged my gaze away, both relieved and disappointed, and the idea occurred to me that I would never be able to expunge that image from the surface of my eyes.

"What is it, actually, that you're trying to find out, in this conversation?" I heard Richard saying to me at that moment, from some endless distance.

"If I could tell you that!"

There was another silence, as if a void was opening before me. I struggled to keep my bearings.

"Go on," said Richard. "Try."

"Would you think," I said, "that I'd gone completely mad, if I told you I wanted to see you purely because I came across a book that traces the designs in the bark paintings of Arnhem Land back to the forms of shells – or if I said that idea had some kind of strength for me, and that the moment I encountered it, it seemed like something true?"

"It wouldn't seem like madness at all," said Richard, in an even, serious voice, as we walked up from the beachfront. "In fact I see things that way myself. The creation of each single shell is a miracle. It's just one part of the mollusc's body that's responsible for making the shell – and yet they create marvels of architecture, more splendid than anything man can make: no wonder if the Aborigines borrow their examples, and use those patterns. The Japanese have, for millennia. Much of the art of Japan is inspired by sea-shell design. I've known for a long time that humans have a natural affinity with shells. But it's a good idea not to get lost in their patterns. There are many authorities who have something very like a fear of them: shells can take you too far into yourself. You need to make sure they lead you back, in the end, to other people." At this, he made a slight, formal gesture with his hand, as though he were drawing a veil across a vault of treasures. "And certainly," he said, "I wish that for you."

\*\*\*

Those words, spoken with such emphasis, like some curse or blessing, stayed with me while I headed into town. On impulse, as I turned off the highway, I decided the time was right for me to pay a call on the writer Andrew McMillan, whom I had not seen since my return.

Our friendship, which had endured many separations and rediscoveries, had come to seem almost a brotherhood to me, if a brotherhood of an unusual kind. I was first thrown together with him in the murky backstreets of Darlinghurst. Even then I was conscious of the similarities between us, rather than the familiar, complementary differences that lie at the heart of more conventional friendships. We shared emotions, thoughts, tastes, enthusiasms – but more than that, I often had the sense that I knew the tone of his mind, and could form a picture of what it felt like to be him. This made his company seem at times superfluous, or even oppressive, and I could read a similar reaction to my presence in his eyes. But if being with him was at times disquieting, how much more so was his way with his words: his similes, chosen almost without regard for logic, his grainy colloquial transcriptions, his jump-cuts, his wildly overtoppling descriptive passages, which run on in diminishing sub-clause chains until the initial subject of his attention has been almost wholly obscured. I remembered my feelings of astonishment on first encountering his youthful articles in music magazines, devoted to the east-coast groups he spent his time with in those days – The Saints and Radio Birdman, both of them marked out by a pure anarchy that defines their retrospective fame. And it must have been his experiences in these years of freelance apprenticeship upon ancient typewriters that led him, long afterwards in Darwin, to set up a music group of his own – 4th Estate, a shifting constellation of journalists, who perform their tunes on miked-up Remingtons and Smith Coronas – instruments that seem to their audiences like artefacts from another world.

Often, as the years passed, I would lose touch with Andrew, only to come across him in the most unexpected places; but even with the episodic quality of our friendship and his penchant for abrupt geographic shifts so firmly established, I was a little startled one day, on return from a spell of foreign corresponding in the Balkans, to hear his voice, soft and hesitant as ever, down a crackling long-distance line. He told me, with an unmistakeable note of pride, that he was in Darwin, a new home he had reached after extravagant adventures documenting an outback tour by

Midnight Oil. How curious I was to see him there, beneath the palms and stringy-barks! Some months later, I embarked on a journey of my own through tropical Australia, and came to Darwin, and found him in his murky lair. After days of prevarications, I was able to entice him out; we set off on a road trip to the Cobourg Peninsula, where I was keen to see the ruins of the British outpost at Port Essington. It was the cool, idyllic dry season. For several nights, we slept in our swags beneath the stars, and from those initial conversations I began to form some picture of the changes in Andrew's life. He regarded himself as a contemporary historian now, but a historian devoted to the fugitive details that conventional history neglects – the grain of the voice, the weight of feeling that hides inside words, the fleeting dreams that reports and documents can never catch.

One evening, at a camp poised on the bauxite cliffs above Victoria Harbour, Andrew offered to read me a handful of passages from the manuscript he was just then bringing to completion – a book which had ramified so uncontrollably that it was turning into several distinct projects.

"What's it going to be called?" I asked.

"*An Intruder's Guide to East Arnhem Land,*" he said. "But of course there's going to have to be a separate volume about the lives and memories of the crew members on the flying boats that were stationed in the Top End during World War II. That's going to be my *Catalina Dreaming.*"

"Good titles," I murmured, and settled back, and let the flow of words transport me. The *Guide* he read to me that night was not merely drenched with the feel and look of our surrounds: it had become one with its subjects. Its words reached out to the sun setting in the green bay before us, and the mauve sky on the far horizon; its paragraphs and pages roamed in the tall stringybarks swaying above our heads. Andrew read on, for hours, unfurling his creation in a loving, protective voice, until the stars were bright, and the little kangaroo mice came out to peer at us by the light of our campfire – and I knew then that my friend's life was at its peak, and that the memory of the time when he composed with such freedom and fluency would haunt him in the years to come.

And so, I am tempted to think, it proved. A few months after that journey of ours into west Arnhem Land, the first edition of *An Intruder's Guide* appeared – but Andrew had revised the text, in keeping with some self-concealing impulses of his own, and his publisher's desires. The new version was shorn of the original's transcendent scenes: scenes I still can call to mind, in which the landscape itself seemed to speak, and the boundary between the writer's voice and the bush in its receding perspectives dissolved. Even without such passages, the *Guide* was sufficiently eccentric and perplexing to guarantee that it would be met with responses of hostility or indifference – and over the time since, utterly untroubled by dreams of worldly triumph, Andrew has devoted himself to higher things: the writing of a long, synoptic novel, somewhat in the style of Xavier Herbert, set in the remote goldmining township of Pine Creek, and the pursuit of his experiments in musical performance with 4th Estate.

I turned in to Stuart Park, an enclave that has managed, despite the usual attempts at gentrification, to preserve much of its delightful shabbiness, with the result that it resembles an open-air museum, through which curious travellers cruise from time to time, marvelling at the proliferation of roundabouts and the rundown charm that Darwin's older suburbs used to offer the passerby at every glance. Andrew's house was an elevated structure with an improvised, louvre-windowed downstairs living space: the Bunker, inside which he had long barricaded himself against the wider world. Frogs were croaking in chorus; Torres Strait pigeons cooed lustily from the trees around the block; there were far-off rolls of thunder. It was Andrew's soundtrack. I pushed through the surrounding palm-tree jungle, and from a distance caught sight of him, framed by the louvres, perched at his desk, feet up, pen poised in his hand like a paintbrush, his eyes staring into space. The Bunker's decoration had changed little during my time away: on the walls there were the same laminated posters advertising 4th Estate concerts; the same detailed topographic maps of Arnhem Land. A motley collection of broken office chairs, some bent into gargoyle shapes, some missing arms or legs, had been lined up inside the front door. From the ceiling above Andrew's work desk hung, suspended by an elaborate pulley system, his row of manuscripts in progress: their pages fluttered in the breeze generated by an enormous fan. I stepped in, past the little ornamental pond and its collection of geckos: they surveyed me, panting, with wide black eyes.

"The traveller returns," said Andrew, in a faintly sardonic tone of voice, although I could hear in it a score of registers: pleasure, and its automatic undertow of regret; excitement, and its hidden companion, despondency; interest, and also indifference; sadness, too, at the passage of time, and the losses that had been piled upon us both and all our friends, in the year that had just passed. There was the desire to speak, the desire to keep silent; to reveal oneself, and to hide one's inmost thoughts. All this lurked inside those first words of his – but within seconds we were both adrift, and far away, on a sea of tales and stories: his adventures that dry season in the obscure bush down near the Daly, his latest implausible literary schemes and projects, his multi-player Scrabble contests at Dinah Beach, the rhythmic rainfall patterns he could now detect in early build-up storms.

I laughed, and felt the magnetic pull of Darwin conversation, in all its mazy, branching, reduplicating charm. Themes and topics would appear and vanish, only to recombine in the most promiscuous fashion, sagas would be told repeatedly, in wholly inconsistent versions, while characters would weave in and out of narratives, and often appear in person in mid-story and continue the telling of the drama in their own voice. At last there was a lull in the Bunker. The other visitors had gone. It was late at night by now: sheet lightning from the storms above Mandorah flashed and flickered in the sky.

"Do you still remember those early days," I asked him, "when you'd just come to Darwin, and you were exploring your way by dinghy across the harbour?"

It was a phase hinted at in the brief, reticent first words of *Catalina Dreaming,* where Andrew describes, in yet another variant, the twisting paths of coincidence that lured him north. When he was a boy in the 1960s, as he writes, he was fascinated by the memory of wartime, and the aircraft that had flown in defence of Australia. He heard stories about them from his father, who served as an instructor and navigator on Beaufighters during the Pacific campaign, and the stories would multiply around the kitchen table, whenever old friends and colleagues of his father's came round: and always the strangest, most vivid adventures were those of the flying-boat squadrons and their crews. Andrew was given a plastic scale model of a Catalina, which he treasured. He began building his own image of the aircraft. In his mind it became the emblem of endurance and perfection, it was lovely in its ungainliness, it could linger airborne for a full twenty-four hours, "crossing oceans and time zones and eras" and then land on water when it came home. These ideas from childhood had lodged in his memory, and when he first passed through Darwin in 1988, he promptly set about discovering the wartime city – a quest that led him to the eastern branches of the harbour, where a picturesque low island, surmounted by a scatter of gum trees, lies athwart the main channel. This island – little more, in truth, than a shifting sandbar – cast a spell over him: a spell that strengthened when he scanned the charts and learned its name. It was marked down as Catalina Island, and it guarded the entrance to the old flying-boat base. Andrew's early passion was reignited: he hunted through the archives of the war memorial, reading all that he could find there, then moved north to delve at first hand into the tales of the Cat boats, and search through the rubble of the East Arm squadron base.

"In those days, before Darwin's new wharf was laid in," he writes, "you could poke around in the scrub and find amber beer bottles date-stamped 1944 and 1945. There were cement slabs, broken pipes, the outlines of long-neglected garden beds, corroding enamel plates and cups, blue enamel water canteens, bullet shells and clips" – and there are still a few remains of this vintage, lost amidst the remote reaches of the mangroves, though now the Catalina base boat ramp is the preserve of recreational fishermen, and the bleakness of the harbour at this point, close by the cranes and barriers of the modern container port, is almost too much for the heart to bear.

"Of course I remember them," said Andrew, getting up, somewhat unsteadily, and emerging from behind his desk, where he had remained for the past several hours, immobile, much like a Mayan altar statue, cradling his ashtray as though it were a votive goblet. He wandered over to the corner of the room, where his talismanic childhood Catalina hung suspended from the ceiling, and gave it a little tap of encouragement: trailing cobwebs from its wings, the flying boat resumed its oscillating journey through the half-light of the Bunker's furthest recess.

"And did you ever, back then, come across a black ship," I asked. "A dark ship, that used to patrol the outer waters of the harbour?"

"What kind of black ship?"

"A ship with an air of miasma and foreboding about it. A ship that looks like the incarnation of death. Dark sides, dark sails, dark rigging, its funnel pouring out a thick smoke like ash..."

"Alright – I think I get the general picture. What a surprise it caught your eye! Maybe you're talking about one of those contract dredgers they used to bring in from time to time. Did you see it close up?"

"Only from far away, for a few moments, at so great a distance at first, in fact, that it might have been one of those chimeras you sometimes think you glimpse in the storm haze, and give form to by yourself."

"Maybe it was just a coastal lugger of some kind," said Andrew, thoughtfully, and showing every sign of receding into one of his lengthy silent reveries.

"And were there luggers like that, on the Darwin run, when you used to travel out by sea to Arnhem Land?"

"You're full of questions, aren't you? I thought you would have learned by now: the North gives you all the things you need to know in its own good time."

"What about the name Karel Kupka?" I tried, changing tack. "Did you ever come across his trail, when you were out at Milingimbi, or Yirrkala? Is he in the *Intruder's Guide?*"

"You mean that collector?"

"The artist."

"If you're interested in him," said Andrew, "maybe you should call in at the Catholic cathedral. When were you last there?"

"I'm not sure I've ever been there."

"I'm shocked; I'm really shocked."

"Because I'm not looking after the salvation of my soul?"

"No – because of the cathedral's association with creative endeavour. It's a temple of art and beauty. Have you really forgotten everything about Darwin's artistic traditions? You've only been away twelve months."

He explored these ideas further, in a hazy set of free associations, and gradually, as he did so, I realised that there, lounging in the Bunker's heat and dust, so late at night, with the geckos cavorting on the walls around me, and the lightning flashing through the leaves of palms and cycads, I had at last the sense of being back, of seeing once more the things I had carried in my mind: people, places, sights, sounds, all in their abrupt, familiar combinations. I told Andrew something of this, and described the impressions that had come over me when I first touched down and spent days exploring about me in the changed heart of the city: the sense that the world I had returned to was further from me than it had been during my absence; the unaccountable feeling that I was walking the streets on sufferance, and my entry ticket to that realm might be revoked at any instant by the vast armies of parking inspectors who now roamed the streets on their grey scooters, exuding enmity towards every spontaneous or freeliving creature in sight. I was speaking in a low voice, and through all this, Andrew listened, a slight, sad smile appearing every now and then on his lips, before remarking that he barely recognised the city anymore, and there were days when he felt absent from the entire course of his existence, and even from the words he wrote – and very few things seemed fixed or solid in his world.

"At least you have the Bunker," I said. "This is the real heart of Darwin for me: the core from which everything else spreads out, and draws its energy. Everything else could be razed, torn down, and the survival of the Bunker would be enough."

"It's strange you should say that, tonight of all nights."

"Why?"

He rolled a cigarette, his movements slow and deliberate. I watched him, quite overcome by the procedure's elegance, as if I had never seen it done before.

"It's the end of the line for this place. I just found out. Development has come to Stuart Park at last. I have to leave. I've got three months, to move – to find somewhere else. Given the frequency of your visits, that probably means this is the last time you'll see me here. I suppose I could go down the highway – to one of those little places that I love. To Larrimah or Pine Creek: it's a different universe down there, it's full of characters. And I like being there. I've spent months happily before now in the Pine Creek hotel – even if the tin roofs of the rooms do get a bit much in the wet season when the rains are falling continuously all through the night."

For some minutes he continued speaking, agonising – but my thoughts had jumped: I saw blurry colours, bleeding into one another, as if in portent of some impending catastrophe. And then, in the depths of my mind, I made out afresh an image which I had glimpsed in a local gallery some days earlier, and which had seemed to me at once an emblem of the time: burning houses, adrift on high waves, beneath stormy skies. It was a well-known print, by the artist Therese Ritchie, whose work combines opposing elements in tension so sharp the eye pleads for release: and those flames, blazing in all their austere, cleansing beauty, twisted and seethed inside me through the silence of the night.

# III

Several days went by, consumed in the upheavals of my return, before I worked up the resolve to cross the threshold of St Mary's Star of the Sea, a building whose wide doors stand invitingly open all day long, so that the tall pews and lines of seats stretched down its nave and transepts can be surveyed during a brisk drivepast along Mitchell Street, and one can half-imagine one knows the place without even venturing inside. But on walking in I was surprised to find most of the wall-space around the entrance covered in children's posters, recording highly coloured interpretations of heaven and hell. In little dispensers were folded leaflets discussing the charitable ambitions of the diocese and describing the various treasures sheltered in the cathedral's chapels and the recesses set aside for prayer. I began a systematic survey of the building and advanced as far as the sanctuary, where I was inspecting the terrazzo stonework of the altar, while reading an account of the overwhelming industry that had gone into its creation: its giltwork was made from alluvial gold panned at the Arltunga mission, in the high ranges east of Alice Springs; the shimmer catching the sun's rays came from pearl shell gathered up by divers on the shallow reef-beds of the Arafura Sea. The cathedral was quite empty – or so I thought, until I heard a soft sound close by me: it was a man's breathing. I turned. There was a slight figure, with a lined face, clutching a white cane, wearing dark glasses, just behind me. His upper body was enfolded in a well-cut jacket several sizes too large: at his neck was a silk scarf.

"Doubtless," he said, "you are seeking the Virgin."

"I am?"

"Of course. Why else would you be here?"

"Couldn't one just come in to see the beauties of the cathedral?" "Only the lost and hopeless come in here," he said, rather firmly. "I may be blind, as you can see – but I'm not weak in the head. The church has no more meaning now: the tide of faith has ebbed away. Those in the flow of life rush by outside. Those without a place come here." He smiled at me, triumphantly. "Those like myself, for instance: exiles."

"From where?"

"East Timor, of course: almost everyone of distinction in Darwin comes from Timor."

"And you were never tempted to return, after the liberation?"

"The Timor I knew will never come back," he said. "The past is safe only in my memory."

He spread his hands, as if to express the elusive sadness of all creatures caught in the flow of time.

"Shall we?"

"Shall we what?"

"Go to see her – the Madonna of the Aborigines." He made me a gesture, to show that I should take his arm; together, at a slow pace, we shuffled soundlessly towards the far transept while my companion told me, in several unfolding streams of narrative at once, the story of the coming of the Catholic faith to his own country, the adventures of the cathedral's wounded, shrapnel-pierced angel, and the saga of the Madonna herself, her theft and her mysterious return. "And you know her most important attribute?"

"I'm afraid I know very little about her."

"She listens. The Madonna listens. That was the intention of the artist who created her, who gave her life: an exile like myself, the Czech painter Kupka: you've heard of him?"

Perhaps at this, I gave a start.

"You're surprised? You know his art? You know his story?"

"Since you ask," I said, "I do feel that things are lining up inside my head – and that I'm coming to know it, bit by bit."

We were in the transept now: my companion pointed up, his arm trembling lightly on mine: "There she is: how beautifully he drew the lines of her face!"

I craned my neck upwards, towards a large canvas, high above us, well out of reach, edged by a thin wood frame. The light was poor; the glare was sharp – so much so that it was almost impossible at first to make out a thing.

"Can you see them?" he asked. "The clan designs – and the look on the Virgin's face: the wisdom and the knowledge in her eyes?" I peered through the murk.

"There seems to be some damage," I said to him. "There's a slash of purple, at her neck, or beneath her arm: it looks almost as if the undercoat has been exposed."

"Not at all! That is the artist's genius: his way of catching the iridescence of her skin. The mother of God is made flesh before you – and she has the body of a young Aboriginal woman. That faint purple is the holy colour – it is Kupka's own way of expressing the grace and shimmer of God's will. I know it. He told me."

"You knew him?"

"When I was much younger. He confided in me: it was as if we were brothers. I know his story well. He felt he was at home here – among friends. We spent time together: I travelled with him on his first journeys, on the mission lugger, out to the Daly and to Bathurst Island. He wrote me letters, long letters, after he left Darwin – for many years. And then – just like that, without warning, or any word to say goodbye – he vanished from my life. You can hear many rumours about this painting, but none of them are true. Karel spoke to me about the Virgin: often. There are people who still say she is a portrait of a woman from the Tiwi Islands, or from Daly River mission."

"And who is she – really?"

"There is a hidden tale that I can tell." He dropped his voice down, and whispered: "A tale few people have heard: it is a love painting!"

And with this he launched into a complex story, clutching at my arm for emphasis whenever he reached a point of special intensity: how Kupka, on one of his first field trips to Yirrkala mission, had met a young woman from north-east Arnhem Land; how her totem, the crested tern, had remained an obsession of his in later life; how this secret romance, which came, like all the greatest loves, to nothing, and had been founded on the vainest of delusions, lay encoded in the patterns of the background behind the Virgin's head; how the Madonna's face, which had so struck the bishop and the priests of the diocese with its calm, contemplative expression, was in truth a portrait, painted with all the care and precision of romantic love.

"So it's a profane painting?"

"If you truly believe love is a profane emotion, then I feel sorry for you," said my companion, with the air of a man recalling a labyrinth of ancient trysts and star-crossed liaisons. He flared his nostrils dramatically.

"And when" – I hesitated – "when did you last see the Virgin?"

"You mean this painting? But I see her internally: with my mind's eyes. Her feelings are communicated directly to me. I have never seen her as you see her – but I can promise you I know her more than you can – and I see her more. I know every line and shading of her face – even though I have been blind since birth."

With a little flourish, he relinquished, at that point, my arm, and lifted up his dark glasses: the skin beneath them was lined and mottled. I could now see the declivities of his eyes, and I could not help myself from trembling slightly as I looked at them, for the lids had been neatly, with fine, even stitches, sewn closed.

***

Weeks passed after this chance meeting, and insensibly Kupka came more and more into my life. I met curators who had studied his collections, and anthropologists who knew his later work; and there were even brief references to his travels in a private memoir I was given from the time when outstations were being set up in the North. Soon, in the Darwin parliamentary library, I found a copy of his doctoral thesis on bark paintings, which had been published, complete with grainy photographs, as an academic text: it had been shelved, seemingly by accident, together with the histories of the Northern Territory Football League. In the musty stacks, perched on a metal stool, I skimmed with mounting frustration through its pages: they were written in the driest and most formal of styles, and betrayed nothing of the writer's inward thoughts during his trajectory through

Arnhem Land. Impelled by this flurry of new findings, and feeling by now almost as if my search for Kupka had become the great task of my return, I called in the next day at the office of the Catholic diocese in Parap. They had no leads: their records, like almost all of Darwin's written past, had been devastated during Cyclone Tracy's onslaught on the Christmas Eve of 1974. At their suggestion, I made a journey out to the Tiwi Islands, to visit the little church at Nguiu and the historical display preserved there by the sisters of the Sacred Heart – but all memory of Kupka's Tiwi days had gone. Even the old missionaries I tracked down from Milingimbi, where he spent months on end, could call to mind little about their artistic visitor, beyond his fondness for French cigarettes and his overbearing ways.

Eventually, the widening circles of this quest brought me to that memory-refuge of last resort, the Commonwealth archives, a low building, almost invisible to the casual passer-by and well defended against the elements. Just beyond its walls runs the sixlane highway skirting Darwin International Airport, but within its cool reading rooms, which are invariably deserted, one has no sense of what lies outside. All seem permanently calm and sylvan: indeed, the central courtyard is thick with ferns and tropical palms, and even the photographs of old Darwin on the walls seem to conjure up the days of creeping vegetation and endless silence, when the town lay, almost unchanging year by year, lost in its own thoughts, and far beyond the boundaries of the active world. This air of pensiveness was reinforced, over the days I spent researching there, by a mood of pervasive grief. The director of the archives, Phyllis Williams, a woman of the most tranquil elegance, and a traditional owner of the rich rock-art sites round Mount Borradaile, was in mourning: her father had recently passed away. Phyllis was still wearing black, and I would catch sight of her from time to time, passing slowly through the research rooms, skirting the desks and microfilm readers, looking around with wide, distracted eyes. Her sadness had transmitted itself to many of her staff, who remained both subdued and silent, as though they had experienced losses of their own – with the result that the archives felt like a temple of reflection, where the past's distance was a cause for continuing and profound lament. One by one, in solemn manner, the research assistants would approach me and hand me new batches of departmental files covering the years of Kupka's visits to Milingimbi, which I studied dutifully, for hours on end, but almost all of them proved of little consequence. Another document, though, caught my eye: it was a brief record, noting Kupka's intention to apply for naturalisation, and to remain in Australia. It dated from the time of his greatest triumph, when he had already gathered up his first collections of Aboriginal paintings and held his early European exhibitions, and the manuscript of *Dawn of Art* was beginning to take form.

That evening I went back to my copy of the book, looking for some trace of this intention, and I noticed for the first time the brief, stiff preface by Elkin, Kupka's great protector, the controlling father-figure of Australian anthropology. Perhaps, I thought to myself, Elkin might have remained in contact, in later years, with his elusive protégé – and I even mentioned this idea to a friend of mine who knew the field.

"Elkin!" he said at once. "Elkin was a force of nature. He was in contact with everybody. No one in the history of this continent ever maintained so wide a correspondence, or preserved it so well. He was obsessional: he kept neat carbon copies of every letter that he sent. You should take a look at the Elkin collection: it's kept at Sydney University – and it's astonishing! It's like a secret repository of every intellectual conversation that took place in the Australian twentieth century – every idea you dreamed of reading, every exchange you know must have happened but you could never find: there are traces of them or clues to them all in there. The librarians have it all kept in smart red boxes and sandcoloured files, as if it was arranged in some supreme order, but in fact it's the wildest mix of dates and domains and subjects – and that produces unusual effects if you just leaf through: it becomes like some anthropological hallucination, full of jump-cuts. You're always going from one mind to another: Strehlow, Thomson, Wentworth, Petri – everybody, from every walk of life, jumbled up together like prisoners in Elkin's social net. Why not give them a call? They would be sure to have some idea of who wrote to the professor, and when."

I took this advice, and was soon in conversation with the University's reference archivist.

"And what exactly are you looking for?" she asked me, in her warm voice, quite kindly: the question reverberated down the line. She asked again.

"The letters of a Czech artist – an obscure, unknown artist."

"You mean Kupka?"

"Maybe he's not that obscure," I said.

"Oh, he's obscure – but that's alright. We're archivists, we like obscurity. And obscure people sometimes become famous."

"Perhaps," I said, feeling drawn in by this exchange, "with enough study, everyone in the past will eventually become famous."

"But that would be the same as being obscure, if fame was a universal condition, wouldn't it? I can put those files aside for you. In fact, more researchers seem to be mentioning Kupka's name these days, although he's been out of the limelight for years. It's almost as if people are starting to realise that he leads on to interesting places."

\*\*\*

Shortly after this, my journalistic duties took me down to Sydney. Once there, I made an appointment to visit the Elkin archives, which are housed in a special suite of rooms on the top floor of the Fisher Library, overlooking the University's lush parklands. Midway through a cool clear morning I took my place there at a narrow desk, alongside several grave-faced researchers who had the air of experts engaged in tasks of many years' duration. A selection of filing boxes, brick red, and elaborately labelled, according to a complex numerical code, exactly as my friend had described them, was waiting for me: "Series 44. Box 222. Box 223." They contained the great professor's general correspondence for a selection of periods, and strewn through them was a scatter of aerogrammes sent to him by Karel Kupka. These stood out at once, for they were hand-written, and in a small, distinctively slanted script, the tops of the letters curving slightly, like fields of windswept corn. I began reading through them, lulled by the sound of pages being turned alongside me and the gentle breathing of the other men and women in the reading room – and often my attention would wander, and be drawn to different sets of letters in the files, until the whole day had passed and I had barely made any inroads into my pile of documents. Only after long hours in that room did the blur of Kupka's life begin to take on a faint definition, in stray remarks appended at the end of his letters, or in the more systematic accounts he offered Elkin of his progress – and I felt something like the joy of a detective whenever I came on one of these little autobiographies. Their fragmentary nature lent them a kind of clarity, in the way details in ill-lit photographic images leap out to the eye. Slowly, from them, the story of Kupka's passage to Australia became plain: he had arrived in hope, and left in shadow; he kept returning, almost in secret, like a ghost, until the last years of his life, which were drenched in the sadness of a constant retrospect. There were letters full of his love for northern landscape, and pleas for Elkin's help in securing academic posts. There was the saga of the collection he amassed in the '60s, and the rivalries that surrounded it. I reached the time of his return to Europe; his Parisian career began. I was reading faster – I found myself caught up in his story; he came alive, I felt the dance and pulse inside his words; then my eyes fell on a letter in broken, uneven script. All about me seemed quiet. I bent over, and traced the lines.

The letter had been written in Kupka's little attic near Saint-Sulpice, and was dated from December 1968: it veered eccentrically between languages, and there was a tormented tone about it, as if its words had been ground out in the entrance to some hidden hell.

"Dear Professor," he begins: "How many months it is I have written to you for the last time. They were so busy for me that I truely don't remember." He winds on into a tale of art: his hopes as a painter, and his fears: his abrupt decision to abandon this path. "I am becoming an apprentice ethnographer," he then announces, but a gloom, by this stage, has taken hold of him, and it is this mood that guides his pen. "If everybody would receive me at least with half of the goodwill and friendliness you have always given to me. More than anything else, I would like to extend my research by filling gaps rather than by searching for the 'new' – which is problematic to find in our days anyway."

Elkin, perhaps as much bemused by the shift in his correspondent's style as the change in his avowed profession, replies in rather non-committal manner, offering up the local news from northeast Arnhem Land. It is not good: a shadow hangs over one of the settlements where Kupka secured his collection's finest gems. "Yirrakalla is going to be overwhelmed with the development of the bauxite mining," the professor writes – and perched as we are now, much further down the track of progress, when an alumina refinery glints in the waters of Melville Bay, it would be hard to dissent too much from this prophecy. Elkin seeks for some upbeat, encouraging words to send his correspondent: "I hope," he continues, "that some day you will return to Australia to see what the artists are doing." But the prospects of such a future unfolding were limited, for Kupka's thoughts were elsewhere now, and he had already, in an increasingly fractured script and broken English, given Elkin a sketch of the events that swept down on him during a brief trip back to his home country in the tumultuous mid-year of 1968: "My summer holiday was not really successful. Going to see, after more than twenty years, the Czechoslovakia, I have chosen the 'right' moment: to see the Russian occupation was a ghastly experience. Yours – very sincerely – Karel."

I leafed on through the remainder of the file. Nothing. I tried the next. For some while, I scanned on, through the ceaseless stream of letters sent to Elkin, all of them promptly answered in the professor's cool, Olympian prose. From time to time, for relief, I would walk out from the reading room to the landing, and stare out through the floor-length window. Far below was the courtyard; the figures of students gathered, clustered and then separated, in sharp, spasmodic rhythms, much like cells growing and dividing in some accelerated scientific film. Across the lawns, and the tops of the trees, I could see the deep sandstone of the university's mock-gothic cloister; it was the haunting colour of low bluffs and ridges in desert country. Elkin wrote again, but no reply came back – for more than a year, until December 1969 – by when the political opening in Kupka's native country had been stifled: Soviet forces restored order; the embrace of the state was slowly re-imposed. Whole lives were played out in the aftershock of those events, which held the world's eyes once, but now seem nothing more than a detail in history's winding channels, a deserted, half-forgotten anabranch in the flow of human time.

"15 December 1969." I gazed down at Kupka's letter: I knew what I was reading even before I made out the words. Stray thoughts ran through my mind: guilt; pleasure; the indifference that comes at the conclusion of the hunt. So here it was: the darkness in my precursor's world. How little a life's course comes down to. How little remains: a few words, a judgment here and there – ideas that form, and scatter, and leave scarcely a trace. All through the early pages of his letter, Kupka struggles for a smooth and tranquil voice. He paints a portrait of his country under martial law; he concentrates his efforts: it is as if he feels the press of Elkin's viewing eyes. He describes to the professor his newest project: an exhibition, just staged in Prague, of Aboriginal bark paintings from Arnhem Land, and its reception, and the relief it offered from the city's daily life. He even sketches his longing to work again in Australia, he dreams of coming back there, as if it was his true and chosen home – but then the other world intrudes, and he is back at once in dark, bleak Prague: "To see the despair of all that good-willing people who were hoping to build a state-utopia, and were so brutally stopped, to find again, after more than twenty years, my family and old friends – and leave them again in their bitterness, was a little bit too much for me. It was no doubt a main reason for a serious nervous trouble which needed recently an energic treatment for about a month. I am recovering slowly, trying to think only about work, and extension of my research."

There is a blank line, then Kupka bids farewell to Elkin: it is his farewell to the tropics, and to northern travels and the pursuit of art. In years to come, he would present himself as a man of rigour and of science; he would rewrite his studies of the first Australian painters; he would be cured at last of his collecting passion, and his desire to find a home. He signs his name, once more, at the end of this letter, which has all the force of a testament, or a confession: "Yours – very sincerely – Karel" – and the correspondence comes to its end.

I listened to the sounds of the archives, flowing round me. I glanced down again at the page; it was smudged. At that moment, the young attendant came over from the far side of the room and bent down beside me, almost kneeling at my desk.

"Please," she whispered, "be careful not to damage the letters."

"What do you mean?" I whispered back.

"You look full of grief," she said. "We can't have tears falling on the page." I touched my fingers to my eyes.

"I'm sorry," I said.

"It's not allowed," she went on, smiling slightly.

"Not allowed?"

"You're not allowed to be sad, in a library, or archive. Didn't you know?"

"I know some," I said, "where sadness seems to be obligatory."

"On the contrary: that's not the way it's meant to be. Archives are where things live on, and memories triumph. This is where the pain of the past is redeemed – and sadness falls into its place."

\*\*\*

A week later, when I came back to Darwin, I found a message from my friend George Chaloupka, the founding genius of north Australian rock-art research, a man of the greatest charm and sweetness, and the mainstay, through both his company and conversation, of my northern life. George had been away on a trip with his grandchildren back to his native Bohemia; I had not seen him since setting out on my brief journey down the Kupka trail. We arranged to meet at one of our regular points of rendezvous, the Sailing Club veranda on the foreshore of Fannie Bay. I found him there, at the appointed hour, seated alone, beyond the crowds, looking out to sea – and at once I began to tell him the news of all my discoveries: the Madonna in the cathedral, the secret story of her origins, the records unknown in the archives, the letters lying like hidden treasure, in distant Sydney, in the Elkin files. I went into fine detail: it was a warm, moist evening, fit for slow, unfurling conversations: the tide was low; the sun, almost wholly masked by clouds and rain veils, was just setting; we had reached that soft, magic time when the light begins to lose its definition and the whole of Darwin seems poised on the brink of vegetal decay.

"And what do you really think you were looking for," George asked me, "in all this story of Kupka's life?"

"A rhyme – a parallel," I said, surprised by the directness of the question, which was most unlike him. I shrugged. I ran on, building great castles of theory for him, as though my own motivations were wholly hidden from me, and they could only be established with the most elaborate analytic efforts. I told him how Kupka had gone down paths that I was following, that he was a forebear, that it was quite natural to want to know the story of a figure of such glamour from the far past.

"The far past," George echoed, with a certain irony.

"Yes: it's natural to seek to reclaim people from the murk of time. Don't you ever feel you can come close to knowing what people have felt; that you can animate them, bring them alive by living in their words? Isn't that something of the secret appeal of history – as much as understanding the past, or knowing the roots of the present, isn't it just a longing to be elsewhere, to ease the burden of the self?"

"No," said George, frowning, and staring at the horizon. "But it does sound like the kind of thing Kupka might have said."

"I didn't realise that you knew him!"

"You never asked. It's true, his name doesn't ever seem to come up. I suppose that's because we generally spend our time talking about Aboriginal issues – like most people in Darwin. But his path and mine crossed, quite frequently, in fact, in the days when he was here. That was only natural: we were both Bohemians, both foreigners, in a small town. We spoke Czech together. I knew him, to the extent he could be known, or wanted to be known. He cut a very distinctive figure, of course, in those days."

"Tell me."

George began, and as he spoke, at last Kupka shimmered into being for me: no longer was he just a printed name, or a fleeting image in old photographs. His tone of voice, his way of speaking, his gait, the set of his hooded eyes – George caught all these things, and his subject's quiet evasiveness. It was a striking portrait; it had the sharp, resistant feel of life.

"He must have made quite an impact on you," I said.

"Of course – he was exotic, when I first met him here, in the '60s. He reminded me very much then of my own father: he was a civilised European, a being from another time. But there was something tormented about him, in that he was far away from his background and had been forced to become an émigré: he didn't want to return home – he knew his own culture was in chains. He told me about his life in Paris, how he moved among the refugees and intellectuals; how he gave one of his pictures as a gift to Picasso. That all made an impression on me: it was very different from the life he was leading in Darwin, staying at the church, or with that big, noisy accountant, Gerry Kostka, who was the town's unofficial Czech ambassador back then, or at the old hostel near the Esplanade. I can still picture him as he was in those days: he was thin, and distinguished, and he knew that he was a striking figure – but there always was a kind of silence at the core of him. I found it quite frightening, the wave of loneliness that came from him sometimes."

"Maybe that was the silence of a man of faith," I hazarded.

"No, no." George laughed. "He didn't impress me as a serious Catholic. He had only one interest in life. He made a religion out of art, and his collecting. That was always what we spoke about: it was impossible to have a conversation with him that didn't veer back to that subject. I can still remember when he had just assembled his first great collection from Arnhem Land: it was 1963 – I saw it all before it left the country. The Methodist Overseas Mission had a storeroom in Knuckey Street, and Kupka displayed his pieces there to the representatives of the Welfare Branch, to show them what he was taking away. Some of the pieces were incredible. One was a forked log, bound with string all the way up: it was seven feet high, and overmodelled with the most intricate designs. It was clearly a ceremonial object. He was a remarkable collector – he got the best of everything – and he even became part of the tradition, in a sense. If you look closely at the pieces that he chose, you can see the change in the work of the artists he was collecting, you can see them developing: he pointed them in the direction they followed later in their lives. He stood at the very outset of the Aboriginal painting movement: and perhaps it was in that way, that diagonal way, only, that he was able to fulfil his ambitions in the world of art."

George fell silent. The noise from the waves, and the voices from the sailing club, washed over us. There was a long pause, in which the past's weight, and the sweetness of recalling it, seemed palpable, and one could almost feel the speed with which our experiences of each moment turn into the stuff of memory, and rush away. "There was one last time that Kupka came to see me here," George said, eventually. "It must have been on the final collecting trip he made. I was in the old house, in my studio downstairs. I was still painting in those days, like him, and he knew by then that I was involved in studying the rock art of Arnhem Land. And by that stage I had collected a handful of early works from Port Keats, and pieces by Midjawu-Midjawu, which he wanted. He had a beautiful sculpture with him. We made an exchange – although I seem to recall that he gave me a carving of a dugong in the end, instead."

"You didn't mind?"

"No – of course not: he was a collector. What else could you expect? It wasn't money that drove him. We stayed in touch – he sent me cards, in Czech, but they're all gone now. They went with the cyclone, like everything from that time. I could never entirely forget about Kupka, though. I had the odd, strong sense that he knew something – some secret thing about the North. At any rate, many years later, when I went back to Europe on a research trip of my own and passed through Paris, I went to visit him. He was living in a garret, on the Left Bank..."

"Place Saint-Sulpice," I said, in triumph.

"Exactly. He seemed to survive there on next to nothing. All the money he spent was on cigarettes: Gauloises, the blue ones – the ones he could never get when he was on his travels in the North. I was only there for a few days. I spent as much time as I could with him, in the galleries, and bookshops, and cafés. He would lead the way on our long walks through the streets, dancing ahead through the boulevard traffic, stopping the cars with his outstretched hands. We spoke a great deal, about the past and our respective journeys out of Czechoslovakia; his longing to go back, and the way all that had come to nothing. One evening, he took me to a restaurant nearby, his favourite. It specialised in the cuisine of the Lorraine: it was very heavy food, dreadful – all sausages and sauerkraut."

"Maybe it helped him to feel at home: it must have been the closest thing to Czech food in that part of Paris."

"Who knows?" said George, rather pointedly failing to leap to the defence of his native land's culinary traditions. "I can only recall brief flashes of what we discussed: it was a talk that left me feeling on edge. He told me how difficult it had been for him to renounce the hopes he had for Australia; to realise that he was at home, at rest, nowhere."

"But he was a cosmopolitan," I said. "Or he became one."

"And I wonder if all that explains something of the appeal he holds for you," George continued. "That longing he had, to remake himself in the image of the northern landscape. That sense of Darwin as the place that might save him, although of course it's a place that tends to take things away: youth, love, hope."

"Life, in the end, in fact?"

"Naturally: but it didn't claim him, although he always used to say he thought those dark mission luggers were machines of fate. And I wonder how his story ended?"

That tale is quickly told. After his breakdown, and slow recovery, there was a shift in Kupka's path through life. He pursued his new vocation: he recast himself as an anthropologist and carried out his researches in Paris, at the Documentation Centre for Oceania, under the flinty eye of the Pacific specialist Jean Guiart. Kupka had already donated most of his private collection of works from Arnhem Land to the Musée des Arts Africains et Océaniens: and it was in a gallery of this museum, filled with these familiar objects, like a room full of approving friends, that he defended his doctoral thesis, which dealt with questions of anonymity in primitive art. In 1972 he gave away the remainder of his sculptures to the museum. Soon afterwards *Aboriginal Painters of Australia,* the austere summation of his studies, appeared in print as a special publication of the Société des Océanistes. It was little read, but greatly prized, and even in recent years one could find copies, kept like some set of Torah scrolls, in the closed recesses of the Musée de l'Homme.

Kupka made trips back to northern Australia, but they were brief: he passed almost unseen. He devoted himself to tracing the genealogies of the artists he had known and encouraged, almost all of whom had died long before – and these researches, and their implications, occupied him for many years, although he published nothing further. His health began to fail; his place in the world of art had long since been eclipsed, and he played no part in the great upsurge of enthusiasm for Aboriginal barks and desert paintings that began in the 1980s and rages to this day. A sketch of Kupka in the last phase of his life was set down in a memoir by his friend Michèle Souef. She was present at his bedside in the Hôpital Cognac-Jay on 14 January 1993, when a team of doctors and nurses came calling, anxiety and compassion in their eyes – but soon, as she describes, they found themselves caught up in conversation with their dying patient. Kupka leaned up on his arm, and outlined for them his last conviction: art, he told them, should not be judged from an aesthetic viewpoint. No, he insisted, fighting for breath: it was nothing more, nor less, than an attempt to communicate. The next day was his last. In his apartment high above the Place Saint-Sulpice a few surviving tokens of his artistic youth were found: a box of paint tubes, a palette and brushes, an empty frame or two, a handful of rough, unfinished portrait sketches, with purple highlights, made during his first trips to Milingimbi mission decades before. Not one work of Aboriginal art remained in his possession: the prince of collectors had kept nothing for himself.

In the first shipment of barks Kupka had brought back with him from Arnhem Land to France, one work stood out in his mind as both the finest and the most unsettling: this was the sorcery bark from Croker Island, which he gave André Breton as a sign of his friendship following the French publication of *Dawn of Art.* It was also very dear to Breton, who loved "these strips of eucalyptus, pollen-dusted," and viewed them as devices that could transport man through time. Indeed, in Breton's eyes this bark was a magic entity, "as discreet as the Mimi spirits of Australian myth, who at the slightest alert breathe on a crack in the rock until it opens to let them pass."

It was one of the jewels in Breton's collection, the dominating, all-consuming centre of his life, a trove of curiosities and wonders without equal in modern times. Breton's studio, filled with masks and surrealist objects, with shells and stuffed animals and tribal carvings, stayed intact for many years after his death, but its contents were eventually sold off, amidst protests, at the Parisian auction house of Drouot-Richelieu. Among the early lots was the sorcery painting of the two spirit figures – the piece which had first opened Karel Kupka's eyes to the potency of Aboriginal art. There was little bidding: as swiftly as a breath, it passed into unknown hands.

# Belief

# I

Even before I went to the middle east, I had spent many hours discussing the Holy Land with various Kimberley friends of mine, who were desert-born and had long since been captivated by the imagery of wilderness they encountered in the pages of the New Testament. Was it sand-dune country over there, like their own, they asked me? Were there many snakes living in the wastes where Jesus underwent his ordeal of forty days and forty nights, and if so what kind; and how exactly did the cloud formations gather and disperse above Bethlehem in the wet season's early days: would I be sure to check? I often promised that I would pay special attention to such questions, and from time to time, during my travels between countries, exchanges like this would come back to me: I would glance out at the harsh landscapes lining the airport freeways, and think back to the sandhills of the western deserts, and the bloodwoods, and the waving pattern of the spinifex.

In quieter spells, if I found myself away from the front-line, in Israel or in Jordan, I sometimes ventured out to ancient ruins or religious sites, and while I made these little explorations I would cast my mind back and try to imagine what might interest that waiting, distant audience: so that much of my immersion in the Bible landscape in those months was through Aboriginal eyes, and whenever I was drawing near some place of Christian pilgrimage, I would feel myself, as if by some fleeting act of magic, returned to the Australian inland. The mountains of Samaria, the ravines of the Jordan rift valley, the coastline of the Dead Sea, the cities of the plain – in my thoughts they all rhymed with the far reaches of the Gibson Desert, and with the gaunt, mirage-torn ranges that lead off from the mid-section of the Canning Stock Route into nothing and the shimmer of the sky.

On many of these biblical excursions, I was careful to take snapshots of the scenery, and I sent these back, in emails, to the Kimberley art centres I knew well, at Turkey Creek or Fitzroy Crossing, marvelling at the incongruity of modern life, that allows one so freely to stitch together worlds and times. Sometimes I would even receive a brief reply, usually with a vast picture file of desert country attached – but as luck would have it, almost always these responses reached me only after long delays, and at moments of tension, in bleak corners of Syria or Iraq. I might be hunched in an internet café, bodyguard at my side, hurrying to transmit some story – or it might be late at night, and I would be leaning halfway out of some back-street hotel window, balancing my satellite receiver on the sill, struggling to keep a signal and turning the angle of its disc to find the best reception, while the wait for the incoming messages stretched on. Then abruptly, there it was on the screen: word from the bush, usually rather peremptory, and including detailed instructions for further pictorial research.

Most often, though, it was Jerusalem that served as backdrop for my forays into the Christian past: each time I was dispatched there I would set off on walks through the old city as soon as my day's reporting tasks were done. Once through the Damascus Gate, the logic of the crowded streets and passages took over: I would find myself heading from busy market squares through run-down, deserted alleyways, past madrasas and monasteries and synagogues arrayed in the most promiscuous confusion alongside each other. There was nothing for it: on those afternoons in old Jerusalem, I resolved to have no aim in mind. I followed my most immediate impulses and inclinations, and almost invariably they were enough to bring me by odd routes to wellknown places: the Via Dolorosa, the Armenian Cathedral, the police fort with its languid throng of taxi-drivers, the gateway to David's Citadel.

But on one of these walks, setting out from the gardens beneath the western fortifications, after several hours in the steep streets of the Jewish quarter meandering between museums and deep excavation digs, I came abruptly on a military checkpoint barring the way. Despite my best intentions, I had strayed too close to the compound of the Al-Aqsa Mosque – the scene, in those months, of frequent protests and confrontations. Suddenly, there was the noise of a crowd, like a wave surging, close ahead;

there was running; voices shouting. I retreated down winding alleys, turning here and there, until I was quite lost. All was silence now, on every side. I noticed, then, an archway set in the stone wall close by me, with a heavy wooden door just ajar. I pushed my way inside and found myself surrounded by the lush, ill-kept beds of a formal garden, choked with flowering jasmines and climbing plants.

*Worshippers,* announced a wooden sign-board, in several languages: *Respect this place: dress modestly: leave all guns and weapons at the entrance.*

Before me rose the flank of an austere church. Its dome was low; its façade was sombre. Beyond this building, the land fell away in a series of embankments, until it plunged down into ruined pits of stonework. There were broken columns, and the remains of stairwells that ended in the air. Indeed, much of this enclosure was made up of cisterns and deep cavities in the ground, across which, at different heights, thin walkways stretched – and only then did I understand that I had come upon a new fragment of the Jerusalem map, though this became clear to me in the most gradual fashion, the way discoveries steal across one in a dream. It was – it could only be – the Church of St Anne, and the Bethesda pool: I had stumbled on a corner of the city linked by the by-ways of tradition with the Virgin Mary and her family home. These were sites that I had longed to see, as much because of the soft sound of their names on the tongue as for their religious charge, and indeed

I had several times set out to find them, only to be defeated by the roadblocks and the labyrinthine turns and dead ends beyond the Wailing Wall. Out of the corner of my eye, as I inspected this lonely spot, I caught sight from time to time of a tall man wearing a white habit, moving somewhat stealthily about, peering on occasion heavenwards. So cryptic and curious was the demeanour of this figure that I was on the point of assuming he was no more than a vague emanation of the buildings, and I was startled when he swerved in his motions and came towards me, perspiring slightly, clutching a green tennis ball in one hand. He greeted me with an air of ecstatic enthusiasm.

"Of course," he inquired, "you are making a pilgrimage?"

"What's that in aid of?" I countered, pointing at the tennis ball.

"Alas," said the man, "it's a long story," and he gave an operatic sigh and produced a card, which he stretched out towards me.

*Fr. Jean Lamourette,* it read: *Missionaries of Africa – White Fathers. P.O.B. 19079 Jerusalem.*

I studied it in silence.

"You have no visiting card?"

"On the whole," I replied, "it's better, in some of the places where I work right now, not to advertise one's identity too much."

"You are surely then a missionary as well!"

"Not exactly."

I explained in greater detail.

"But that makes you almost a social visitor!" declared the priest. "You can't imagine how weary one becomes of religious guests, when one lives here in the holy city. Although, to be truthful, in these days of crisis hardly anyone comes calling on us any more. We must mark the moment. Some tea – something stronger?"

He led me into a sparsely furnished dining room, dominated by a long refectory table. We sat facing each other there, as the cool light, broken by the shade of the jasmines, filtered in. He leaned back; there was an immediate curiosity between us, we began talking, we talked for hours, and though I returned several times, in the months ahead, to the Church of St Anne and became friendly with Lamourette, never did he speak again with the freedom he displayed that afternoon of our first meeting, as he described to me the trajectory which had brought him to Jerusalem at the mid-point of his life.

He was born and raised, he told me, in provincial Quebec, in a religious family. There had not been any uncertainty in his mind about his faith: it had never wavered, it had been as clear to him as the pillar of cloud that led the Israelites from Egypt. How, though, should he fulfil his vocation? What was the precise task the Almighty had laid down for him? While he was still casting about for the answers to these questions, he received an unusual recommendation from a childhood friend of his, who had entered the

Benedictine order, and, as part of his novitiate, had made a brief trip to its most distant outpost: an Australian one.

I smiled a little at this, for I had been developing, as a result of just such coincidences, the thought that a link of some kind existed between the far reaches of the Outback and the country of the Bible, in the way that certain places incessantly call up memories of distant landscapes, to which they seem quite unconnected by either geographic resemblance or historic bonds – and I had come to feel that this pattern of links, like some doubling in nature, endures and even strengthens the longer one refuses to admit its existence.

"Perhaps you yourself," said Lamourette, "with your story, would even know the place: the mission of Kalumburu, in the Kimberley, on the north-west coastline? Perhaps it was that connection that guided your steps here?"

It was one of the few communities in the North that I had not visited. I told him this: he received the news almost as if it was a personal betrayal.

"You must go!" he insisted. "I was a young man when I went there: my life was changed by those experiences."

"It's not a mission any more," I said. "And it doesn't have that great a reputation nowadays."

"Fulfilment," said Lamourette, "lurks in strange locations. I still remember the journey I made there, even though it lies thirty years away in time. How dense and harsh the country was: those twisted, ragged mountains; the unmoving rivers that were no more than pools of standing water; the mocking, turquoise sea! It wasn't the landscape, though, that drew me there."

"What, then?"

"This was a time, remember," he said, his voice somewhat distanced, "when I was still on the brink of committing myself to the missionary life – a path that is not without its rigours. I'd heard about the Spanish monk who served for many years as the Superior of Kalumburu: Dom Serafim Sanz. He was well known, once, he was a commanding personality – though doubtless he died many years ago, and has long since been forgotten. I had heard such wondrous things of him. It occurred to me that I could learn from the example of such a man! You could almost say it was a kind of youthful pilgrimage that I made, in those days, to the farthest corner of the earth, to test myself. I spent months there. I came to know the people of the mission well, and now I look back, I realise I had the sensation, all the while I stayed in Kalumburu, that I was staring into the heart of life."

"And what did you learn?" I asked him.

He shrugged and made a little gesture with both hands, as if to suggest the elusiveness of all inward experience. Then he began to describe the mission, to paint it with his words: its lines, its colours, the folds of the valley, the broken cliffs and crenellations of the ranges all around. I half-closed my eyes, drowsily, as if I could take wing on his breath and travel there, and steep myself in the far North Kimberley, and not return.

"The monks had made it their first task, of course," said Lamourette, "to build a little church: a structure with its own simplicity and elegance. And I still had a young man's fervour; I prayed there, a great deal, seeking for some guidance. Everything made the strongest impression on me: the heat of the day in the buildup season; the smoke plumes from the fires in the bush that burned for weeks on end. I spoke to Sanz, and listened to him, whenever I could claim his attention. He was very fit. He loved arm-wrestling: it was one of the great passions of his youth, in Spain. He used to challenge me to contests: 'Ready?' he would say, and give a little smile, and slam my hand down on the table as if his life depended on it: he beat me every single time. But he loved work above everything: he was a typical Benedictine! He had the dream of building up a cattle station, in hard country on the plateau to the south of Kalumburu, and often I would drive out there with him. There was no road to speak of; no shelter – we slept in swags beneath the stars: they were so clear and close you felt you had to brush them from your eyes. And it was there that Sanz told me about his adventures during wartime, when the mission was attacked by the Japanese Air Force, and several members of the congregation were killed by the bombs dropped at point-blank range. It was very late one evening, when at last I plucked up the courage to put to Sanz the question I had come so far to have answered. I asked him if he felt he had chosen the right path in life: if service among the Aboriginal people had met some need in his heart."

"I think I can guess the reply," I said.

"I wonder! He leaned towards me: I saw his eyes glitter in the light of the fire. He told me that it was not the need of his heart that mattered to him, of course, but God's will. And what he said next determined the path I chose to follow from that day. I remember the exact words: 'It is the intent that God sees, before the act. Even if I had failed to convert a single Aborigine, to save a single soul, I would regard my life as well spent.' We spoke no more that night."

"That's a hard line to take," I said.

"Religion is an extremism. Hasn't being in Jerusalem taught you that? When the morning came, I saw another side of Sanz. He loved exploring through the bush, and seeking out the traces of vanished cultures that had once flourished in that landscape: he was a great aficionado of rock art..."

"I think that's almost a universal condition for missionaries and men of God in the Kimberley," I put in – but Lamourette ignored this and continued, in phrases of mounting sweep and poise, to tell his tale: how the two of them had hiked through the ranges above the Carson River, through gorges and ravines where unknown waterfalls came tumbling down, until they reached a valley, deep, surrounded by red, granitic cliffs. Sanz led the way up, along the flank of a tabletop peak; beneath its crowning mesa was the slightest of overhangs, guarded by white gum trees, and there, cut into the rampart wall, was a piece of rock art unlike anything that Lamourette had seen.

"That country must be full of Bradshaw figures," I interrupted, a touch impatiently. "They're extraordinary the first time you catch sight of them: lithe, precise, mute, mysterious."

"Of course there were Bradshaws. There were so many of them in those rocks we stopped noticing them. And there are the famous Wandjina sites as well, in the stone platforms further south. This was something different. It was a single carving engraved in the hard rock: a human figure, in profile, blurred, as though it was being copied from some distant pattern in the memory – but it was clear at once to my eyes what it was. Ever since, I have described it to myself as the carving of the armoured knight: a man in armour, wearing a helmet and breastplate; I see it now as an emblem, in the harsh world, of enduring faith. Sanz told me he had found it several years before, on a trip along that escarpment – and it was as if someone had guided his path to that very overhang, for how else could he have found it, in all that unending wildness of thorn and rock? We inspected it very closely. To both of us, it seemed old. Who knows what hand placed it there? I used to turn over in my mind whether some lost explorer carved it, or whether it was the last trace of a forgotten empire, some civilisation vanished in the pits of time. But soon enough I realised there were many things about that silent world that I would never know. When we retraced our route, along the valley floors and river channels, we barely spoke; I had the sense that both of us felt crushed, then, by the intensity of being in those ranges. It was hard not to have strong intimations of some presence, some force greater than the purely human, there. Back we drove down the dirt track to Kalumburu. How neat, and clean, and frail the mission seemed, after that spell in the wilderness! The stone buildings set at right angles, the lawns and flowers, the herd of cattle by the lagoon. I was very quiet within myself for several days: I had taken those words from Sanz as a kind of emblem for my life. I wondered, even, if I should stay there, and fulfil my vocation in the North Kimberley, so far from the world I knew. One afternoon, when these internal storms were at their height, I drove out in the truck, alone, to Pago, near the beach where the early settlement was built. The ruins are still there; and beyond them, the coastline, the mangroves and the curve of the bay. You look out, and you seem to look at nothingness: the shape of the low islands in the distance merges with the water and the sky: the view becomes an abstract space. I stayed there until late that evening, turning over many things. I was afraid that pride would always stay with me; that it would prevent me from doing the will of God. I felt life's futility at every turn. I knew I was too weak to help those for whom a hopeless future stretches ahead. I wanted a sign to come to me. There I was, waiting, at the end of the world, unknown, unseen by any eye."

I found it hard not to be affected by this recital, which had gained greatly in pathos as he spoke. In fact Lamourette's voice, by now, was trembling.

"And did any sign come?"

"Of course not!" He laughed, and shook his head. "No! These are modern times. But as the hours passed, I remembered what had brought me to that point in my journey: I saw that self-doubt is itself a form of pride. I remembered the grace in life that balances its bleakness. I trusted once more in forces greater than myself. I was resolved: I was at peace – and then, as I was looking upwards at the strange stars of the southern sky, I saw a point of light."

"A meteor?"

"No – it was a satellite: slow-moving, very brilliant. It passed above me, and I felt singled out."

"Not exactly the most conventional way for a divine message to be passed."

"In this world, where signs of God's presence are so infrequent, I don't think we should rule anything out. But the whole story has become for me a set of symbols and resonances; a parable about finding a true path ahead – otherwise I would never have thought of telling it."

At which point, there were footsteps, hurried, the door was thrown open. A young man appeared, clutching the bloodied carcass of a small, brownish bird, and laid it, without a word, on the wooden slats of the table between us, then took a step back and stared, somewhat reproachfully, down. Lamourette covered his eyes with his hands and let out a groan.

"Not another of these cursed annihilations! Take it away, Yusuf – and give it a Christian burial like all the rest."

"Is that the orthodox approach to animal fatalities here?" I asked, after a few moments.

"We seem to have fallen into a spiral of blood sacrifice," said Lamourette, with a note of drama in his voice. "Come with me."

He led the way out towards the church, outlining as he went in vivid terms the dilemma he confronted: a plague of pigeons, fast-multiplying creatures, had descended on the holy city, and St Anne's, lying as it did so close to the Crusader Wall, with its convenient roosting places, had become one of their favourite spots.

"I know they're unsightly, unappealing birds, but is that really such a disaster?" I asked.

"It isn't their unsightliness that vexes me," replied Lamourette. "Not at all. We find ourselves troubled by a cascade of unintended consequences: of collateral damage, in fact, if truth be told."

"A very Middle Eastern kind of problem," I could not refrain from saying.

"That's not a helpful response! It's unavoidable."

The seeds of this crisis, as he explained, had been sown long before, in the Middle Ages, in fact, when the church was built, with eyelet windows piercing the high reaches of its bare white walls: apertures ideal for avian ingress, and much used by the newly arrived flights of domestic pigeons, which had developed the habit of perching on the broad ledge of the cupola, directly above the altar of the church.

"And it is here that they choose to defecate, of course," Lamourette exclaimed. "I know they are God's creatures – but what acidic excrement they have! The moment it lands, phht! – it burns right through: you have to throw the altar-cloth away. I promise you, there's no humane remedy we haven't tried. I had the idea of disturbing the birds by throwing tennis balls up at their roosting perch – but they know very well how safe they are, so far up and out of reach. I brought in a speaker system and played recordings with the hunting calls of birds of prey – but the calls were from European falcons, and the pigeons didn't recognise them."

"So you had to escalate your reaction? That's the way it always goes."

"It was a dark night of the soul! I could see no alternative to a strategy of pest eradication. You can imagine I don't approve of taking life: I couldn't even kill a chicken. That was when I first heard about a non-lethal solution. I went to a meeting of the churches of the city: we have informal talks, from time to time, about the challenges we face in common. And I learned there that the Franciscans across the valley, in the Church of All Nations, had discovered a chemical technology. Maybe you've heard of it?"

He rummaged in his pocket and produced a little packet, bluish in colour, with a beatific image on it of a sleeping, sleek-winged bird, its long eyelashes closed.

"Tardimon," he said, dramatically. "The answer!"

"What is it?"

"The Arabs use it. It's a stun-poison – it comes from Egypt. It only costs five new Israeli shekels a pack. I've developed a special recipe: a few handfuls of grain, a scatter of the powdered Tardimon, and some good olive oil – to bind the mix together and give it the right consistency."

"And all the churches of Jerusalem are following this route?"

"No – I don't think they would dare use it at the Church of the Holy Sepulchre, with all the pilgrim groups about. They have too many competing religious orders there anyway, and the different factions can never agree on anything. And I believe the White Russians refused, too."

"The White Russians?"

"Don't you know about them? That lovely Russian church that you can see, standing out so prominently with gilded domes, on the slope above the Garden of Gethsemane. It's a very interesting place; I go there, sometimes, when I feel the need for some flash of salvation in life. They don't really approve of Catholics, but they let me in. It's the quintessence of Jerusalem: menace and tranquillity. There's no need for pest control over there, anyway: they're fatalists. We, though, have an obligation to try to preserve life."

"So why isn't it working?"

"It works perfectly: on the pigeons, at least. It puts them to sleep for a while, and it's certainly not a pleasant experience for them: they stagger around, looking distressed, and then they fly away and make their nests elsewhere. I would say it's proved very effective – but it only lasts about four weeks – then fresh birds move in, and you have to repeat. The real problem, though, is with the smaller birds – the sparrows. They're much more susceptible to the effects of the poison. It knocks them out, or they try to fly off but don't have the strength. They flutter about or they're just immobilised, and that leaves me very ill at ease. You see, the cats come to get them."

"The cats?"

"The cats of Jerusalem! They have a banquet – those creatures from the mouth of hell."

"Your love of animals doesn't extend as far as them?"

"I like cats – but these are savage street cats. Surely you must have noticed how fierce they are? You never see a mouse or rat anywhere in Jerusalem: they eat them all. And they eat the sparrows too – they pounce on them. See," – he gestured accusingly over at a thin, grey tabby that was stretched out on the far side of the church portico, sunning itself – "they're waiting, just like vultures: they have come to associate me with death! The harshness of the natural kingdom!"

"I don't know," I said, retreating and trying to choose my words with a degree of care, "that life in a remote Aboriginal community would really have been ideal for you."

"You're going?" said Lamourette. "So soon? Don't be put off by all the blood and slaughter."

I was careful, in a few words, to reassure him on that front, and explain to him that I had other tasks, which went beyond the work of memory.

"Of course," he said indulgently, a touch of sadness coming into his voice. "How close the past is, when we look for it. You almost made me feel that I was back once again in those lost days, standing in the shadow of the trees and peaks, on the edge of the world – at Kalumburu."

***

Some weeks later, after assignments in Iraq, I came back to Jerusalem, and one of my first expeditions took me along the promenade beneath the walls of the old city, down into the Kidron Valley and its tombs. I paused at the walled enclosure of Gethsemane: a row of narrow, green-painted benches had been installed beneath the ancient, twisted olive trees. For much of the afternoon I stayed there, turning over the events I had witnessed in the days just passed, and leaving a space inside myself, to see if some mood or memory from biblical times could still be felt in that spot: some grief, some sense of vigil or nocturnal fear. I walked around the gardens and the religious buildings close by, and allowed my thoughts to roam unchecked. Despite these exalted surroundings, they unfurled down well-worn avenues: recollection, surmise, regret. I was on the point of heading back towards West Jerusalem when my eye was caught by a group of gleaming, gilded domes. I realised that I was near the White Russian monastery, which stands halfway up the mountain slope and looms above the buildings lining the valley floor. On an impulse, avoiding the trinket salesmen and clutches of sadfaced tourist guides, I walked up the steep, narrow road behind the garden, until I reached the wrought-iron monastery gate. It was still open: a handful of pilgrims and black-clad nuns were strolling about. I went in and made my way along a winding path, through the trees, up to a wide courtyard before the church entrance steps. There was a belvedere across Jerusalem: one looked down into the ravine and saw the Jewish tombstones, like a scree of barren, broken rocks upon the hillside, and, beyond them, the Arab houses in the valley, and the fall of the land towards the plains of Israel, and the distant sea. There was something fearful about that view; staring at it felt like falling: too long there would surely pull one over the precipice. I drew away, uneasily, and went into the church and buried myself in the story of its foundation. It was a tale rich in history's familiar reversals: hopes crushed, intentions fulfilled in mocking fashion, the slow, unyielding advance of death and time.

Late in the nineteenth century, during the last years of his long reign, Emperor Alexander III of Russia, a ruler of the most authoritarian instincts, had formed a resolve to commemorate his mother by raising a church in her name in the Holy Land. He put this plan into practice: his agents set out for Jerusalem. The olive groves above Gethsemane were bought, and the church that stands there to this day was built in their midst, and consecrated, in 1888, in honour of the gentlest and most appealing character in the gospel narratives, Saint Mary Magdalene. To preside over the ceremony, the emperor dispatched his brother, Grand Duke Sergei, and the German-born Grand Duchess Elizaveta Fedorovna, who found herself much inspired by the austere landscape and the flash of the new domes against the grey-leaved olive trees. "How I would like to be buried here," she exclaimed on first seeing the prospect from the church across the valley, which was untouched, then, by the marks of war and nation-building. Her experiences in Palestine moved her to convert from the Protestantism of her homeland to the Orthodox faith. When, some years later, her husband was assassinated by a terrorist, the grand duchess decided to withdraw from court society and abandon all worldly concerns. With her fortune, which was considerable, she founded a convent in the heart of Moscow, dedicated to the sister saints, Martha and Mary, and founded upon the twin principles of mercy and love. Those principles, though, were not in the ascendant in the wake of the Bolshevik uprising, and in 1918, the grand duchess, together with her faithful cell attendant, the nun Varvara Yakovleva, was dragged from the monastery, held captive by revolutionary forces and eventually transported to the Ural mountains. Here, in the vicinity of the town of Alapayevsk, together with other members of the royal family, the prisoners were thrown down a deep mineshaft to their death. But this was far from being the end of their displacements. Reports of their fate soon reached White Russian forces, which gained control of the district and were able to retrieve the corpses. For some months the bodies of the victims lay in state in the cathedral of Alapayevsk, until the balance of the civil war turned definitively. The White armies retreated, bearing the slain members of the royal family in their baggage train. They were carried all the way to the south-eastern Siberian town of Chita; from here, across empty steppes, they were transferred to Peking, and thence, by the most circuitous of routes, after further delays and negotiations, two of the coffins – those of the grand duchess and Varvara Yakovleva – were conveyed to the Holy Land. It was 1921 before their remains were at last laid to rest, in the crypt beneath the Church of St Mary Magdalene, and in this tortuous way the wish of Elizaveta Fedorovna, first expressed three decades earlier, was fulfilled.

Sunk in this story, I quite failed to register the presence of a young nun, who was in attendance inside the church, performing her devotions, kneeling before the altar and gazing up towards the icons displayed in their precious frames. After some while, she rose, adjusted the incense-burners, then came towards me.

"It's closing time," she said, "for visitors."

I felt a sudden yearning to stay there, in the low entrance chamber of the church, in the glow of that late, soft light.

"You seem to be a little agitated," she said, and stared at me, frowning a little, her brow furrowed, her expression strengthened by the framing blackness of her veil.

"It's just the normal setting on the dial, Sister," I said.

"Sophia," said she. "Sister Sophia."

"That's a striking name."

"Yes – it was given to me by the abbess."

"And what were you called, before?"

"We leave all that behind, you know," she said, with a look of vagueness, as if she found it hard to remember, and then, more enthusiastically: "Would you like to pray?"

"You were just praying a moment ago."

"That's true: we do a lot of praying here. We pray for the world, constantly, to ward off its fate. 'Watch and pray,' we tell ourselves. But I didn't really mean me: I meant you. I thought you might like to pray alongside someone."

We knelt down; I closed my eyes. A silence ensued. Folds of colour drifted across my darkened field of vision. There were birdcalls in the trees outside; the noises from the city filtered in.

"I'm afraid it's not really working for me, Sister," I said, after a few minutes.

"Truly? It was fantastic for me. I love praying beside other people, especially if they have good souls. I find it gives me freshness, and strength."

She had a Bostonian accent, which was becoming more noticeable as we spoke on.

"You don't sound very Russian," I said.

"Being Russian isn't an entry requirement of the Russian Orthodox Church," she replied, a touch reprovingly.

"So then – how did you find your way here?"

At this question, Sister Sophia stood up, in rather regal style, and began walking round the church, preparing for the evening service, letting fall, in the midst of this activity which she performed with gestures of the utmost ease and grace, a detail or two about the shaping moments of her life, and I made attempts to answer her with brief stories of my own. Soon, as this exchange, which was tentative in the extreme, drew on, the light began to shift: we went outside and watched the mauve haze of sunset spread across the horizon, and I pieced together the fragments of her tale. It seemed marked by spasms of the most baroque disaster – deep sicknesses, nightmare car crashes, all of which Sister Sophia had learned, in retrospect, to read as so many urgent, prompting signals from the divine. After much questing and searching, and fruitless study of the world's most recondite religions, at the very moment when she stood upon the verge of entry into the race of life, she visited an Orthodox church and encountered an abbess, whose influence guided her. And then it was as if a strong wind began blowing, deep inside her being: she was swept onto a new path, she felt chains lifting away.

"You were free?"

"It was simply that I realised: I wanted knowledge of the truth. Not the surface knowledge that flows freely and cheaply through the world – I wanted reality."

"And everyone who doesn't follow a religious life is lacking reality?"

"I'm sorry to say so, yes! And there's something about being here, in the holy city. Don't you feel it? A special atmosphere: a sense of calm that reaches into you."

"I find it troubling and oppressive," I said. "In fact, when I'm walking through the old city, and catch that mood of bleakness that it has, I sometimes imagine that all the crimes and horrors of the world began here, and they're still radiating and spreading outwards."

Sister Sophia listened to this outburst with an even, slightly pained expression.

"My experience has been the opposite," she said. "If you stay here, things start coming out. Your power becomes unhidden, it becomes re-vealed: all the passions and emotions that you've hidden in your life."

"Really?"

"Really. The deepest emotions."

Even as she said this, she swooned and swayed back beside me, before recovering herself.

"Forgive me," she said. "I didn't get much sleep: that's one of the drawbacks of deep meditation and nocturnal prayer. And I have low blood sugar – ever since ... ever since an incident, some while ago, in Jericho. My pulse sometimes just seems to fade away."

I reached over to her wrist, which she had raised up demonstratively, as if to check it. She pulled her hand away from my touch, rubbing it gently, as though it had just undergone some faint contamination, and smiled.

"That's kind of you," she said. "But it's not really recommended. I am a nun, you know. And this is a convent. We endure intrusions from the outside, rather than welcoming them."

I said nothing, and allowed this crushing remark to echo in my thoughts. Sister Sophia stood up, hands clasped, and surveyed me.

"There's something I'd like to show you," she said. "Before you go. Something that comes from your part of the world. It's in my cell."

"Your cell!"

"Yes – what did you think? That we have luxury accommodation? Wait here a moment. Ping will keep you company."

"And who exactly is Ping?"

"The monastery cat – right there." She pointed to a large, indolent-looking grey cat, which had been moving stealthily about, much like a small-scale version of a stalking panther, all through this conversation.

"I bet he's killed a few sparrows in his time," I said.

"What a dreadful thought," said Sister Sophia. "We feed him well. Don't we?"

The cat approached, purring beatifically.

"Anyway, Ping's fifteen years old: I think his hunting days are over."

She turned and went down the winding path, holding her habit to her body, breaking after a few steps into a light, skipping, bird-like run. I let my eyes rest on the domes and spires across the valley. The routines and patterns of my life hung before me in those silent seconds: they seemed like arcane shapes in some strange script. Soon Sister Sophia was back, panting slightly and holding in one hand a small square of canvas, wooden-framed, no larger than a hard-backed book.

"Surprised?" she said. "It's a painting!"

She was beaming: she gazed down at the canvas, then lifted it up and held it close before her eyes.

"It's an image that's come to mean a great deal to me. I stare at it, and travel into it; I can get lost in it for hours. It was given to me by an abbess, and she was given it by one of her sisters, who travelled very widely. I keep it on the mantelpiece, next to my icon of Saint Nicholas. And that's a real place of honour."

She fell silent an instant, then began reciting in a low voice: "Oh blessed Nicholas, show compassion to me who fall down praying to thee; and enlighten the eyes of my soul, O wise one, that I may clearly behold the Light-Giver and Compassionate One..."

"I'm afraid I don't know very much about icons, Sister," I said.

"But this isn't an icon! It's a landscape. I call it 'The Promised Land' – it's like an image of paradise for me, an austere and lovely paradise, and I've always longed to find out what it shows: where it really is. Maybe you can help. All we know is that it came from northern Australia."

"That's quite a large area," I said. "Would you actually go and make a visit, if you could pin it down? I thought everyone agreed that paradise wasn't a place on Earth."

"It's just to know. Remember, we like knowledge."

She stared down at the little canvas with a slight, appraising frown, then spun it lightly with her fingertips, until the painted image was facing me.

"So," she said. "Do you recognise it?"

I looked at the painting. I laughed, and smiled. I felt a slight pressure at the corners of my eyes. I glanced away. It was a Kimberley horizon – red ranges, sand, bright flowers, the blue vault of dry-season sky.

"I know the artist," I said, "and I know the place – I know both of them well."

"I was sure of it: I had an intuition. I understood, the moment you walked into our church, that your steps were being guided: that there was something you were sent to give us."

"God's will in action?"

"We see signs of it everywhere: we can tell: a whisper on the wind; a gleam inside the light."

"I would have to say, Sister, it was pure coincidence that brought me here."

She looked at me with wide, sad eyes.

"There are never coincidences that seem full of meaning in your life? It's all just the movements of colliding atoms? Even this?"

Her voice softened: she drew one hand across the surface of the canvas.

"Perhaps there are times," I said, "when life's course seems to take on a shape and definition, and chance cues point you in a certain way: when memories rise up and lead you back to times you've lived through, or people far away whom you know and love – or even stretches of country that live inside your heart. Of course I often think that: it would be inhuman of me not to – and maybe this is such a time."

I took the little canvas in my hands. In a few words, I sketched the story of the painting for her. It was by Daisy Andrews, an artist from Fitzroy Crossing, whose works, which are much sought after, always depict a single landscape: blood-coloured ranges that rise up sharply like domes, shimmering in the desert light. They show the country known as Lumbulumbu – obscure, ill-charted, lying beyond easy reach, down bush tracks on the fringes of the Sandy Desert. For Daisy, a woman of Walmajarri parentage who was born in exile on the banks of the Fitzroy River, close by old Cherrabun Station, this has always been a landscape with special resonances, though she had not even seen it when she made it the chosen and constant subject of her work, and years later, when I travelled in her company out to those silent ranges, the voyage proved almost too much for her to bear.

"I wish you would tell me the story of the painting – and that journey."

"I don't think you'd thank me," I said. "It's a fairly dark story."

"You believe we don't have any dark stories, of grief and betrayal, here? We're in the Garden of Gethsemane: that's the reason why I want to know."

"It's not exactly a Christian painting," I tried.

"Please!" said Sister Sophia, clasping her hands together tightly in annoyance.

I began, in cautious fashion, with the familiar, despairing sense that the bush escapes all capture in the net of words. I tried to portray that stretch of desert: its look, its changes between dawn and dusk, the shifting moods that it conveys. Daisy herself, as well: how I first met her and heard her often talking of her country, and how the idea of making a brief trip back there took hold in her thoughts. It was early one dry season, after long months of planning and scheming, when at last I drove in to Fitzroy, collected my friend Karen Dayman, who was still in those days the co-ordinator at the Mangkaja Arts Centre, and picked up Daisy and her companion for that journey, her fellow-artist Dolly Snell. We headed off at speed and made our way through station country, driving south, until the range systems of the backland loomed ahead. They were purple, and bare of vegetation: their cones and fluted cliffs rose sheer from the plain. We passed by broken windmills and the gaunt remains of abandoned stockyards: the sandhills and the yellow patterns of spinifex began to show. Daisy was singing to herself by now, and launching into long exchanges with Dolly in Walma-jarri language: the two of them were side by side in the back seats, pointing eagerly out through the windows of the troop carrier at stray lizards or incautious bush turkeys – and it was only towards sunset, after we had crossed a set of stony desert watercourses, that the ladies at last fell quiet. There was a line of peaks, running westwards.

"Lumbulumbu," said Daisy, in a low voice.

I glanced in the rear-view mirror, and saw her lovely face, and her eyes wet with tears. That night, we camped in the shadow of a low mesa. Karen and I walked slowly up its flank and watched the last traces of the sun fading from the sky, and she told me the story of the ranges, and something of what had happened there. Daisy's beloved cousin-brother, Boxer Yancar, had been brought to that country often as a child by his family. Late one afternoon, the youngest children were swimming with their parents in the deep, shaded waterhole, when a party of white stockmen from a far-off station came riding up. The horsemen were moving along the creek line, suddenly there was shooting – it was an ambush, the sound of the bullets echoed between the rocks. Boxer ran to hide beside his grandmother; they crouched down together in the spinifex; before his eyes his father fell to the ground: the waterhole turned red with blood. The white men rode off again; there were bodies, dead and wounded, lying everywhere; one of the children had been thrown alive onto the fire.

"That story made a great impact on Daisy," said Karen. "Boxer Yancar, who only died recently, told me about those days often. He was a delightful man: I miss him very much."

I spent a sleepless night in my swag, tracking the stars in their motions, and the sweep of the Milky Way across the sky. At dawn, I saw Daisy sitting alone, cross-legged before the fire. I went over to her. We spoke about her memories of life as a girl at Cherrabun Station: the day she saw the Japanese bombers come over, low, during wartime; the time she started painting, on paper, at the school in Fitzroy Crossing; all the triumphs of her artistic life. The sun came up; the desert finches twittered; the crickets began their hum.

"I just sit and think, when I paint," said Daisy to me after a few moments. "In all my paintings, I'm thinking about Lumbulumbu, about these mountains – and when I paint them, it makes me happy, and sad at the same time, for the memory. And you can see now: I'm painting it the way it is – red, and the blue sky, and flowers, everywhere: purple, and pink – and the rocks, and the grass. Beautiful, good country – but it makes me sad at heart, to think of all the old people who were living there."

The hours stretched away; we drove on, further towards the desert, until I pulled up beside a creek bed that ran towards the ranges and asked Daisy if she wanted to go closer in: to visit the waterhole once again.

"I see it always in my mind," she said, and made a sign to drive on, and buried her head in her hands. "Keep going," she said. "Keep going; I don't need to walk in there."

"And that's it?" said Sister Sophia. "That's the story of the painted paradise – my promised land?"

I felt her eyes resting on me: they were wide, and framed in the half-light in dramatic fashion by her jet-black veil. The church bell began ringing just then for the evening service. Its sound shook and trembled in the air.

"I could tell you much more in the same vein," I said. "A hundred other stories. Of course it doesn't change the painting: and there are many people who like to think that life in the desert country, in those days, before the Europeans came, was a paradise: a hard paradise – and they believe it's that time that Daisy is remembering in her art. But after I knew that story, I must say I found it more and more difficult to look at those paintings of hers and not remember what had happened, Sister – in that Eden you're holding in your hands."

# II

Several months went by after these encounters in Jerusalem, but in my thoughts they stayed vivid, marked out as they were, against life's haze and murk, by the bright, seductive gleam of coincidence. And it was at least in part at the prompting of these memories that I made plans, soon after I came back from the Middle East, to travel from Darwin to the Kimberley and see the Fitzroy River valley and my friends there once again. I took the Air North flight across to Broome one morning, then headed eastwards into the glare of the day. The familiar landmarks came and went: the river bridge at Willare, the roadhouse, the lone boab beside the Derby turn. I counted down the station sidetracks: Camballin and Ellendale, Quanbun and Noonkanbah. The road ahead had little traffic, and what there was came towards me in satisfying rhythm: caravans, ancient troop-carriers loaded with Aboriginal families, Greyhound buses, ore trucks wavering across the centreline. There was the way into Windjana, and the gorges, and Leopold Downs: the flanks of the Oscar Range began to glow before me in the afternoon sun. Throughout the last hour of that journey, I had the sense of brushing through a thick, resistant curtain, back into the landscape and the country, while a dreamlike, insubstantial tone now seemed to colour all my recollections of the year that I had spent away.

It was twilight by the time I drew near to Fitzroy Crossing and made out its traces across the green plain. I picked out the water tower, the service stations on the edge of town, the lights and powerlines. I could just make out the old mission compound in the distance, and, close by, the sweep and jumble of houses at the community of Junjuwa. At last I pulled up at the supermarket car park: the door to the Mangkaja Arts Centre was open; the pale fluorescent strip lights were still on.

At her desk, in her favourite attitude, staring into some unseen middle distance, was Karen Dayman, surrounded by the remains of a busy day of meetings. She glanced up at me distractedly: her expression, as always, was one of calm amazement, as though the mere texture of life in Fitzroy was cause enough for wonder at the world's intricacy and depth – and, as always on seeing her after a long interval, I looked at her in admiration: how beautiful she still was; how little, in the decade I had known her, she had changed: and yet the marks of time, and the lash of the Fitzroy climate, the unyielding pressure of its build-up season, its scouring dry-season winds and fiery sun had all stamped their signs upon her: they were etched like a patina into her face, so that the nature of that face's elegance had slowly altered: its beauty had become a commentary on the idea of beauty, it spoke of time, and fondness for the past, and an acceptance of its own end: those aspects completed it, and lent Karen a remote, unassailable quality, as if she was becoming increasingly immured within herself, hemmed in by her mounting awareness of man's fate. Many of these themes hovered in the margins of our conversation, once we had exchanged greetings and felt the shock of closeness that comes when friendships are picked up afresh.

The talk ranged far and wide, and much of it was sparked by the paintings piled up in loose rolls on the trestle table next to her, or stretched out in various stages of progress on the floor. There had been illnesses among the artists; there had been deaths as well. Karen told me about the recent funeral of an old woman she had felt especially close to, and the thoughts that came to her over the succeeding days. It had become clear to her, she said, that the time was drawing close when she would have to leave Mangkaja, which had been the heart and centre of her life, and that soon her oldest friends among the artists, who had sat with her for so long, cross-legged, painting, unfurling new worlds of thought and splendour before her eyes, would not be there. A new chapter lay ahead, of retrospect: she would be called on to record her experiences and paint in words the lives of the artists she loved most. Karen had already begun thinking, with some dread, about the monograph that she would have to write, devoted to the bestknown painter from the river country, Butcher Cherel Janangoo, whose health was failing – and to that end she had just made a visit to the nearby station, Fossil Downs, where Butcher had worked as a stockman many years before.

"Do you know that place?" she asked me, and went on, rapidly, in a light voice, with the details of her story – but my thoughts, for a moment, lagged behind. Fossil, the Central Kimberley's oldest and most celebrated station, stands just outside the modern site of Fitzroy, on a bluff close by the Margaret River's broad and sandy bed. The gate into its grounds is marked by a stone pillar bearing the heraldic emblem of the MacDonalds, the family that established the land holding in the late nineteenth century's pioneering days. The main house, which has the air of a country palace in the Veneto, is approached down an alley of boab trees, and is flanked on both sides by rows of out-buildings, all of them, including the grader shed, painted a delicate blush-pink. Like the other long-established homesteads of the Fitzroy Valley, Fossil is invisible from the highway and rarely seen by outside eyes: and yet its history is woven into that of Fitzroy Crossing, its mood and tone affect the town, it exhales a mingled breath of pride and sadness that seems to spread, like a hidden plume of radiation, following the winding channel of the river downstream, slowly, persistently, until it loses its definition in the muddy waters of King Sound.

I listened, as Karen described her visit to the Fossil homestead and the lengthy research trip she had gone on to make with Butcher, out to Imanara, his birthplace, during the year that I had been away: the pair of them had travelled north-east from Fitzroy, down remote, half-remembered tracks, following what they could piece together of old ceremonial trails. During those days she had seen peaks and gorges she knew only from the paintings of her artists; she had penetrated deep into the back country of Bedford Downs and Tablelands, underneath the spine of the King Leopold Range. It had been a time of joy and fascination – but both she and Butcher had been unable to rid their thoughts of the secret purpose behind the expedition: they knew it was the last time that he would be strong enough to travel through that landscape and read its hidden features with his eyes.

"And Daisy?" I asked.

"The beauty queen? She's been ill, too," said Karen, almost vengefully. "In fact, you're lucky to find her still alive. You know, if you go away, the worst thing tends to happen. You'll find her down the road, at Junjuwa – or she still comes here, sometimes, in the mornings. It's been a dark year or two for her: her husband passed away not long ago; and Elizabeth, her daughter, whom she loved very dearly, whom she saw, I used to feel, as a continuation of herself, and who looked so like her, died as well, and after that funeral Daisy mourned for a long time, very deeply. Then she fell ill herself. She's quite weak now: she's had a series of operations."

"For what?"

"She'll explain, I'm sure. She's been back in Fitzroy a few weeks now. It's been an interesting time: I find myself often thinking of the days, long ago, when she and I were down in Perth together and she was painting the sets for that production of *Alcina* – do you remember that?"

"The opera? I suppose it was quite an appropriate choice for a Walmajarri set designer – all that love magic."

"Exactly – although I think Daisy was more interested by the idea of the enchanted island in the story – and she painted river scenes, rivers running through forests and through red range country, and it looked like the landscape round old Cherrabun Station to me. She dreamed a great deal then, and she used to tell me about her dreams – and these days that's started happening again. Almost every time she comes in she has more dreams: great, arching dreams that take in everything: her family, the Broome supermarket and post office, the creation of the world. She had a dream, too, just around the time of her medical dramas, and it was so striking I made sure to remember it, even though I usually forget the details of hers at once, almost as if they're my own."

"And what happened, in that dream?"

"There's a boab tree," said Karen, "just outside her house, and its seed came from the country around Lumbulumbu, where we went with her. And when she collapsed on the pavement in Perth, and fainted away, and was rushed to hospital, she went into a dream-state. She was aware of standing in the shade of that boab and looking up at its highest branches, but her daughter came to her and told her she couldn't go yet, it wasn't her time, she had to stay – and then there was a break in the dream's flow, as if the scene had changed, and she saw her daughter once again, flying gently in the air and strewing the white flowers of the boab tree all over the country around Junjuwa. Isn't that the most beautiful, haunting dream-story?"

"If you have to have a near-death experience," I said, "that's probably the kind to have. And what did it mean?"

"That's just typical of you! It was a beautiful dream in itself – apart from the meaning. And that was the meaning!"

"That life is precious?"

"The meaning is the dream," said Karen, ill-concealing her displeasure at this continued quest for literalism. "More and more, I feel desert people are put here to have our dreams for us, and tell them to us, and keep our hearts alive. And with every day that passes, I feel grateful to know them, and grateful to have lived with them so long."

\*\*\*

When morning came, I drove out to the Crossing Inn and down a sidetrack to a lookout that catches the morning sun. I watched the water in the main channel, far below the sandy bank, churn by; cockatoos were shrieking in the white gums; an eagle wheeled overhead. For some while I stayed there, until the landscape's scale and silence had emptied all my thoughts, and I was barely present to myself – and I remembered, as I drove on, the time when I was first making my way through that landscape, and abstract reveries of this kind would swoop down on me and last for hours and days on end. I swung back, past the Inn, down old short cuts, along the airstrip road, by schools and run-down houses, until I reached the rutted turn to Junjuwa. There, little had changed. Near the entrance to the community, a morning card game was in progress, under the branches of an ex- iguous shade-tree. I circled round and soon found Daisy, sitting alone, on a broken-backed chair on the concrete veranda of her house. She was wearing a black lace dress of extreme elegance and a black bandana around her neck; her face, framed by her long straight hair, was tranquil; her hands were rest- ing on her knees.

"My boy," she said, softly, and made a sign to me to pull up a chair beside her.

I glanced about: there was a large, half-wrecked hospital bed marooned in the front yard, and next door a couple of green plastic seats in advanced stages of disintegration. I selected one of these, brought it across and leaned back.

"I was thinking to myself," said Daisy, "when's he going to come? He's been away too long."

I began explaining: she cut me off. "Too long," she said, in a stricken voice, "too long, too long."

I felt the right time had come to proffer the dress I had bought as a present for her. It was purple- coloured, and decorated with large bluish tropical birds. Daisy glanced at it, nodded in seigneurial fash- ion and stowed it beside the bag at her feet.

"What now?" she said, after a long, dramatic pause. "I've been dying," she went on. "I died, and then came back."

"I heard," I said, taking her hand, pressing it tight and feeling a stab of overwhelming sadness.

Daisy looked at me – a wry, measuring look.

"People go away too long," she ventured, after a further silence. "And never come back."

"You look wonderful," I said, in a vague bid to shift the subject.

"I knew you were coming."

"You heard from Karen, at Mangkaja?"

"No. I knew. That's why I put this dress on."

"It's fantastic. And the pink espadrilles, too."

Daisy glanced down at her long, stick-thin legs, and swung them out, and inspected her brand-new shoes.

"I was a good-looking woman, once," she said.

"You still are. The best-looking woman in Fitzroy Crossing. You always will be. Karen and I call you the beauty queen."

Daisy, at this, smiled, and the air of inwardness that had mantled her since the beginning of the conversation dissipated. She began, in a low voice, talking about the bush and her childhood, and the youth of her parents, and the journey they had made, north, from the desert country of the Canning Stock Route, to rockholes with sonorous Walmajarri names, until they reached as far as Lumbulumbu.

"And they were having their own ceremonies there, and everything; they killed bullocks at the waterhole, and then they waited there, for all the other people to come in. And that's when the stockmen came to get them: they came from Christmas Creek, with guns – they were killing all the old people."

Daisy was leaning forward now: she was frowning; her hands were clenched.

"I know," I said. "That story's become famous. In fact I even saw one of your pictures of that country while I was away."

I told her, in a few words, about my experiences in the Russian monastery: I described the church, and Sister Sophia, and the dreams and bitter fate of the grand duchess. Daisy nodded and gave some thought to this episode of foreign violence, and to the international dissemination of her work, then went on talking, very quietly, almost whispering, so I had to lean towards her. Eventually she adopted the expedient of murmuring into my ear, one hand to her lips, as though recounting a great secret. She was describing Boxer, her cousin-brother, at the waterhole: his fear, his flight, his feelings, all caught so vividly they sounded like her own: "Run away, get away, that's what he was saying, that's what he told me."

She copied his voice; she mimed his boyish gestures – then she sighed. "That's why I can't leave that place. That's why I always paint that place. Because my brother Boxer told me. I think of it, and the story, I can see it all the time, I'm looking at it in my mind."

At last she leaned back. The scene switched to Cherrabun Station and her childhood; her brief schooldays, and then her move to Moola Bulla, the old native reserve, which lay in lush pastoral country just west of Halls Creek.

"I never knew you went there," I said.

"You want to see me, what I looked like, when I was young?"

"Of course."

"There's a photo of me from there. It looks like my daughter."

"Who took it?"

"Some old white man: it's at Mangkaja right now. Karen has it on the wall beside her desk. And it was at Moola Bulla that I met my husband."

Daisy smiled. The tale swirled on; then, with a sharp, savage motion of the hand, she brought it to an end.

"My husband's gone. My daughter's gone – I'm still here."

She gazed straight ahead, and went on speaking, evenly: "For a long time, after I was sick, I stayed in Perth. Then, when I came back from hospital, I couldn't do anything. I was crying all the time; my heart was broken. And I had three operations – look!"

She pulled the bandana round her neck to one side: there was a pale vertical line above her throat.

"And here," – she pulled open her dress: operation scars, with stitch-marks running evenly along them, covered her chest. She took my hand again.

"I wish we could go back there once again, to Lumbulumbu – all together, just like before – me and Dolly, and Karen and you. Something about that place is calling me back. I haven't been there for a long time now, and it's calling me back there. I hear the voice."

"And what does it say?"

Daisy turned, and rested her deep, liquid eyes on mine, and held my gaze: "It's telling me – the same thing for everyone. There's a place that calls, for everyone. We'll all be laid out there, like sticks of firewood. You'll hear the voice calling, one day, in your life: and it says the road is coming to an end."

\*\*\*

After some while, I drove back into town and called in again at Mangkaja. The familiar bush art-centre atmospherics had descended: the studio room was full. Old desert men in ancient hats were reclining in the tattered armchairs, watching grainy, hand-held footage of dances and ceremonies, while their wives sat close by and leafed through the piles of illustrated exhibition catalogues. Little knots of tourists ghosted about in their midst from time to time, smiling politely, examining the artworks in desultory, faintly embarrassed fashion. On the concrete veranda just outside the door, tiny children were at play, pushing prams about, giving occasional percussive howls. The phones were ringing out; the air conditioners wheezed in soporific rhythm. Karen was at her desk, surrounded by a throng of artists; a diary-book, its pages covered by neat hieroglyphs and complex arrowed messages, lay open before her. It was some hours before this human tide abated. I gained her attention.

"The photograph," she said. "What photograph? There are hundreds of photos of artists, you know that. What's come over you, anyway – you've become extremely visual since you went away. Why were you sending back that stream of picture files from the Middle East? Just because of the biblical associations?"

"Were they a success?" I asked her.

"Initially, of course, yes: people like to feel as if they're in your thoughts – but after the first few hundred, I'd have to say I think the interest began to tail off. The ones that seemed popular were the images of deep desert country – I don't think there was that much excitement about churches or mosques."

I allowed this summary to sink in.

"Perhaps," said Karen, "you're talking about the Tindale photo? I thought you'd seen it before."

"Tindale the anthropologist? I didn't realise he was a photographer." "Tindale was everything: not just a photographer, but a code breaker, a map maker, a butterfly collector. He even lost an eye to photography, when there was a gas explosion while he was helping his father take pictures: that was what decided him against becoming a professional entomologist. It would be hard, really, don't you imagine, to specialise in little flying insects when you're half blind. But he loved cameras: right from the start, he photographed and classified all his informants, and he drew up detailed genealogical records. They've become quite well known now in the Kimberley: people consult them all the time. He must have been travelling though this country just after the end of the war, when Daisy was taken away from Cherrabun and moved over to the reserve at Moola Bulla."

Karen reached down into one of her desk's drawers, produced a file and leafed through it. She found the picture; her eyes softened. "Wasn't she beautiful," she murmured dreamily, almost to herself.

"She still is," I said. "Beauty doesn't die. Sometimes it doesn't even fade: it simply changes in state."

"Yes, I know that proposition's become very important to you, over the years. But why? Are you hanging on to the only good thing you see in the world? Are you turning into an aesthete, or something? Of course beauty fades: it's a human attribute: it lives in time, and in time it tarnishes and dies. Let me tell you about it!"

As she delivered this little sally, Karen gave me a particularly swan-like, sidelong glance. I felt we were getting into contentious terrain. I stretched out a hand; she passed across the file. The image it contained was black and white, printed on fine photographic paper with a glossy sheen. Daisy was posed, almost in the style of a prisoner, eyes staring straight ahead. She was sitting, wearing a black and white striped mission dress, her black hair neatly combed to one side, her thin arms held before her, her hands wrung together between her knees. Her face had its familiar, ethereal perfection. Her expression, though, was the striking thing: it was hurt, and candid; self-contained, and trusting; troubled, and abashed. In it lay all the grace and sweetness of the desert world, revealed, spread out before the viewing eye – and the gaze of the camera, even decades after it had fallen on her, still held the force and potency of gunshot, anatomising, pulverising all it saw.

*＊＊*

I spent the next days on the road alone, in an attempt to leach away the more disquieting memories of my Middle Eastern sojourn and fill myself with the desert's sights and sounds. I drove out on the highway to Halls Creek, then south, on the broad track that leads to Billiluna and Balgo, through subtle, elusive hill country which seems to merge in fine gradations into the horizon and the sky. During the long, humid afternoons, I would pull up and rest for hours in the shade of old station buildings, or explore the workings of abandoned mines. When darkness fell, the gleam from the moon and stars picked out the bloodwoods and the stands of burnt grevillea in the landscape and gave them the air of armies invading by the stealth of night. One morning, early, I came upon a side road that leads down a corridor between sand dunes towards Mount Bannerman – a track so faint one's eye loses it for kilometres at a stretch, until driving becomes an exercise of pure imagination and it almost seems as though the best efforts of one's will are necessary to conjure the path back into life. After some days in that landscape of sandstone bluffs and salt lakes, trying to align my thoughts with the country and its chords and echoes, I retraced my steps. I camped at Carranya ruins, and walked, late in the afternoon, across to the meteorite crater at Wolfe Creek, and watched the sun setting on its jagged rim, its rays blazing fiery red, in much the way that it might set on the last day of time. When, exhausted, half-starved, I completed this bush escapade and turned back onto the bitumen of the Great Northern Highway, it was mid-evening. I sped back to Fitzroy, and, on the whim of the moment, checked into the Lodge just outside town – a curiously designed hotel, elevated, built almost entirely on a structure of steel girders, with the result that even at the best of times it seems to be swaying gently, as though its elevation had set it out of true with the motions of the earth below. The main channel of the river runs to one side, flanked by tall, spreading gums, while to the east, beyond the caravan bays and powered camping sites, the country of Fossil Downs stretches away.

Morning came. I woke in my hotel room from a run of broken dreams, and made my way in to the reception, a vast hall with the air of a military commissariat, dominated by masterpieces of Daisy Andrews that depict the red ranges and the white trees along the creeks at Cherrabun. The front desk was besieged by throngs of tourists clamouring for attention. I found an unoccupied corner of the breakfast room and watched my fellow guests eating through their meals of eggs and grilled sausages, and, after so many days in the silence of the landscape, hearing only the whispers and the secrets of the air, I contemplated once more the noise and sword-clash of human life. It was the transition: it was inevitable: it was as wrenching as every time. Just as I passed the order counter, I noticed that a lavishly framed historical panel had been hung since my last visit, alongside the collection of faded, glass-covered photographs from the early station days. This panel told, in distinctly heroic manner, the life story of Maxine Mac-Donald, the celebrated chatelaine of Fossil Downs.

Maxine was a glamorous air hostess, who married the heir to Fossil and transformed the station into the Versailles of the North, awash with parties, incidents and intrigues, and I had already heard several tales from those hectic days – but a passing knowledge of the Fossil saga was not enough to prepare me for this ornate feast of narrative. It began with the basics: "Born 27 January 1914" – but very quickly the author rose up to the heights, and it was hard not to wonder who this stylist of the Central Kimberley might be, so florid were the tropes of the account, so lush the profusion of its images. At times, it was terse, even sharp; at times, it lost itself in ambiguities. Its grammar was vague; it hinted at tragic depths; it struck, at several moments, a strange, off-key bush sublime. "It may take a few years," the anonymous author mused at one point in his tale, "for us to understand the genius of Maxine" – although the significance of Fossil itself, as a "monument to courage, which had given hospitality to prince and pauper alike" was already plain. "Maxine's love for that hot, sometimes drowned, sometimes burnt, seldom peaceful crust of earth is a part of her soul. A generation of youngsters, weaned from their homes in the south, started their careers on Fossil and fell under Maxine's spell. She became their second mother, and taught them it was possible to live, to rear a family on such an unforgiving stage as the Kimberley, without becoming heartless stereotypes." I read on, caught by the tale, right through its dewy version of the chatelaine's ties with the Aborigines of Mudludja outcamp, until it reached its peroration, replete with the most alarming grace notes: "Maxine," it ended, "endured half a century of Mother Nature's wild objection to human presence on her Kimberley estate..."

These words, with their threatening rhythms, reverberating inside me, I took my seat beneath the grainy photographs of fencing teams and bogged bullock drays and consumed a plate of leaden eggs, and bacon that seemed coated with the concentrated salts of the Dead Sea, before heading off to check out and travel on, towards Kununurra and Turkey Creek.

"Hello, stranger!" came, at that instant, a voice, at once warm and piercing, from the far side of the Lodge's entrance hall. A woman, keen-eyed, with blonde hair cut to shoulder length, wearing clothes of high bush chic, surrounded by an array of expensive suitcases, stood at the door. Susan Bradley, the mistress of Doongan Station, the queen of the Kimberley, a woman whose network of intimacies and friendships, of convolutions and connections, spanned every last inch of terrain from Broome to Kununurra, stared me up and down.

"You look awful," she pronounced after a few moments. "That year away didn't do you any good! Do you want to drive up with me to Kalumburu? I'm setting off right now."

"I can't think of anything I'd like to do more," I said, catching at once the rhyme with Father Lamourette, and feeling exceptionally light-headed, as though a shape was declaring itself inside my life.

"I'll only be a second — I'll just go and get my things."

"Goodness!" exclaimed Susan.

"What's the matter?"

"Well, it is the remotest Aboriginal community in Australia, and I don't know you all that well — I didn't think you'd say yes. I'll have to rearrange everything: it's lucky I always expect the unexpected!"

She went outside, leaving me, with a faint directional nod to show that I should carry down her cases. Outside, parked in the driveway, was a lavishly accessorised Landcruiser, metallic grey, its roof glinting in the sun. She opened its rear door and began shifting a set of leather trunks and large picnic hampers about. We drove off. The hawks wheeling in the air above the town receded; the plain stretched away. Once I had replied to, or parried, her first fusillade of questions, Susan speeded up a little and produced a pair of white cotton gloves. With elaborate, almost pantomime gestures, she put them on, lifting first one hand then the next from the wheel.

"They're very formal for the Kimberley," I said.

"You can never be too formal," she replied, very firmly. "Civilisation, here, hangs by a thread. I must say I'm always pleased to see the back of Fitzroy Crossing."

"It does feel as though it's in a down phase just now," I said, cautiously. "But there's still a kind of vigour here and there, if you know where to look for it."

"I know Fitzroy very well," said Susan, with a touch of indignation. "Much better than you, I'd imagine."

"How come?"

"I lived in Fitzroy for years – or rather with Maxine, at Fossil. I saw you reading that strange history placard they've just put up in the Lodge's dining room. Do you want to hear the real version?"

Susan was a superb narrator – she gave herself fully to her performances. They were operatic, full of abrupt ascents and savage reversals of fortune – and even the most obscure detail, which seemed at first flung out as a pure piece of colour, would be braided into the denouement of the plot, and lend its particular frisson to the outcome – so much so that her listeners often longed for her to repeat a story she had told before, and when this happened, they were well placed to study the storyteller's art and spot the zones of the narrative that were improvised and those that formed the core of her accounts.

"I'd love to hear it," I said. "You know everyone talks about your stories."

I settled back; she accelerated; the country flashed by.

When she was a very young woman, she began, she happened to go to the Perth Cup races one New Year's Day: it was the event of the season. There she was introduced to Maxine MacDonald, who by then was widowed and was looking for a secretary to work with her at Fossil Downs. Susan, whose complex personality was still emerging from its chrysalis, had already worked in the North, at Brunette Downs Station on the Barkly Tableland; she volunteered at once for the job.

"I was pretty struck, I must confess, by Maxine, back then," said Susan, almost wistfully. "She was an unusual act. She would only have been about sixty, and she was very much the glamorous star: red hair, long red nails, bright eyes. She was a good-time woman, she loved life, and people. She lacked, per-haps, a certain style – she looked like a barmaid who'd made good."

"Susan! I thought she was going to turn out to be your role model."

"Only in some respects. She had the look, in fact, of a classy sort of madam. Of course she was my kind of person – when you were with her, you always had a wonderful time. I flew up the week after the races. I can still remember what I had on when I landed at Derby off the MMA plane from Hedland and Broome; it was a blazing, humid Kimberley day. I was wearing ultrafashionable yellow shoes and a long, white-but-toned shift dress – I've never felt so hot in all my life."

At Fossil, Susan soon learned the routines of this new world. Maxine loved soirées and amusements; she surrounded herself with a tense, constantly maintained gaiety, and that atmosphere drew visitors from all around and made Fossil the core of the Fitzroy Valley's close, somewhat incestuous social life.

"That house was the emblem of an era," said Susan, "an era that was passing into history at quite a rate. Fossil was the model, and the gravitational centre as well. There was a permanent flux of minor royalty passing through. Maxine loved being the mistress of a million acres, the queen of all she surveyed. But the evenings she presided over were always eventful – she had a tendency to degenerate towards the end of the night, and that only made her more entertaining. In fact, sometimes the transformation would begin quite early: after I'd done the second weather schedule, she used to turn to me and say: 'Susie, darling, it's time for the lemon juice' – we'd have a couple of gin and lemons, in crystal glasses with vine-leaf patterns, and then we'd go off and have a sleep in the green room, on purple-covered mattresses. It was a wonderful existence, like a succession of scenes from dreams: there were always impromptu parties, and Maxine would go upstairs to change into one of her kaftans. We could calibrate the scale of the coming excitement by the number of beauty spots she was wearing when she came down the stairs: one, two or three. There was a particularly turbulent phase, of course, when she was being courted by Bishop Jobst."

"By whom?"

"The Catholic bishop of the Kimberley in those days – an important figure. Don't you know about him?"

"I don't think I do. Is that normal conduct, for a Catholic bishop, up here?"

"Almost *de rigueur,* I imagine! Anyway, Bishop Jobst, who had won the Iron Cross in the war, was very handsome in those days. I'm sure he is still, in fact: he eventually left the church, and he's just celebrated his eightieth birthday. I believe he lives with a woman now, somewhere in Cottesloe. We always knew it would be a busy weekend at Fossil when his plane flew over and came circling in to land. I remember one night, very late, looking up from a sofa and catching sight of the Bishop strolling into the main room, his cheeks stained red with the imprints of lipstick kisses, like something out of a cartoon – and that wasn't in the least unusual. On one particular evening, with another admirer, I can still picture the most dramatic scene, being played out on the grand staircase, involving a large bottle of Dram buie..."

Susan's voice tailed evocatively away. We had driven the length of the Windjana back road; the wide landscape of the Leopolds stretched ahead. I gazed out at the even, hazy contours: those running peaks and green, unfolding valleys seemed like harbingers of an unmapped world. The turn on to the Gibb River Road loomed up before us. We took it and drove in

silence, shaken by the pleasing drumbeat of the corrugations, until Susan picked up her thread.

"Ah, Fossil," she sighed, and gave a little laugh.
"The Kimberley was a real collection of misfits back
then."

"As opposed to now?"

"Well, I'm the queen, now," said Susan. "You've
got to be careful what you say!"

I remembered her special trick of concealing her
intent in a wash of ironies, and phrasing her words
to imply at the same time both their literal interpreta-
tion and the direct opposite. She paused, frowning,
as a kind of punishment for my indiscretion, then
finished off the tale.

"Maxine died, of course. There was a huge funeral,
with the MacDonald tartan very much in evidence.
They buried her on the hill, next to the windmill, beside her husband's grave. I realise now that I was up
there in the Indian summer of her reign, and I loved
it: it was like being in a theatre, on stage all the time.
I lived fully – I had several wild affairs."

"So why did you leave: and why don't you like
Fitzroy?"

"It's not that I don't like it, or care for it. It's just
that it's so full of memories – like all the bush, which
we always seem to pretend is empty. It's not: it's full
of the past – both happy and sad at once. But Fitzroy,
for me, is too confused and jumbled up, and all the
different echoes are still present in my head."

I digested this for a while, until Susan asked me to reach back into the large travelling bag behind us, made of a soft grey leather, so smooth it looked like the hide of baby elephants.

"You'll find a little book in there," she said. "Hard-covered: a book of stories. I just found it again, the other day, and brought it with me to read through. Pull it out."

I did so: it was a frail, slender thing, quarter-bound in burgundy leather, with faint gilt letters on its spine: *The Drover's Cook and Other Verses,* by Tom Quilty. I leafed through: it was a selection of Kimberley ballads, rhyming gently, full of the usual rough whimsy and hard times. On the title page was a short inscription, and, in Susan's neat, upright hand, her maiden name.

"So," I said, "what's the story?"

To my surprise, for a few moments Susan said nothing. She gave a little, distant smile: a smile at herself, I would have guessed, and at her own capacity for sentiment, and the way emotions and memories take their place in the passing run of life.

"A sad one, of course," she said at last. "Sad, but not because it had to do with romance – sad, because it was so long ago now, and fate still seems so hard. The bush was different in those days: people who come here now can't have any idea just how lovely and how sweet the life once was."

"Before the revolution, in a way?"

"Absolutely – of course everything had to change, and it did change. But I wonder if there weren't many people, across the whole reach of the Kimberley, station people, Aborigines, drovers, labourers, who didn't feel themselves happier back then. All the old cattle empires were still in place, although they were beginning to crack apart. The Emanuels still had several of the great stations of the Fitzroy Valley – Cherrabun, and Gogo, and even Christmas Creek – and my friend Vic Jones was the man in charge of Gogo. We were very close, he and I: real soul mates. I spent a lot of time with him in Fitzroy – until the day, in July 1971, when he decided that his life was over. He was going blind: the darkness was coming over him. He used to tell me that he'd be useless when he could no longer tell a good bullock from the top rail. The Emanuels knew all about it: they offered him a desk job at the head office, in Perth, but that would never do for him. He decided he would only leave the Kimberley feet first. And that was what he did. It was the race day at Fitzroy Crossing."

"A lot of things happen to you on race days," I put in.

"Do you want me to tell you the story?"

I apologised, and Susan frowned and took a few sharp bends in silence, before continuing in a quiet, collected voice.

"I still remember the moment when he produced that book: he handed it to me, in a very courtly way. We were having a drink together, in the back bar of the Crossing Inn. There was a lot of fond talk, and banter about me saving the first dance that evening for him: and then he went back to Gogo, and took a Luger from his pocket, and shot himself through the head, right at the front gate. He loved me – I loved him. I enjoyed spending time with him."

There was a pause in the conversation: the entrances to Gibb River and Mount Elizabeth went by; I stared out, into the curtain of fan palms and bloodwoods, and the play of sunshine on the parched, yellow stands of cane grass.

"I worked out later," said Susan, "that I was the last person he'd spoken to. He said, 'Don't wait for me for that dance, I might be late' – and then off he went."

I glanced down at the book in my hands.

"This book is published," I read out loud, "to assist the Australian Inland Mission."

"I've become quite interested in publishing, myself, actually," said Susan.

"It doesn't sound as though you'd have too much trouble finding enough material for your memoirs."

"Not to publish anything by me! No – I've made a promise to Father Sanz, at Kalumburu, to print his autobiography before he dies."

I was startled to hear that name: I felt the memory-chime again.

"I had no idea he was still alive," I said.

"Very much so," said Susan. "He's a force of nature. He's full of spark and energy: he's just invented an anti-snoring device, made out of tyre rubber. He's ninety-four years old now. He left the mission in the early 1980s, when the state government took over the running of the community from the monks. He moved down to the Benedictine monastery at New Norcia – but early this year, he told the abbot there that he was drawing to the close of his life, and he wanted permission to go back to the place he loved most on earth. I've come to know him well. I go up to Kalumburu quite often these days. I like to keep an eye on things there."

"Well, it's natural – after all, you're almost neighbours. It's only 250 kilometres away from where you live, across the wildest country in north Australia, up a famously awful, stony plateau track, with nothing else to tempt you at the end of the road."

"It's not that bad," said Susan. "And I'm glad we've got onto Kalumburu: it's at about this point on the journey, with a few hours still to go, that I mentally convert to Catholicism."

"I hadn't realised confessional allegiance could be a matter of geography."

"It is for me – I think one should always be pragmatic about questions of faith. There's just no point in going to Kalumburu without attending evening mass. It's an experience everyone should have at least once in their life. You're in luck – we'll be there in time tonight."

"Wasn't that the Drysdale crossing back there – that green underworld of river gums, and white sand, with all the kingfishers, and pelicans, and brolgas?" The river was lost already in the dust trail. I craned my head back; we swept on.

"It was," said Susan, staring ahead with the fixed gaze that comes over all long-distance drivers. "But there's not really any time for worship of the natural kingdom: you can do all that kind of thing at the mission, on the King Edward Lagoon. Perhaps I should give you a quick run-down on what we're driving into. I suppose it's for the best if you realise in advance that everyone in Kalumburu is slightly cracked."

"Everyone?"

"Everyone – it's almost a condition of entry."

She ran through the list, in brisk, precise fashion. There was Father Anscar, the twelfth son of a twelfth son, a collector of spiritual memorabilia, a man of the most engaging personality, with a tinkling, upward-rising laugh and a habit, useful in Kalumburu, of looking on the bright side of life: although Anscar's mood had been somewhat downcast recently, perhaps because of his neartotal blindness, caused by the inroads the disease of lupus was making on his organism. There was Sister Scholastica, who had been in the Kimberley for five decades, and was closing in on her ninetieth birthday, and had lost almost all feeling in her legs, with the result that she now used a form of motorised quad-bike for transport about the mission compound, though this handicap had yet to stop her from pursuing her culinary endeavours, which often produced outbreaks of food poisoning and bitter protests from her colleagues. There was Brother John, of course, who was in regular communication with Our Lady, and who had been engaged in the most complex negotiations with Susan over his prayers for a white late '90s-model Suzuki trayback to cart the mission rubbish – prayers which had been miraculously answered, due to Susan's chance attendance at a Perth car yard.

"You mean to say you bought him a Suzuki four-wheel-drive – just because he told you he needed one?"

"As I said, it was a miracle – and now we're in discussions over his wish for a dog to replace the old blue heeler, which succumbed to the attentions of a king brown. But Brother John's still trying to determine Our Lady's precise instructions on that front: breed, gender, so on. And naturally one always comes across the administrators, who arrive and depart with great regularity, because of the stresses of the life up there."

Susan's portrait of this little realm had all the energy and adjectival profligacy of a Jacobean drama, and it was set, too, on a tight, constrained stage: the mission, in her telling, was a square of ordered space, fringed by lush, towering mango trees, jammed hard against the wider Aboriginal community of Kalumburu, which lapped against its low stone walls like a heaving ocean. Between the two was the narrowest of frontier strips, formed by a grassy reserve where the sacred grotto, topped by a statue of Our Lady of the Assumption, stood. The monks, on their devotional visits to this image of the Virgin, would patiently gather up the remains of half-smoked joints discarded in the grotto's furthermost recesses and dispose of the used condoms they found, shaking their heads all the while, wondering at the new-found interest in balloons being displayed by the more youthful members of the congregation, and utterly perplexed by the ways of the teenage world. Beyond this buffer zone, the community proper began. It was the standard mix of run-down houses, front yards full of half-dismantled cars, and roadways leading nowhere, down which little groups of young women would drift with slow, tranquil strides. Susan's friendships, though, were with the few surviving older inhabitants, who remembered the early mission days. Each time she drove up, she would call in on the artists Jack and Lily Karedada, produce a folding chair from her Landcruiser, sit beside them in the fetid room where they lay on their beds, and listen to their papery voices as they ran through the tribulations of their lives. But before anything, she liked to exchange greetings with Dolores Djinmora, a woman of preternatural grace and beauty, a mother of thirteen children, and a Christian of the most intense beliefs.

"In fact," said Susan, "she's the co-author, with Father Sanz, of another book I'm publishing: an anthropological study of the Kalumburu people in the time before the mission came."

"It's going to be the best-documented community in all Australia," I said. "Maybe you should think of starting up a special imprint: Kalumburu University Press!"

"That's a splendid idea – but we might have to do something about the literacy levels first. Father Sanz is quite depressed about the educational picture: he talks about it in his memoirs."

"And what are they like?"

"It's not exactly a standard story of faith: there's a lot about the Aboriginal politics of the Kimberley, and his arguments with the state government. He describes the wartime attack by the Japanese, and his adventures on the coastal supply luggers, and his days as a young postulant in Spain, when he ate raw mice and insects to prepare himself for his missionary tasks. There's a big cast of animals, as well. Father Sanz wanted to start up a croc farm at Kalumburu: he kept a family of pet crocodiles and became very close to the dominant male: he used to pat it and stroke it every day. And he was keen on fantail pigeons: he liked to play musical pieces on the harmonium, accompanied by his favourite bird. The book's structure presented some problems, though."

"What kind?"

"It had about eight different endings – but I think we've found a way of dealing with that: it has a kind of diminuendo conclusion now, like waves ebbing on a shoreline; fading away."

The sun had dropped down to the western horizon: its beams came slanting like a spotlight through the trees. We left the plateau country and began descending. Beneath us, between red cliffs, ran the King Edward River channel; its pools caught the sun, gleamed and curved into the distance and out of sight. Soon the corrugations deepened; the road branched and widened: it switched to bitumen, the scrub gave way, water tanks and the low roofs of houses appeared.

"Kalumburu," said Susan, proprietorially. "The end of the line."

We glided in, past a large police station. Off to one side was a floodlit basketball court; the stone buildings of the mission and its low walls lay ahead.

"Familiar?" she asked. "What you were expecting?"

I gazed out: a sweet, transfixing tone of longing stirred inside me. I had the sense of seeing once more a place I had known in some forgotten episode of childhood – or of watching a filmic adaptation of a much-loved book: snatches of Jerusalem and Lamourette's descriptions came back to me, and I could see him once more, trying to paint the portrait of the mission and its country, his face assuming an expression of tense delight.

"Aren't all remote Aboriginal communities of a kind?" I said, carefully. "That tone of drama without purpose; of listlessness and expectancy without end?"

"Of course," said Susan. "But there are local variations. I sometimes like to think of Kalumburu as the best and the worst all jammed up tight together."

"How does it rate on the accommodation front? Five-star?"

"They've got a small motel – for the contractors. In fact it's more of an ATCO container set-up. I'm sure we'll find you something there."

"And you?"

"Oh, I tend to stay in the guest quarters in the bishop's house," she replied, rather airily. At that moment, we passed a large painted sign: *Kalumburu – Our Lady of the Assumption Catholic Parish: May the Lord Preserve You.* Susan turned into a gated driveway: "Look, there's Father Anscar. I'm glad to see him up and active: he's been knocked about by all his cortisone treatments. His Auntie Bridgie in Melbourne told him they could dry the blood of a horse."

She waved and drove slowly past a man with white hair and an even, slightly unfocused expression in his eyes – but he paid no attention, perhaps unsurprisingly, because he was wearing a large pair of orange industrial ear muffs and was headed, in purposeful manner, towards a small tower at the far corner of the walled garden.

"What on earth is he doing?" I asked.

"He's about to ring the bell for mass – perfect timing: we can go straight into church."

Susan pulled up before the low stone façade of the monastery's main building. With an air of great ceremony, she gazed into the rear-view mirror and applied a fresh coat of lipstick. I glanced about and took in the surroundings, which had the air of a set from some radical operatic production in which opposites are provocatively combined. There, set in a smooth expanse of lawn, was the little church, and nearby stood the storerooms and outbuildings, each topped with a neat wrought-iron cross. Beyond them, along the bank of the river lagoon, vast raintrees towered upwards, and in their topmost branches white cockatoos were shrieking, and cavorting, and hurtling through the air. The front grounds were being watered by large, noisy sprinklers, which threw out sharp, scudding jets of water. Strewn about the gardens were decorative assemblages of bent, rusted metal and old saw-toothed wheels arranged in geometric shapes. In the distance a generator was humming; at the front gate, dogs scuffled and yelped like condemned souls being thrust down into the maw of hell.

"Let's go," called Susan. "Mustn't be late – think of our spiritual health!" She led the way, providing a running commentary, offering brief biographic sketches of the various individuals who crossed our path, in quite a loud voice, seemingly oblivious to their reactions.

"Here's Cyril, who was hit on the head with an iron bar, and comes to mass every day, and does the gardens. There's Brother John over there – I wonder if he's had any more communications from Our Lady about his dog. And that's Brother Tomas, who's visiting from Poland, and doesn't speak much English – dinner can be a bit tricky if you get stuck next to him."

A handful of young mothers, tall, in bright-coloured dresses, holding their babies on one arm, stood in the doorway of the stone-fronted church. I followed Susan in, sat beside her in the back pew and examined the interior. Above the arched entrance was a fresco executed in a wild profusion of conflicting styles, incorporating Wandjina faces, hieroglyphs and occasional biblical scenes. A wooden head of Christ, carved with disquieting verismo, stood on a plinth before the lectern. Behind the altar hung a painted image of a black Madonna, posed before a lush rendition of the Mitchell Falls. The service unfolded: prayers and gospel readings came and went, but it was hard to keep one's thoughts focused on the mysteries of the divine, so noisy and protracted were the struggles between the little children playing on the low steps outside the entrance, or running up and down before the altar.

"What's that odd contraption over there," I asked Susan, after some while.

"An overhead transparency projector, of course," she whispered back. "For displaying the texts of the hymns. It may be a bit noisy now – but when we get to the singing, the voices are beautiful. Just go with the flow."

"And who are those two?"

I pointed at a couple of figures, hunched, kneeling at the front of the congregation.

"Can't you tell? That's Father Sanz, and Sister Scholastica: she came up on her quad. I thought I described everyone to you so well you'd have no trouble recognising them."

I spent the rest of the service studying the man before me, bent, hands clasped together, at the altar rail. He was wearing vestments of gold and turquoise; his hair was white, and combed back from his broad forehead; his eyes were veiled by thick, lantern-like glasses. And how did the decades figure in his thoughts, I wondered: what of those days I had heard recounted in such detail, when he was the arbiter of inter-tribal spear fights and he mounted boat trips to save the crews of crash-landed American bombers; or his two years of pure solitude, in the bush at Pago, tending the black luggers, on the wide, humid coast-line of Mission Bay? Were they the clues to any understanding now: did they make a pattern or shape of the past?

"Wasn't that a wonderful, uplifting mass?" said Susan as we filed out. "Although I do sometimes ask myself what the locals think of the more obscure passages in Father Anscar's sermons. I couldn't see what he was getting at with all those comparisons between Nelson Mandela and the leaders of the Kalumburu Council."

"Nor me," I said, absently. "And there was that odd lesson from the New Testament: dying to oneself?"

"Absolutely," Susan replied. "I've often thought there should be a slight revision of the Christian scriptures, in favour of ease of understanding. It's lucky, isn't it, that we're able to have dinner tonight with so many experts on Catholic doctrine. I'll make sure to seat you beside Father Sanz."

And she was as good as her word. Half an hour later, the monks, the nuns and their guests were gathered round a long veranda table, with Susan at its end and Father Sanz between us, holding court. I bent my head, and listened to him speaking, and tried to screen out all other sounds – but his voice was high, and his Spanish accent strong, and his words were like the rustle of reeds in the wind, so that it was only late in the proceedings, long after the arrival and departure of the plates of dark boiled beef and pale vegetables looking like deep-sea creatures, that I began to decode anything of what he had to say. We seemed to be in the midst of a story of religious ordeal, relating to the early years of the Benedictine mission, when it was still located near the mouth of the winding Drysdale River.

"Did you just mention something about levitation?" I asked him. Everyone, by now, was leaning over and listening to his monologue.

"That's right: the founding missionary father, Father Vincent, had the misfortune to shoot, with a warning shot, one of the marauding Aboriginal warriors during the first days of settlement, when attacks on the monks were still very common. He said prayers of penance every day for the rest of his life, and slept in a coffin every night, and very regularly he would levitate, and his brother monks would see him, and this proof of his holiness, and God's approval of his penitence."

"It must be disappointing, in a way, Father," I ventured, after this vignette, "that you don't live in such hectic times, and see such proofs of divine intent."

"Proofs!" Father Sanz turned to look at me with an air of indignation. "My life in Kalumburu has given me all the proofs I need of God's will. I know how God made the world. Do you want to hear?"

"Of course. Who wouldn't?"

"God is infinite goodness – and happiness, because perceiving goodness creates happiness. He was aware of himself, his goodness was by nature effusive – it spread out, and through his infinite power, in a single instant, he made the whole world, in its complexity, its interrelatedness and splendour: he is an eternal now."

"It's a kind of wave theory of creation," I suggested. "An expanding Big Bang. Quite in tune with modern thinking."

"It's not a theory," said Father Sanz in his papery voice. "Not at all! Sometimes I look up at the sky, and I see its beauty – sometimes I look up, and I see a kite, hovering in the sky, moving its tail, adjusting its flight, meticulous, still, and I marvel anew at the splendour of God: how could he have made such a wondrous thing? A single kite is enough to prove to me the splendour of creation."

Those words might have been chosen to quiet the race of my imaginings. I waited – the talk flowed on: the richness of the mission's banana harvests in former times; its lush orchards of orange trees; the duels with nine-foot hammerheads that were fought out in the shallows of Vansittart Bay. The stars wheeled above our heads; the candles burned down low. I was on the verge, repeatedly, of asking Father Sanz more about his memories and the days when a young Canadian named Lamourette came to Kalumburu – but something made me draw back, as if the past had found its place, and being there, where the story-line began, was completion enough. At length, Sanz rested his hands on the table and got up.

"Time," he said, "for us young men to retire to bed."

"One moment, Father," I said, "before you go!" Intuitions seemed, in those seconds, to guide me; soft, light words came from my lips. "One moment more: I have a little challenge for you."

"A challenge?"

"An arm-wrestling contest!"

He looked at me rather quizzically.

"I think you know something," he said, after a pause, his eyes through his glasses magnified into an owl's stare. "That was all a long time ago – a very long time!"

"But you just said you were young. One bout. Why not? I'm sure you'll win: you always do."

"You're just humouring me," said he, in a slow, suspicious voice. "You're just trying to give pleasure to an old man."

"Maybe," I said. "But maybe not."

And at that Father Sanz sat down again, with all the gravity of his nine decades. He balanced himself in his seat, he assumed the poised position of an experienced contestant; he placed the broad, dry palm of his hand in mine.

"Ready?" he said, with a slight, sardonic smile. He gripped, tensed and applied a clean, sharp pressure, which I resisted for some seconds, until I felt my forearm trembling, weakening, yielding: an iron force pushed against me: it ground down on me with all the harshness and the strength of time.

***

Days went by, after this; we travelled further, across the Leopolds; my trip drew near its end. I drove on from Fitzroy slowly, making detours as I went eastwards, through the quiet expanse of station country, past Moola Bulla and the hills round Springvale, until I came to the red escarpments of Turkey Creek. At the entrance to the roadhouse, just beyond the helicopter landing pads and the gaudy placards advertising Bungle Bungle scenic flights, I turned off the highway. A pair of campervans had drawn up along the verge, beneath the shade trees; marooned in front of the fuel bowsers was a small flotilla of Aboriginal cars: old Falcons and Kingswoods, Datsun hatchbacks, all of them in advanced states of disrepair, all empty of passengers. Country music was playing softly over the forecourt speaker system; the sun beat down. I wandered in and soon lost myself among the shelves of intriguing bargain items: diecast toy fire-engines, beef and camel jerky valuepacks, discount CDs of hits by Beyoncé and Tina Turner. The poetry of the roadhouse, I said to myself, in abstracted fashion. There was a cavalcade of customers: German tourists, old couples, passing government officials. I was pondering the array of soft drinks, and the dazzling illuminations that gave the refrigerator the look of a Times Square billboard, and the vast expense such facilities must entail, when a man with an open, easy face came across.

"Are you a regular?" he asked.

"In a sense," I said.

"Dave – from Queensland," he announced. "We've just taken over. We're keen to expand."

I noticed, then, that the sea-green polo shirt he wore had a stylish, neatly stitched logo: *Turkey Creek – heart of the Kimberley.*

"Expand?"

"Yes – you know: improve the operation. We were at Marlborough near Rockhampton before. You might have seen it if you've driven up that coast: they've got a tremendous little chrysoprase museum."

"And are you thinking of a museum here?"

"Well, this place already is a museum, isn't it? It's full of history. Look at the bowsers, after all, and the paintings on them: they're all masterpieces, and all by the artists from the community. I'll bet you're here for the art, aren't you? You probably know those advisers, down at the art centre."

"I was just drifting, really," I said.

"Drifting! You need a purpose in life!"

"I find it can be quite purgative, not knowing where you're going."

"But you still need sustenance, don't you? I'll bet you'd like it if you could order a few lattes in the morning? We'll have a good espresso machine soon. And look," – he moved his hands, with sinuous, stroking motions – "I can see a whole new counter, there. Elegant Italian steel, running the entire length of the building. We're going to remodel: it's a new dawn."

"Clearly," I murmured.

Dave swept on: "We're already baking our own fresh bread each morning, and we sell maybe two dozen rolls: we're going to get into croissants, focaccia breads. You have to think big in the Kimberley. But of course, if you're a roadhouse, you have to have the staples, too, don't you? You have to sell grease in a roadhouse," and he nodded, somewhat dismissively, towards the glass-fronted, steel-trayed hot-food counter, which was sheltering an array of batter-coated, shadowed, deep-brown shapes.

"I quite liked the old order, you know, to be truthful."

"What about it?" said my companion, in a voice of mild incredulity.

"I used to come here very often," I went on. "This was very much a part of the old Kimberley – and it was always a special roadhouse for me. In fact I can still remember the first time I drove in here. I parked in the wrong place, in that engineering area round the back, where the forklifts and the pallets are. There was a big pile of rotting dairy products, and the air was full of that rancid, half-fermented, medicinal smell of industrial disinfectant: giant triple road trains were clattering past; the sky was a perfect blue; there was the faintest impress of a single cirrus cloud, like a fossil, or a feather, very high up."

"And that's a happy memory?"

"A clear one. I went inside, and there was nothing on the shelves at all to buy, except for yearling steaks, and impact wrench kits, and frozen presentation boxes of Milk Tray. It was the middle of the wet season. There was no diesel fuel: I had to wait for days – and there were kite-hawks everywhere – just like now."

"They're carrion, I know," said Dave, grimacing. "There's nothing we can do about them."

"I've always loved them," I said. "In fact, their being here is what makes this roadhouse into a version of heaven for me: perhaps its only rival is the fuel stop at Timber Creek."

"What's so wonderful about a bunch of hawks?"

"The way they're always circling, hovering, swooping, spiralling, with the sun shining on them, catching the different patterns of their feathers as they glide and turn."

Another Kingswood, midnight blue, dilapidated, its trunk held closed with elasticised ties and knotted snatch-straps, drove up at this point, spewing dark clouds of particulate from its exhaust pipe. Its back seats were full of children. They waved at us enthusiastically.

"What is this?" said Dave, in tones of outrage. "A bloody 1970s Holden convention?"

"You could take a more broad-minded view," I said. "Don't you think there's something rather touching about the way all these unloved old cars which have been sold off and tossed aside come back for another stint of life in remote Australia, and get nursed and coaxed on for a few hundred thousand more kilometres – and then they die in the deep bush, and they're abandoned next to some remote desert track, and they decay gently, into the redness of the soil."

"Hey you," called out one of the girls in the back of the Kingswood. She jumped out and came over, smiling. "Do you know me?"

Her face was familiar, in a distant way; she was poised, and angular; there were deep scabies scars on both her legs.

"Where are you from?" I parried.

"She's from Bow River," cried the other girls in the back of the car, in unison. "She wants you to drive her to Wyndham! Her cousin-brother's there!"

"It's only two hours away," pleaded the girl.

I felt the strange, assertive harmony of chance again.

"Well, why not?" I said, almost to myself.

"You're not going to take her, are you?" exclaimed Dave. "That far – you must be crazy!"

"I don't know," I said. "I've always had a soft spot for Wyndham: the salt flats, the tidal systems, the ruins and cemeteries. And there's a croc farm, with a breeding pair of komodo dragons, as well."

I opened the door for my new passenger: we drove off. The music I had been listening to for several days without interruption clicked automatically on.

"What's your name?" I asked her after a few kilometres.

"Don't you know?" she said, reproachfully. "You know my family. You used to come to Bow River, when we were there: I'm Cherandra!"

"That's a lovely name," I said. "I've often wondered where the names come from up here – they're so unusual."

"We make them up," she said, staring at me as if this was obvious. "We have to: we need new ones all the time."

"Why?"

"Because we die so often! We die so much – and then all the old names have to go underground."

"Of course," I said. "That makes sense."

I pondered the wreckage of the lineage systems of the East Kimberley, the mortality rates, the collapse of families and kinship structures, the frequency of the car crashes and catastrophes that sweep down on Aboriginal populations all across the North like biblical plagues. On our right, the red walls of the Carr-Boyd Range stretched into the distance; the stepped cuts of the Argyle diamond mine, as neatly defined as contour markers, shimmered in the air.

"What's this music?" said Cherandra, wrinkling her nose in an appraising way.

"Don't you like it?"

"It's deadly," she said in an enthusiastic voice.

"I've often felt that myself," I said, and began telling her, in succinct fashion, the story of the Haydn string quartets and their place in Western music; how much they meant to me, how I first discovered them.

"And where did he live?" asked Cherandra.

"He came from Vienna," I said, "in the heart of Europe – but he lived in a palace, for many years, in a town called Eisenstadt. In fact, I loved this music so much I went there once, on a kind of pilgrimage. Shall I tell you about it?"

She nodded, rather uncertainly, and I began describing to her the journey I had made, one bleak winter morning, by slow train, through the empty backlands of lower Austria, along the shores of the Neusiedlersee, which seemed to my eyes as bleached and glittering as those of a desert salt lake, until I reached the little terminus at Eisenstadt. The sky was a grey monochrome; the landscape was flat; the town was ringed with high-rise blocks. I walked slowly up the main avenue to the Schloss, and inspected its gardens. They had been the envy of Central Europe, and the delight of the Viennese court – but much of the woodland and the streams and meadows that once stretched through the park had been destroyed, and modern houses thrown up in their place. The arches of the Gloriette and the Leopoldine temple now stood well beyond the surviving garden walls, while the front elevation of the palace, for all its scale and swagger, was very different from the façade I had pictured in my dreams. There was a sombre menace in the carved heads of the Magyar generals; the stucco was cracked and peeling; the false balconies and shuttered windows gave off an air of mournful neglect. Inside, up several flights of dusty stairs, in a corner of the building, were the Haydn rooms, where episodes from the composer's years of creative fervour were recounted, amidst memorabilia and musical scores, displayed in squat, ill-lit glass cases. The museum was deserted: the floorboards creaked beneath my feet. There was a small side room devoted to the chamber music Haydn composed for his princely masters: it had his portrait and a handful of instruments from his day.

"I'd love to see those things," murmured Cherandra.

"But I found I could barely focus on them," I said. "It's always that way – when you have your heart's desire – when you see something you've lived to see. I was looking at those old handwritten scores and paintings, and pouring myself into them, and nothing came back: it was just a chill, dead suite of rooms, full of objects that had no strength in them, no presence for my eyes. The only thing that I remember from that day in any detail is the story of the Esterhazy family, and the last prince, Paul, who chose Hungarian citizenship and fell in love with Melinda Ottrubay, the prima ballerina assoluta of the Budapest ballet."

"Was she beautiful?"

"Of course she was – she was a woman of unearthly beauty – it wouldn't be a proper story otherwise!"

"And what happened then?"

"Can't you guess? He married her – but they were living in dark times. His estates in Hungary were taken over by the communists."

"They took his land!"

Cherandra stared at me, eyes wide with horror.

"That's right. In fact, the way that governments in Central Europe behaved in those days might sound quite familiar to you. And then he was put on trial for high treason, and sentenced, and thrown into jail. But seven years later, there was an uprising, in Budapest. He was released; he left the country, with his wife, and emigrated to Switzerland: they lived together there for many years in exile, in Zurich – the place where I went to school, actually, when I was a boy."

"And did you know them?"

"No – it's quite a big place."

"Oh," said Cherandra, sounding disappointed. "I see."

"There's another twist. They loved each other very much, but they had no children: not one – so he was the last descendant of the line. He died in the same year, and almost in the same month, that the regime in Hungary began to disintegrate. He never saw the dawn he had waited for all through his life. There are pictures of him and the prima ballerina in the museum at Eisenstadt. They always look very composed and elegant, in fact they look like mirrors of nobility and beauty – and they never, ever smile."

The last movement of the quartets came to an end; the sound of the gypsy suite, which leaves its listeners perched on the very edge of nightmare, hung between us for a second and fell away; then there was nothing but the muffled roar of the Landcruiser as we swept on. We crossed the last of the single-lane flood channels. I veered around an ore truck which was driving slowly and keeping almost on the centre-line.

"Oh, please," I said, rhetorically, as we went by.

"Oh, please," mimicked Cherandra, catching my voice with weird perfection.

"Are you copying whatever I say now?" I glanced at her. "That might be quite a stretch: there's still a long run ahead."

"Why did you come back?" she said then, very directly. "You were away a long time."

The Wyndham T-junction was close ahead of us. I slowed, and puzzled over what to answer: to her, and to myself. Ahead, above the haze of bush-fire plumes, the mass of the Cockburn Ranges, grandest and loneliest of all the mountains in northen Australia, rose up in spurs and battlements to a pale blue sky.

"I could tell you several things," I said, rather tentatively. I had the sense of discovering my thoughts even as I described them. "I could tell you I came back because I missed the country, and because I promised myself, when I was away, that I would drive alone across the Kimberley again. Or I could say that I heard several stories while I was in the Middle East – stories that linked up with here, and so I made myself a secret promise to go back to the places they were set in, because one has to answer those kinds of signals and calls in life – and life's like music, anyway, it has its songs, and rhythms, and repetitions that one shouldn't fight against. And I could tell you I missed the people I know, in Kununurra, and Broome, and Fitzroy, and that I wanted to see them: I'd been carrying them in my thoughts and wondering about my friendships with them all the time that I was away – and those things would be true. But there are other reasons that don't really come with words: they're more to do with dreams and feelings, underneath the surface of the mind. And beyond that, there's the last reason, the one no one likes to talk about: I half believe, these days, that people who come to northern Australia come here because they're lost,  or searching, or on the edge of life, and silence, and they're chasing after some kind of pattern, some redemption they think might be lurking, on the line of the horizon, out in the faint, receding perspectives of the bush."

"I see," said Cherandra, in a very solemn voice.

"Shall we have some sound again?" I said, and I switched the radio on, and at once picked up the signal for Radio Waringarri in Kununurra.

"So what is strongyloides?" inquired the announcer's upbeat, smoky voice. "Listen up, brothers and sisters – because it could be you we're talking about! It's a parasitic worm, and you can catch it easily: it's spread in droplets through the air. It affects the heart and decreases immunity, according to this health department handout that I've got in front of me. So if you're set up with glandular fever at an early age, and you have this worm that can impact on your heart or kidneys, then you'll have long-term damage! The good news is it's easy to get rid of – one, two, three. But the bad news is there's cross-infection all the time, because of the overcrowding – and dogs pick up the parasite when they eat human faeces..."

I turned the voice down.

"I've got that," said Cherandra, proudly.

"Is it very overcrowded, in the house where you live?"

"Not really."

"How many people, would you say: rough guess?"

She counted up on her fingers in methodical fashion, moving her lips silently: the counting went on for some while.

"Twenty-eight," she announced eventually, in triumph. "Or sometimes I get to stay in my cousin's house, with twenty-five."

"Look," I said, in some perplexity. "There! The Bastion: up ahead, and all the salt flats, and the cemeteries. Tide's out."

"The tide's always out in Wyndham," said Cherandra.

We drove in slowly, past the outlying blocks with their shade trees and shacks of corrugated iron, past the Six Mile houses. The airport came, and the race track, with its rails and furlong markers stretching away across the mud beds, dancing and wavering in the reflected dazzle of the sun. I pulled up at the little shopping centre, next to the giant concrete crocodile.

"Not here!" said Cherandra, shaking her head, as if unable to believe my stupidity.

"Keep going? To where? Old Wyndham? What's there?"

"The Port Hotel, of course: that's where everyone is, in daytime." "But is it really the best place for you? You're only a child."

"I'm twelve years old! That's grown up."

"Maybe it is," I said, "around here. And what did you actually want to come to Wyndham for?"

"A funeral – on Temptation Island."

"Where?"

"Oombi."

"You mean Oombulgarri, across the Gulf?"

"That's what I said!"

"Why do they call it that: Temptation Island?"

"Oh – I don't know," said Cherandra, looking tactfully down at her knees.

We had crossed the last of the salt flats by now; I drove up the avenue of boabs, between the shuttered houses and old stores, and paused, engine running, opposite the car park of the Port Hotel. Loud music was blaring from the front bar. Beneath a shade awning, just past the side entrance, a handful of men were engaged in a drunken, desultory scuffle. They flailed their arms and clenched their fists, their gestures unfolding with an agonising slowness, as if the emotions within them had somehow produced an immobilising effect.

"Are you sure," I began asking, "that this is really the ideal place for me to leave you?"

"There's my cousin's car," cried out Cherandra, pointing to a crooked, antiquated trayback, which was caked in a thick coat of red dust and was missing a large part of its radiator grille and bullbar. I drove up to it, parked alongside and marvelled at the extent of the damage it had sustained.

"And is he," I asked, still more sceptically, "the ideal carer?"

"Too many questions!" said Cherandra, and jumped out, and waved; then, much like some animal returning, after brief detention by research scientists, to its natural habitat, she scampered back in the direction of the hotel.

I glanced up and down the main street. It was mid-afternoon: the sun's rays were burning down. Close by was a low-slung building, its little garden choked with discarded pieces of industrial equipment. I took shelter beneath its veranda. A discreet sign, laminated, peeling slightly, was on the door.

*To make it easier,* it declared, *for you to understand our history, please look at our pictorial panels as you would a book. (Mystery novel addicts please refrain from peeking at the last page first!)*

How to resist such an invitation? Inside, a set of old photographs and mementos from Wyndham's days of prosperity had been arranged in a tight, compelling hang. Desks and tables were piled with reference volumes and heritage reports. One back room had been reserved for telephone switchboards and radio sets; the entrance hallway was decorated with carved shields, and nose pegs from camel trains, and a black cast-iron dingo trap. Perhaps those objects, with their antique aura, had removed me from the immediate present; perhaps the heat and stillness inside the building had gone some way to stupefying me: at any rate, it was not until I had done a quick circuit of the display that I noticed a man with long, elegant silvery hair, reading quietly in a small front office. He was smoking a roll-up cigarette, which was couched precariously inside a thin black cigarette holder. His pose was reflective. He looked up, then stared at me with quiet, measuring eyes. There was a silence, which lasted for almost a minute.

"That's an interesting motorcycle you've got outside there," I said, in desperation.

"Isn't it," he replied at once, with abrupt enthusiasm. "Isn't it just! It's an old Indian – before 1913, we think. We're going to make a bit of a stand for it – and I want to make sure that wheel doesn't keep falling off."

"What is this place?" I asked.

"The Historical Society, of course. Haven't you been here before?"

"Years ago," I said.

"I thought so," he replied. "I thought your face was familiar. I told myself I knew you."

"And I remember you," I said.

We shook hands, very ceremoniously, and although there was not the slightest further evidence brought forward to support this theory of a former encounter, we began speaking much more freely: of the society, its dreams, its goals, its prospects, the way ahead for Wyndham.

"Oh, this place is holding up like fury," said my new acquaintance, almost shaking with excitement as he ran through the signs of the regional revival. "It's the only viable port between Darwin and Broome, after all. And it's cyclone-free: well, nearly. We've had the world's second-largest cattle boat in here; the nickel's going to be coming into port on road trains, and if they do bring in the iron ore, they'll have to open up the old Durack Road. It'll be like something out of Texas! That big warehouse on the block next door's for sale, if you're interested. It would be a good investment. A lot of people have seen the potential in Wyndham, you know. The Japanese had their eye on it."

"That's why they bombed it, presumably."

"Yes – but they didn't bomb the jetty: and they were very careful with the town. In fact I'm pretty sure, myself, that they sent out landing parties across the top of the Kimberley, just the way they did along the Gulf of Carpentaria."

"True?"

"Never a truer word! We know one of their forward subs dropped off a shore team on the coastline, at Point Warrender, north of the Mitchell Plateau."

"And what happened to them? They're not in the history books."

"No, that's right – that landing party just disappeared. Although the monks at Kalumburu did notice that some of the locals had nice new knapsacks, but they all said they didn't know anything."

I allowed this startling reinterpretation of northern history to filter through my thoughts. I glanced at the man before me with increased curiosity. "Hot in here, isn't it?" he said, wiping his forehead with his wrist.

"Pestilential."

"We could talk about all this more," he offered, "over a drink or two, if you like, in the back bar of the hotel."

"You mean the one that has the old-timer buried underneath it?"

"The very one. It's a good atmosphere in there. I just hope it doesn't get too crowded. The town's filling up – and I'll be here, of course, the next two or three hundred years."

"Are you sure?"

"For a certainty: that's the length of time it takes for all evidence of corporeal life to vanish into the ground. If you're doubtful about that, just take a drive out to the pioneer cemetery: the washaways have done their work, and the salt from the flats is leaching up and corroding everything that's left there in the soil. You can see quite clearly what happens in a coffin, after a century or so."

"I don't know that's really for me," I said.

"Well, at least have a glance at our special display, about the meatworks. I've always thought that Wyndham was a kind of holy city – and the meatworks were the temple, or the sacred site. They were the heart of everything, in their day: the pulsing heart. It was industrialised extermination on the grand scale. I was watching one of those documentary programs on the TV last night: you know, Germany, World War II, all that. You could see the parallels. It's just in that room over there, our exhibition. Take a look. I think you'll find it bloody impressive!"

Without a word, I did as he advised, and after some searching, I noticed on the back wall a sequence of photographs, each one enclosed by an understated wooden frame. They were black and white, shot with strong contrast, and marked out by the most dramatic lighting effects. The compiler of the display had clearly  intended to build up, through these multiple images, a portrait of daily life inside the meatworks, and simultaneously to describe, in the same brief visual narrative, the journey of an individual carcass, from the moment of its first arrival in the processing room until its transfer to the chilled hold of a waiting cargo ship. Each photograph showed men with frank, open faces, engaged in their distinctive tasks. In the first, two figures sat at a long wooden table, bent studiously over a pair of severed ribcages, while behind them stretched a curtain of eviscerated torsos, gleaming white. The adjacent image caught three tall men, bare-armed and barefooted, their legs reflected in the wet flooring of the meatworks, as they manipulated whole, new-skinned carcasses, thrusting their hands deep into the haunches and chest cavities of the dead beasts. And in the most elaborate of these scenes, bathed by soft illumination, a team of workers moved amidst a forest of dangling bodies, each casting long shadows, which were in turn set off by the patterning of wire-mesh window frames. To one side of the men, an overseer, fully clothed, wearing a smart, broad-brimmed hat, stared on impassively, a hand resting beneath his chin. At several points this pictorial sequence was interrupted by supplementary notes, hand-written in neat, cursive script: *Bullock approx. 450kgs (990 lbs). Fronted out (insides removed) then onto splitting saw. Further for trimmers and finally, intochillers.*

Beneath the photographic gallery, the history of the meatworks, which had been central for almost seven decades to the economy of Wyndham, was given in a series of fragmented cameos. These had been strung together and neatly typed up, somewhat in the guise of a formal report, complete with paragraphs and regular bullet points, although they were in fact subjective recollections of the most jagged kind, full of cinematic intensity. Some described the workers' huts, with their hessian roofing made from washed and opened salt bags; some re-called the moon's gleam on the boning chamber's walls of corrugated iron. There was, as these accounts made plain, a deep camaraderie among the workers, and a completeness to their life, which was amply matched by the thoroughness of the production cycle: for each bullock that entered the meatworks had a defined value, and every scrap of the carcasses was put to use. Even the horns and tail tips of the slain creatures were processed and bulk packaged: they went off by sea to the subcontinent, where they were transformed into brooms and suit buttons for the domestic trade.

But the days of this Kimberley Elysium were numbered: a deep downturn in the pastoral industry, coupled with the persistent growth of the export market for live cattle, brought about in mid-1985 a closure that had long been inevitable. Two years later, at an auction held on the site, much of the structure of the meatworks was dismantled and sold off. The production rooms, which had been cloaked for decades in darkness, were uncovered for all to pick over. The furniture and equipment was dispersed, and much of it found new life in the iron sheds and machine workshops that sprang up round Wyndham in those days.

For some while, I studied these images and documents, aware of the utter silence around me, until my eyes chanced on a little plaque, of brass or some similar dull metal, which was mounted on a wooden plinth and had been positioned so it was facing the wall. I leant down and turned it round. The surface was engraved with golden letters: its words paid tribute to the men who had laboured in the meatworks, from the first season in 1919 onwards, until the very end. *In that period of time,* the plaque recorded, with striking precision, *the works processed 2,072,049 cattle.*

"Remarkable, isn't it?" The museum's guardian had come up behind me: he was standing at my shoulder. "What men could do: what they achieved back then! Two million head of cattle: it sets one's dreams in flight."

My thoughts, though, had been stilled by that figure. It fell through me like a stone. I turned away, keen to seek the daylight, and quite unable to strike from my mind the images that were forming there: road trains, in their dusty livery, driving beneath the Bastion; a line of docile bullocks, stepping forward; blood, coursing through the mangroves, blood pouring in continuous flow from the meatworks drains.

# Vision

—

# I

A few days after leaving Wyndham, I set off on a trip to Central Australia, in part to attend a native-title handover in the community of Mantamaru, in part because of an enduring, elusive sense of connection to that stretch of country. For ever since I started frequenting the Centre I have felt that there are certain sites in Alice Springs, and in the ranges reaching westwards, which play some concealed role in the unfolding of my life – and so much had this conviction strengthened in me over the year of my absence that I was almost living in that landscape in my mind during my last months away. I felt caught up, wherever I was, with the desert world, I haunted Alice Springs: it was part of me, like some perfect simulacrum carried in my head. Often the idea came to me that I should abstract myself from my hotel room in Beirut or Baghdad and travel in a sweeping instant, across oceans and continents, towards the red line of the MacDonnell Ranges, to the peak of Mount Gillen and down, until I was beside the banks of the Todd River, or in the shaded gardens of the Silver Bullet, beneath the grevilleas and the cypress pines. It would be still and calm there, the kites would be circling, and the zebra finches calling; I would fall into conversations with men and women whose company I felt myself deprived of, as surely as a patient knows himself deprived of some life-preserving medicine – and this imagined sense of closeness was enough to breed a distinct apprehension about what I might find on my return.

It was sunset when I arrived on the late flight from Darwin: the jet came gliding in through banks of cloud. I stared down through the aircraft window at the street grid spread out beneath me; the redness of the glow on the ground looked like a coat of fire. Early next morning, as my first port of call, I paid a visit to the Panorama Guth, an unusual structure on Hartley Street, set back, with a crenellated, white-painted central tower, which gave it the air of a hieratic temple, though it was designed by its creator, the Dutch artist Henk Guth, to serve as a tourist attraction and as a repository for his own renditions of the desert landscape.

Guth was born in 1921 in the city of Arnhem, on the lower Rhine. His training as an art student was interrupted by the outbreak of World War II and the German invasion of his country. For some months he was active in the Resistance and worked in a little studio near the Rijksmuseum in Amsterdam. Guth was a gifted draughtsman. This skill was put to practical use: he specialised in removing the incriminating yellow stars from the identity papers of Dutch Jews threatened with deportation to the death camps of Eastern Europe – but he was himself detained in the course of a Gestapo sweep, jailed for half a year and then dispatched to a concentration camp in the north of Holland, near the German frontier. Very probably this was the transit camp at Westerbork, a place of great sufferings, though Guth was always reluctant to discuss in any detail this episode of his life, his experiences there and his subsequent escape. During the lengthy oral history interviews he submitted to with questioners from the Territory Archives, he skates quickly over those months and turns instead to his days in hiding, a time of pure adventure, when he lived in the underground alongside French, Belgian and Dutch partisans.

After the war was over, Guth dedicated himself once more to painting, and above all to the study of the Dutch masters: he spent his summers travelling in Switzerland, where he became convinced that the landscape artist's true task and challenge lay in catching the look of light, in recording the exact colour, the depth and variation of the sky. In 1960, driven by a desire for fresh horizons, he emigrated to Melbourne and tried there, for several years, to build a new life for himself. He worked as a house painter and as a teacher of deaf and dumb children; he explored his way around the Western District of Victoria; he held exhibitions of his Dutch landscapes, with moderate success.

He was on the verge of returning to Europe when he made a visit to the Centre, thinking that he should at least see the heart of the continent before leaving it for good. For a week, he stayed in Alice Springs, which in those days was a remote township with an air of pronounced isolation about it; then he drove west, on the station road skirting the line of the MacDonnell Range. By chance, Guth arrived at the entrance to Ormiston Gorge round sunset, when the light picks out the finest variations in the colours of the rocks. On the horizon loomed the mauve silhouette of Mount Sonder; before him were slant shadows and shining, white-barked gums. He had fallen on a stretch of country that combined the remote grace of alpine peaks with the textures of the woods in Gelderland, round Arnhem, where his childhood years were spent. Guth felt himself reached, and summoned: he saw, in that darkening sunset gleam, the pattern of his future stretching ahead. At once he moved to Alice Springs and set up a studio, which gradually became a gallery not just of his own canvases, but of Aboriginal artefacts, entrusted to his care by Aranda men he came to know. After several years, the idea formed in him that he should create a monument to the landscape of the Centre and the desert peaks, which were still, in those days, far beyond the reach of most visitors to Alice Springs. Guth decided to paint a panorama, along the lines of the famous Panorama Mesdag in the Hague – an enormous cylindrical painting by the late nineteenth-century marine artist Hendrik Mesdag, which records with the utmost accuracy the streets and coastal dunes of Scheveningen on the Dutch coast. But many early visitors to Guth's panorama were reminded instead of the Waterloo monument, a work of similar design and proportions, intended to memorialise the battle that decided, for several decades, the fate of Europe – and in the days when I first discovered the Panorama Guth and began visiting it regularly, drawn by its quiet and air of artifice, I found myself receptive to a note of melancholy that seemed to lurk within it: a mood of grief and remembrance, which I assumed by instinct, even before I knew anything of its creator's biography, must be bound up with some experience of ordeal and loss.

Guth's painting style, if one can judge by the works he put on permanent display in the Panorama galleries, tended towards the soft and sentimental. He was a fluent portraitist; his desert vistas teemed with stagecraft and incident, with water, wind and gauzy light – but the exception was the Panorama itself, a vast, sombre affair, made up of thirty-three strips of Irish linen joined together by aluminium struts and hung from a circular rail in an elevated lantern, purpose-built to house the work. Guth engaged a friend of his from Holland, Frits Pieters, to help him paint the panorama. Pieters arrived in Alice Springs in February 1975, and the two men spent three months side by side, on wheeled scaffolding, at work in the summer heat, sketching in the topography of the landscape and laying down the undercoat. Guth then devoted three more months to the detail of the painting and the creation of its foreground – a sloping platform, covered in red sand and dry tufts of spinifex and designed to blend seamlessly into the lower reaches of the encircling canvas.

The conception was simple: the visitor would ascend a spiral stair case to view the panorama, and country would surround him. There, spread out wherever one faced, was landscape, a softly curving wall of desert, in exact perspective, receding towards a horizon marked out by the great tors and ranges of the Centre. The eye would be drawn by the long, straight mesa of Mount Connor, then move towards the hazy outline of the Olgas and the flank of Ayers Rock, while at the opposite point of the panorama, behind two straight ghost gums, one could make out the sharp ridge of the MacDonnells and the landmarks near Alice Springs: Standley Chasm, Simpson's Gap, the Old Telegraph Station. Dry riverbeds coursed through the painting in loose meanders, there were rock piles and dead branches; there was the hint of a rundown homestead, and a Southern Cross windmill in the distance; while close up were lines of coolibahs and ironwoods, and even a grove or two of distinctly unpersuasive desert oaks. It was a chapel dedicated to the landscape – and it was impossible: there was no one place from which a traveller could hope to see the peaks and gorges Guth had joined together: they were separated from each other by hundreds of kilometres of intervening range and sand plain. Nor was the painted country, for all the accuracy of the transcription, remotely like the real landscape of the Centre. Guth used the palette of the old Dutch masters – deep, rich sepia earths, dark greens and wheat-sheaf yellows, which lent the scene the glow and lustre of a Ruysdael. Something of the tone of a Dutch work of the seventeenth century was conveyed by its brushstrokes as well: the sky was lightly clouded over, the mountains were tinged with haze, and one half expected a hay wagon pulled by straining cart horses to appear beside the riverbanks, dry though they were, or playful peasant boys to leap out from the golden undergrowth.

I still remember my first visit to the Panorama gallery, years ago, during one of my early explorations through the Centre, when I was just beginning to find my way around Alice Springs. I had been told about the building often, and I had often felt there was something disapproving in the voices of the old hands in town whenever it was mentioned or Henk Guth's name came up. "Just look for the fake castle turret, if you really want to see it, and there's a row of flags on the street outside as well: Australian, Territory and Dutch." Three flagpoles – there they were, before a lowslung, white-painted building with a wide veranda shading its front. I went in. The entrance hallway, with its little reception counter and display of books and trinkets, was intensely air conditioned and quite deserted. I wandered through the first rooms, where Guth's collection of works by Albert Namatjira and the Hermannsburg school was hanging, together with a number of his own desert landscapes. To one side, a recreation of the artist's studio was being set up, with odd items Guth had amassed on his travels: coins, rare stamps, Dutch schoolbooks from his childhood days in Arnhem. One advanced into a narrow chamber, which led into a much larger gallery lined with tall, glass-fronted wooden cabinets, each illuminated by pairs of green-shaded lamps in Tiffany style. These cabinets, as I soon realised, were filled with a collection of archaeological curiosities, and with Aboriginal sacred stones and boards. I paused before each case in turn and gazed through the glass. A vague sense of trespass took shape inside me. I was seeing for the first time objects I had heard described in whispers, or had read about in the obscure footnotes of anthropological classics. There were headdresses made from the feathers of wedge-tailed eagles and black cockatoos, there were cords of hair once worn as armbands by avenging warriors; pearl-shell pendants for rainmaking, stones and wooden boards engraved with circles and arrowed lines – all the secrets of the desert, spread out before my eyes. My unease mounted. I felt on the edge of laughter: I was close to trembling. I tried to copy down in my notebook the texts of the neat, hand-written labels on the display-case shelves. At that instant a whirring noise came from behind me; there was a click, then the noise of a twangy guitar soundtrack.

*At sunset, Ayers Rock seems to glow with a light of its own,* declared a voice in a velvety English accent, comically old-fashioned.

A tourism video had sprung to life on a television screen placed in a position of honour at the centre of the gallery.

"Is it loud enough for you?" asked a man, long-haired, with a fixed smile, standing in the doorway.

I had been kneeling down before a cabinet which held flat, white stones with faint concentric patterns carved upon them. I was so close my breath had fogged the glass. I wiped it away.

"Who are you?" I asked, and as I did so I knew the answer.

"I am the artist," he said in an even voice, not without a little touch of satisfaction, and brushed back his mane of silvery hair.

*In places like this, where the rainfall is slight, the oxides remain and build up, giving the desert its reddish colour,* declared the voice-over sonorously.

"It's quite a collection," I said, and listened to the echo of my words.

"I am happy if you like it," said Guth and spread his hands: "my Aboriginal museum."

He approached with small steps and inspected me through wide, lantern-like glasses. He began escorting me round, waving gently at the cabinets, describing the way the pieces in them had come to him. Sometimes he went into the most punctilious detail; sometimes he lost the thread of his narrative and hesitated, until his attention was drawn by another object in the display. His voice was soft; he had a light, lilting accent. He kept pace beside me and even guided me with his hand, touching my shoulder or elbow to orient me here and there.

"You have seen, of course, the panorama?"

I was still gazing round at the glass-fronted cabinets. The patterns of the stones remained like an afterimage in my field of vision. I found it hard to take in his words.

"Not yet, I must confess."

"You should see it," he insisted. "It's the main attraction."

He gestured towards a spiral staircase, which led up into the lantern.

"I liked the fortifications round the tower," I said. "As if it was a castle."

"It is a castle," he replied. "You should always defend what you love."

I climbed the staircase, moving in a circle above him, looking down into his face, until I was at the level of the great painting. Its wide sky seemed to shimmer in the bright daylight filtering in.

"What does it remind you of?" asked Guth, who had come up behind me. Then he began pointing out the landmarks, one by one. "Mount Hermannsburg, Glen Helen, there – Mount Sonder, Ormiston Gorge. Ormiston," he repeated, softly, "Ormiston – where the dingos howl."

"It reminds me," I replied, "of a Dutch landscape, I'd have to say: Delft, Haarlem – or at least what I remember of them."

"I used to think it was a long way from Europe, here," Guth then said. "I wanted to leave it behind, when I emigrated, when I discovered Central Australia. But you never leave the past – never forget – never remake yourself. I am still the man I was. And you?"

He smiled, and that smile is how I remember him, and he too seems to have regarded that expression, puckish, full of confiding candour, as a kind of mirror into his heart, for he caught it in an engaging self-portrait, which shows him clasping a sheaf of fine paintbrushes in his hands and gazing steadfastly outwards at the world.

That first visit, distant in time, was in my thoughts when I walked back into the panorama building and through its downstairs galleries, past the display cases with their freight of sacred objects, from which I was careful to avert my eyes – not merely out of some vague respect for their sacred resonance and the power they once held, but more from a conviction, which has gradually deepened in me, that things of beauty are best seen once, and never looked at again. The smaller exhibition rooms, with their walls full of watercolours, were closed off and plunged in shadow; the television which once played the tourist video had been taken away. I climbed the spiral staircase leading to the lantern and the panorama with a strong sense that I was repeating, in exact fashion, the movements I had made so long ago, and that

I was rejoining a trajectory through the past. While I was standing in front of the panorama, examining its meticulously painted details, that appealing idea lingered, although the thought also crossed my mind that something more than a mere landscape might be needed to transport one effectively in time. How pale the sky before me was, like the blue of eggshell; how full of depth the ribbons of the cloud. I gazed into the distance of the horizon for some minutes, and only then noticed that I was staring at the low, sloping line of Ormiston Pound, where the gorge entrance cuts through the rock. Ormiston, I remembered, where the wild dogs howl. Guth had painted it as a faint, mauve blur, nearly obscured by a large, twisted corkwood tree in the panorama's foreground. As I looked, new details of the landscape struck me: burnt trees; cloud shadow; a discontinuity, of line and colour, where two sheets of the canvas were joined. And have I truly been here before, I wondered, half-whispering. Is memory repetition; is there any part of me still the same as all those years ago? Why does the sky in its paleness remind me so much of Europe, and the cold, clear air above camps and battlefields? I turned and retraced my steps, down the spiral staircase, which now seemed to me like the stone steps inside castle towers, and went back through the empty galleries until I reached the chill, over-air-conditioned entrance hall. An attendant was standing there, poised behind the counter desk, his hands resting on its surface, his eyes fixed on the street outside. He glanced at me with a faint air of irritation, as if I was interrupting him at some religious task.

"They always make us wait," he said eventually, in a resigned voice.

"They do?"

"The coach parties."

We began talking. I glanced over his shoulder at the row of half-filled shelves: the selection of booklets and items for sale were so dated they could have served, without the slightest modification, as a historical display.

"There's been a drop-off in our visitor numbers, of course," the man went on. "There's that many indigenous tours now, out into the ranges. People prefer going out and seeing for themselves, not just looking at pretty pictures. And Henk's passing away, that put a shadow over things too there for a while."

"I didn't realise," I said. "I'm sorry."

"It happens to the best of us. It was a while ago now. Did you know him at all? You might want to have a look in there: in that side room. He had a pretty interesting kind of life. It tells some of the story."

The studio gallery had been made into a little shrine. Guth's self-portrait was on the easel: his palette and paint box were at its side. Near the door was an obituary notice, together with a selection of brief articles from the local newspapers, describing his funeral. I studied them, and lost myself in the quietness that print, with its formality, brings. Guth had developed a keen desire to be buried in the bush, rather than in the bleak, scorched cemetery of Alice Springs. This wish had preoccupied him so much that he negotiated an agreement to that effect, both with the traditional Aboriginal landowners of the West MacDonnells and the Northern Territory government's Parks and Wildlife Service. His grave lies near the entrance to Ormiston Gorge, where the landscape first disclosed its splendour to his eyes. As with most features in the rangelands of the Centre, the gorge's name, despite its soft and fitting cadence, is quite arbitrary: it is borrowed from an outer suburb of Brisbane, overlooking Moreton Bay, where Louis Hope, the seventh son of the Earl of Hopetoun and the father of the sugar industry in Queensland, lived. It was one of the pioneers of pastoral settlement in the MacDonnells, Richard Egerton Warburton, the son of the famous explorer, who bestowed the name on a creek line near his first homestead, with the thought that it might encourage Hope's interest in the area. Warburton himself had long been open to the call of the inland: when he was still young, he had travelled in his father's camel expedition, the first successful crossing of the western deserts, which left Alice Springs in 1873, and reached the Oakover River near Roebourne ten months later, after a journey of extreme privations. And so Henk Guth, who thought himself a latecomer, but who was in truth a pioneer, and who felt the depth of colour in the canyons and the gorges, and the fear and mystery that lurked inside them, and built a temple dedicated to them, linked himself, by this brief, unconscious relay of association, with the steps of the first explorers bound for the silent ranges of the west.

$$* * *$$

That obscure region, with its desert oaks and bloodwoods, and its abrupt hills which rise like island archipelagos in a red sea of sand dunes and loom on the horizon, mauve from distance, had been often in my thoughts over my year away, for when I left, I chose, almost at random, one book to take with me: one book as a talisman and emblem, a mirror of the Australian landscape, and a prism for my dreams. It was my companion on scores of journeys, I sank myself in its pages nightly, I could recite its climactic passages almost by heart, I came to know it as intimately as any text I studied in my schooldays. *The Red Centre* is a short, rhapsodic account of the deserts and the rangelands west of Alice Springs, written in the 1930s by a naturalist, H.H. Finlayson, and largely cast as the narrative of the author's quest for small, endangered marsupials, chief among them the engaging rat-kangaroo of the desert plains, *Caloprymnus campestris,* now long extinct. Finlayson, about whom I knew, at that time, next to nothing, was clearly an individual of romantic sensibilities, whose dreamy cast of mind was barely held in check by a fierce devotion to the task of biological surveying and sample collecting.

*The Red Centre* shows all the signs of having been thrown off in a few short spells of inspiration: it soars and swoops, it is both succinct and open-ended, its ideas and intuitions shimmer into being like mirages on the page, only to dissipate and vanish in the onrushing stream of species descriptions and desert anecdotes. Much about its presentation is misleading: a surface tone of gentle humour serves to hide its deeper mood of wonderment and free-floating melancholy; it is divided into sections, yet its chapters bleed into each other; it makes liberal use of black and white photographs, which at first seem well chosen to illustrate the author's arguments, but which soon reveal themselves as evocations of landscape, as linked studies in pattern, shape and light. Finlayson begins his narrative with dour pages of historical background and reflections on method, before his true subject makes its first appearance. Metaphors of disruption and imbalance at once invade his thinking: his language, which has been, until this point, smooth and tranquil, takes on a dark, prophetic tone.

The old Australia, he declares, is passing: the landscape is beset on all sides by forces that are reducing it to a scatter of semiartificial environments, mere islands in which the original plan is lost. They are no more, in fact, than fragments of the initial country, frail shards whose fate no man may predict.

If there is authentic terrain to be found, it lies in the far deserts, and above all in the mountain chains, which are the goal of all his travels, and the constant focus of his words. Finlayson scarcely hides his scorn for the flat, wrecked pastoral runs surrounding Alice Springs, he yearns for remoter country: the Petermanns and the Musgrave Ranges. He lingers on their look, he dwells constantly on the causes of their beauty in his eyes: "In spite of their insignificant dimensions they are curiously impressive; and the first sight of a blue line of distant hills breaking the horizon of scrub is seldom without a pleasurable thrill." This, he decides, is in great part because these mountain chains are refuges, shelters from the harsh, oppressive flats of sand and spinifex, and because each of them has its own special character: the Everards with their bare smooth domes and rock slides; the George Gill range, all canyon gorges and smooth rock basins; the Rawlinsons, where quartz screes lie like a mantle of hail beneath the dark mulga surrounds. There is one destination, though, that most draws him, and he returns there in a haze of exaltation: Ernabella, in Glen Ferdinand, where the peaks, after seasons of heavy rain, are covered in bright green waving grasses – and even today, when a large Pitjantjatjara community fills the valley, and its houses straggle along the creek line, there is still a sharp splendour to the landscape, and the soft hills form a striking contrast with the straight church tower raised in mission times.

Finlayson loved to lose himself in memories of country, to summon up the texture of particular places in his mind. There is an almost painful immediacy in his descriptions, yet he seems to be writing of a world already gone. Though *The Red Centre* was composed soon after his survey trips into the far western deserts, and they were then largely intact, the book reads as a retrospect: it is steeped in an awareness of time's passage, its words vanish from one's reach. Finlayson had absorbed a mood and spirit from the landscape: the ranges seemed to him aloof from the country surrounding them. "They look out," he writes, "over a world which has seen great changes, in which they have had no part. To walk alone into their gorges by moonlight; to look into the clear depths of their splendid pools when the noon sun flares on the rocks and the world is unbelievably still; or to listen to the dawn wind singing in the pines on their tops brings always the same suggestion: a sense of things about them once familiar, but now long forgotten; a haunting nostalgia that will not be shaken off."

Even today, such passages, with their air of internal storms first mastered then projected outwards, leave me without bearings. But in the months when I was turning to them and reading through them late at night, in the back rooms of small hotels in the Syrian desert, or in the highway hostels of southern Turkey on the road into Kurdistan, they took on the force of spells, or incantations. How much more strongly then did Finlayson's sense of things ending, collapsing, changing ineluctably from one state to their next strike home! In the pages of *The Red Centre* I came to hear a distant whisper speaking to me, murmuring that life is never what we see, and even we ourselves are not what we believe. I found a logic to Finlayson's word pictures; his voice always seemed with me, like a secret companion – and the suspicion that he had somehow remained by my side all through my travels came back to me strongly later that same day in Alice Springs.

Towards the end of the afternoon, after various visits and encounters, each one marked by the unease of return and all its restitching of broken ties, I called in at the Strehlow Centre, a curved, barn-like structure, several stories high, built from rammed earth, which stands at one corner of the cultural complex in the western part of town. In addition to the anthropologist's papers and other closed collections, the building houses the Museum of Central Australia, or its visible portion: a handful of giant fossils, cases of rock samples, display panels of the usual kind. On my previous visits, the museum had been almost empty, but this time a guided tour of some description was underway, a curator was speaking, his voice reached me from the far corner of the gallery. I listened, and only after some minutes of vague interest did I realise that the story's details were familiar and that I must be hearing a succinct account of the life and times of Finlayson, who was the subject of a new scientific exhibition – though it was nothing more elaborate than a display of his photographs and taxidermic specimens, since he was a long way from being a figure of renown. I drifted over and attached myself to the group of tourists.

"Those were certainly enlightened attitudes," the expert was just saying, with a striking warmth and intent, "at least for the time. Finlayson made a strong impact on everyone who knew him. He was the Centre's most significant mammal biologist – he was the last scientist to see the desert fauna before the wave of extinctions that swept through the region in the 1930s. Had he not made his great collecting journeys, we would have nothing. And this, you could say, is the pride and joy of our display." Obediently, the group gathered close. Before us was a tiny, ungainly skeleton.

"*Caloprymnus campestris,*" said the man, in reverential voice. "The desert rat-kangaroo. There are no more than 120 records all told of this animal. Very few people actually saw it – and anyone who's read Finlayson's account of how he found it will remember how he ran it down. His team chased it; it ran until it dropped dead. It gave its life for science."

"It's a wonder, really, there are any native animals left," said one of the group.

"There aren't that many," said the man. "But look at this sample: it was almost worth it!"

I lingered and gazed at the rat-kangaroo's skull: it had wide, deep eye cavities and frail struts like scaffolding within its jaw. Alongside it were the mottled pelts of other rare marsupials: bilbies, bettongs, bandicoots. The tour moved away, and soon came to its end. Eventually the curator came up beside me and looked approvingly on.

"Lovely creatures, aren't they?" he said. "It's amazing he was able to collect anything at all."

"Why?" I asked.

He cleared his throat and stroked his beard. "Do you want to know the story? Not the abbreviated version?"

"Put like that, who wouldn't?"

The curator stepped back and fixed his eyes on mine with a rather alarming intensity.

"They called him H2F," he began, dramatically. "Hedley Herbert Finlayson – he was a man of high degree..."

It was an unusual tale, made more striking by the building's sudden emptiness and the sombre presence of the skeletons, whose skulls seemed all to be turned in our direction. Finlayson had been born in Adelaide, into a large family; his mother bore the lovely name Finette, and sang in opera; his father, Ebenezer, who began his career as a Murray River paddle-steamer crewman, rose to dizzying journalistic heights, becoming the finance editor of the *Adelaide Register.* Finlayson was a student of unusual gifts, fascinated by chemistry. At the age of eighteen, he embarked on a series of experiments involving explosive compounds of his own invention. He chose a warm morning in early May for an allimportant test explosion, and travelled out to Glen Osmond, in the lee of the Adelaide Hills, at that time a remote spot. He was screwing in the percussion cap; it detonated prematurely: his left hand was shattered, the left side of his face was gravely damaged, he lost one eye, his hearing was impaired for the rest of his life. Such, said the curator, in solemn voice, was the condition in which Finlayson went out on his pioneering surveys of the western desert.

"You mean he was a wounded healer!" I interrupted.

"What?"

"Isn't it obvious? He was half blind, and he saw more than others. He suffered, and came close to death, and he devoted himself to studying creatures that were themselves endangered and on the edge of extinction. He travelled into the remotest country, and he could read its pattern and look into its heart. Don't you see? It all fits, perfectly. His weaknesses were what made him strong."

"I don't know I'd be applying some spiritual grid to Finlayson," said the curator. "He was very much a man of science. There's a new book out: it's like a biography, a life sketch, told through the diaries he kept during the time he was out here in the '30s, making those expeditions by camel to the Petermanns and Musgraves. Do you know that country at all? Out where Docker River and Warakurna are today?"

"A little."

"Everyone says they do, now. Everyone thinks they've seen the western deserts, if they've been out by Landcruiser and hurtled down the Great Central Road, and maybe stopped at the Docker campground overnight, or called in at Giles and seen the old grader used by Len Beadell's construction team. But those diaries give you a sense of how things really were out there along the ranges, when the first scientific surveys and expeditions were going through. You'll find the book easily. It's got a very striking cover: it shows Finlayson looking almost like Errol Flynn. There's a blurry photograph of him. His bad eye's in shadow, he's cradling a rifle on his shoulder, he's wearing a fedora hat. It's called *A Truly Remarkable Man.*"

"A mass appeal title, I'm sure!"

"It's everywhere in town, don't worry. Alice Springs is a very history-minded kind of place. As a book, though, it's strong meat: it's not for everyone. I don't know too many bush stories that pack that kind of punch."

*∗∗∗*

I stayed in my hotel room over the following days, which were ones of intense heat and summer storm, and took up this implicit challenge. Soon I was immersed in the diaries and the book's curiously episodic record of its subject's career, compiled, after several years of dedicated sleuthing, by Don Tonkin, a historian based in Adelaide. Parts of the narrative related Tonkin's quest, which required long months of outback travel in his subject's footsteps. Since the book was only lightly glued together, and disintegrated almost immediately after purchase, I recomposed it into several piles of pages, divided by the regions of Finlayson's adventures. These I arranged around me on the floor before the plate-glass window, and I ran through them one by one, looking out towards the flank of the MacDonnells, where the clouds loomed and the rains poured down – and though I had expected to find myself caught up in landscape descriptions, or closely observed encounters with Aboriginal groups, of the kind that fill *The Red Centre,* I was struck, instead, by passages with very different themes. In early 1932, shortly after his rediscovery of *Caloprymnus,* Finlayson boarded the Old Ghan at Marree and set off on a trip north, making for Tempe Downs on the Palmer River, where he hoped to continue his collecting of rare marsupial specimens. As his diary entries recount, he falls in with a lively cast of characters: an amateur anthropologist, a newly transferred police constable, a sister from the Inland Mission at Abminga – but as the day draws on, the rising temperature quickly drowns out his social instincts. Finlayson was travelling at the height of a great heatwave, which devastated the wildlife of the Centre, and his account of what he was witnessing swiftly takes on a tone of horror. The temperature of the region stayed over 38 degrees for nearly two months, as records show. The dreadful blanket of the heat lay across the inland from Tarcoola, on the edge of the Great Victoria Desert, as far east as the Gawler Ranges; it stretched north to Birdsville and Goyder's Lagoon. When Finlayson at last crossed the Territory border and arrived at Rumbalara, in range country, he saw zebra finches and budgerigars in their hundreds massed in the shade of the shelter shed beside the line, or perched beneath the train carriages, or gasping on the rails: birds were dying all around him. He prepared a brief scientific note upon the phenomenon, in which his intense feeling for wildlife comes through.

"From Horseshoe Bend, Central Aus., Jan 10, 1932: it was 120 degrees F in the shade at 1 PM: the hottest day in the Centre for many years. At Rumbalara Siding, when the train pulled in at about 3.30 PM, the dining car and sleeper were invaded by scores of waxbills. They fluttered about, gasping with wide-open mouths. Many flew into the fans and were killed or maimed. Under the carriages and on the floor of the shelter shed were massed hundreds of birds in various stages of incapacitation, and scores were lying dead."

The condition of these creatures was undoubtedly a true temperature effect, he was able to conclude, and had nothing to do with thirst, for the railway workers had put out several pans of water and only a handful of the birds were seen trying to drink. They seemed incapable of the slightest movement: when the train pulled out, scores more birds were crushed where they were stretched out prostrate on the rails. That afternoon, there was a sharp storm. Finlayson walked out in the evening along the sandy bed of the Finke River, following the foot of the curved clay cliffs which rose high above him. Zebra finches were still dying on the cliff tops; their bodies rolled noiselessly down into the sand bed at his feet. Some weeks later, he was able to confirm that bird deaths on the same scale had been observed that month across the western desert wherever there was a European camp or presence: in the Basedow Range, at the Olgas and Ayers Rock. He travelled on, through red-sand country, by heavily laden truck, in the company of Gus Elliot, the portly, cigar-smoking hotelkeeper from Horseshoe Bend, and the pair of them eventually reached the sanctuary of Erldunda station, where a large aviary had been constructed for the survivors of the holocaust: it was filled with bright-coloured songbirds. Among them Finlayson noticed a few crimson chats, delicate creatures, black-faced, finebeaked, which portend disaster in various story cycles of the desert lands.

Such signs, though, were quite hidden from him: his eyes were on the distant west. Like all writers in the Centre, he had fallen under the literary spell of his precursor, Ernest Giles, and he longed to travel through the mountain chains where the great explorer had suffered, and nearly perished, six decades before. Finlayson made collecting trips through the nearer ranges over the next two summers; he befriended

Pitjantjatjara people, and met frontier bushmen in their camps. He made solo probes by riding camel, and came within faint, distant view of his goal, the Schwerin Mural Crescent. He was almost stranded in remote bush on his return journey when his support team pulled back from their advance camp and left him to ride back to Ernabella alone. Through all these travails, his longing to reach the far country only endured and deepened. In the cool seasons he would retreat to Adelaide and his professional duties. In the first days of January 1935 he returned, ready for a last attempt on Giles's country – the Rawlinson Range, and all the romantic campsites the explorer had made famous in the pages of *Australia Twice Traversed* – the Circus Water, with its tall surrounding cliffs; the Pass of the Abencerrages, Desolation Glen. Finlayson stopped first at the remote station of Tempe Downs, in the hope that its manager, the "dilapidated, obstinate and irritable" Bryan Bowman, would ride with him. But Bowman offered him instead a stranger, H., "who knew the west country."

So began an ordeal that can only be pieced together in the most broken fashion in the pages of the journal: an ordeal as fierce and jagged as any in the brief, tormented annals of Australian exploration, of which this trip, a camel trek undertaken in the age of the car, marks the final, bizarre flourish. The diary entries record only occasional scenes in the duel between the men: the effect is like watching lightning strikes fitfully illuminating a landscape through which one is passing at speed. Finlayson takes an immediate dislike to H., who has an "evil aspect" – tall, stoop-shouldered, black-haired, green-eyed, without teeth, with a prominent scar on one hand. And what, then, must H. have thought of Finlayson, with his own scars, and his academic brilliance and flood of words, and his one good eye, and mutilated hand? Were they not a pair, branded by their shared initial, marked down for rivalry? The two head out, with their camels and supporting cast of Aboriginal guides, through familiar country, past the Cleland Hills and Mount Solitary; they skirt Lake Amadeus and reach the Blood Range, and the desert oak groves that line the Docker River – but already Finlayson has wearied of his companion's vain, vaunting self-obsession, his constant boasting and talking and wild fabrications. H. told Finlayson early on in their trip that he was Scottish and had come to Australia in the Victorian goldrush years, but he was said to be a Spanish and a German speaker, and his past was distinctly chequered: "Though he was evidently familiar with a large part of eastern Australia, and was a master of all the bush arts, his time seems to have been spent largely in the Sydney underworld, and his anecdotes and talk were extraordinarily foul, and had a strong city cast." Finlayson rode with his new companion, at first, at the tail of their camel-string; but soon he resolved to keep his distance, repulsed by the periodic, spasmodic rages to which H. was prone; struck surely, too, by the strange way H. and his abilities were the black match to his own. "He was all evil," wrote Finlayson, "and long-forgotten ideas about people who sold themselves to the devil came back, without sense of their absurdity. There was a sense of driving power about the creature, partly a natural consequence of his egotism, but partly derived from his energy and resource and natural abilities, all of which were of a very high order."

It was with this travelling partner, who by this stage had confided an intimate knowledge of Lasseter's lost gold reef, that Finlayson rode at last into the country of his dreams. The wind was hot, there were wild storms, the bush was thick with fruit and waving spinifex. They explored their way through the Rawlinsons; they found Circus Water, the Pass and Glen – but at this point, the tone of the undertaking suddenly shifts, as so often on bush journeys when one's goals are too easily reached. The Aboriginal guides, deep in strange country, make their escape; H. vanishes from sight for days, then re-appears, full of stories about a mysterious quest he is engaged in, and mortuary caves far to the north, and great lakes in the desert, still unknown to the mapping eye. He is in the grip of a renewed obsession with Lasseter, who had died in the nearby ranges, close by Docker River, only a few years before. Grievances between the two men deepen. H. has by this time revealed his trump card: he is in fact, he says, none other than the famous "Sapphire Bill," a writer for the *Chronicle* newspaper, and he plans to tell the unexpurgated story of the expedition – writing, on the frontier, being all. Finlayson, by this stage, regards his companion as mad, but with a "desperate and calculating madness." How vulnerable he is. He sees himself without help, half-blind, one-armed. There is a confrontation, it is described in the merest dabs and sketch notes. Finlayson raises his gun: he is quickly, cunningly disarmed. It serves as a catharsis. Peace descends, if not brotherhood: reflection; a hint of remorse. The pair reach Tempe Downs, their starting point. Finlayson, by now, has heard the bush story about H. – that this bleak man, with all his understanding, his intimacy with the sand dunes and the secret, far-off ranges, is in fact none other than the lost, crazed, dead Harold Lasseter in some strange reincarnated form. A ghost; a devil; a mirror of some common darkness? He turns over his trip to his chosen country in his mind, and edges towards the realisation that it was H. he had been seeking in the desert, and had been forced to confront. Not science, and knowledge, not the beauty of the landscape, but the chasms of humanity – and himself. He gives this thought brief houseroom before turning from it, definitively. There will be another completed line on the map of his expeditions, he declares, the journey is over, and his "little book" – *The Red Centre,* which is based in great part on the worked-up jottings of his diaries – will go out now with enough experience of the country to give the most carping of critics pause.

And with that – one can almost feel his heart racing, as he fends away the dark, and nightmare – Finlayson resumes his scientific activities, and it is very noticeable that he makes no return to those ranges on collecting trips until the 1950s, when the frontier is closed and settled, when missions and reserves have divided up the landscape, and the desert is criss-crossed by networks of graded tracks. Nor, at any point in the hypnotic, image-glutted chapters of *The Red Centre* is there mention of his bleak, disquieting alter ego or their duel of wills, not a word – although the submerged trace of that encounter lingers, like a pause before a breath, for those who know the landscape, and its silences, and can feel the anguish hiding in the author's voice.

\*\*\*

So caught was I by this story – its pace, its unfolding, its unravelling – that it seemed quite natural, the morning after I had reached its end, when I woke before the dawn to find a storm front breaking against the MacDonnells – a storm so fierce, fast-moving and spasmodic that it could have come straight from Finlayson's most overwrought and troubled pages. Thunder crashed and echoed from the peaks; lightning was flashing and striking in jagged patterns across the sky. Through my hotel window I could hear the wind blowing and see it tearing at the leaves of the nearby gum trees, gusting wildly then dropping momentarily away. I went outside, into the lee of the long, low hotel building. The flyscreens on the guest-room balconies shook and rattled; the shadows of the trees moved with a dreamlike, rippling rhythm. The storm drew nearer; daybreak came: the sun's gleam hit the range tops. It touched the lowest layers of the clouds, from which rain plumes, stained pale pink, were now falling. They hung like curtains in the air, vanishing whenever lightning sheets lit up the land-scape, then reappearing almost instantaneously, their drift and colour changing with each of these sudden re-animations, as though they were betraying brief discontinuities in the flow of time. Raindrops spattered in sudden surges, and stopped: thunder rolled again between the walls of the ranges. Then all fell quiet; the centre of the storm was passing overhead. I gazed up: its fluid shadows moved in silence. For some minutes, I watched, as the patterns wound and coiled above me. That sight summoned to the surface of my thoughts a memory fragment, a scene from a film I saw in childhood, a scene that struck me, in the darkened auditorium, with an intensity so sharp that, years on, it is one of the only instants from that time of my life I still preserve in my mind's eye. It was the brief sequence in *Ran,* the Japanese version of the Lear story, when the director, Akira Kurosawa, cuts, and turns his camera upwards to the sky, where the cloud formations seen against the sunshine convey an image of fate and its obscure unfoldings: the king's fate; the kingdom's; the flow and indifference of time.

After some while watching the clouds in their motions, and letting my thoughts run unguided, dwelling on themselves, until they had taken on a maze-like, wordless quality, I resolved to pay a call on my friend Mike Gillam, the photographer of the inland, a man whose life seems ruled and measured solely by gradations of light. I drove through town, past the bleak motels that form the centre of the desert art trade, past the lines of car yards and service stations, until I reached the highway turn-off at Hele Crescent. There, set back, was the Silver Bullet Café, with its forbidding, fortress-like entrance and its thick canopy of overarching pines. The lights were on in the low-slung side building, where Gillam, doubtless, was bent at his work desk, engaged in his painstaking tasks. I pulled up and looked around. I called out. Nothing. All the old totemic structures that marked out his property were still in place: the Ansett aircraft steps, the ancient goldmining cyclone, the Blitz truck from Newhaven station, the decommissioned, blue-painted double-decker bus, the Silver Bullet caravans themselves.

The perimeter defences, though, had been noticeably strengthened during my time away. For some minutes I probed here and there, trying various padlocks, searching for a way in, until I found an unguarded chink between an AUSCO container wall and a wire-mesh tangle, and edged through, expecting to find myself in familiar surrounds. I walked up beside the two Silver Bullet cabins, beneath the camouflage-cloth shade covers – but the gardens, which had been a bushland haven all through the time that I had known them, were quite transformed. New shapes met my eyes at every turn: curved steel rods, decorated car bonnets, ironwork sculptures and various wire-mesh animals had been interspersed amidst the grevilleas and the mallee trees, as if some second, purely metallic episode of creation had occurred there over the past year. I explored along the winding pathways. A pale, rose-coloured light was in the sky; the storm was to the north now; the thunder had ebbed away. I was just completing a circuit of the grounds when I spotted Gillam, standing at his veranda doorway in shadow, staring at me. He was wearing his standard uniform: dark work shirt, shorts, boots, an old Akubra pulled down almost over his eyes.

"What are you doing here?" he said in a voice of pure astonishment, as if only divine intervention could explain my presence there – and in truth, I reflected, it was an odd time to come calling and announce one's return, although the atmospherics seemed well suited to the moment. There was a flash of lightning, just then, in the distance. It shimmered, and forked above the range line; it cast the country into false colours, and stabbed down to the ground.

"Well, it's a social call," I said. "You are one of my closest friends in Central Australia, and I have been away for a while."

"Couldn't you have rung in advance? I would have set aside some time. We might have been able to go on the long bush trip we always talk about."

"That's something that's been very much on my thoughts. In fact I was hoping we might go out together this time – out to the west. And I have called you. Maybe six, eight, times. I've left several messages. If you ever cleared your answering machine, or checked your emails, you'd find them."

"Good point," said Gillam, reflectively, stroking his chin. "So what do you think of the exhibition? My whole life's energy is in it. It's called *Scrapyard Magicians.*"

He gestured vaguely at the forest of wire and metal structures. We fell into an exchange of news. We went inside, past the main room full of bookshelves and desert paintings, to the narrow kitchen, where Gillam took up station at his wooden bench and embarked on an elaborate ritual of coffee preparation.

"And you," I asked, eventually. "As bleak as ever?"

"Oh, on the contrary," he said. "I don't dignify despair with more than a fleeting second of my time. Everything may be dark in the Centre and Alice Springs, but on this block we're full of light and hope. Take a look at this – it's the catalogue."

He handed over a sheaf of photocopied paper with an elaborate survey drawing of the site on its cover.

My eyes fell on one paragraph: it had a certain spring to it.

*Most of this year's scrapyard magicians,* it announced, *make furniture or ornaments to challenge or hone their skills, to decorate their own homes; as an alternative pastime to shopping, watching television, or, perhaps, drinking to excess.*

"What do you think?"

"Very distinctive. Maybe we should do a walk-through. In fact, a walk-through of the whole Silver Bullet. It's a work of art itself, it always has been: the purest in all the Centre. I've always been curious about the ideas behind this place."

"Have you? You never asked before."

"Sometimes going away and coming back changes your slant on things."

"And what if those ideas were a secret?"

"What's the good of a secret nobody knows?"

"Good point, again. But they're not, of course. Everything about this place is a logical response to the landscape: every artwork, every found object; every curve in every path. There's nothing here that hasn't been re-engineered, and remade. See that table over there, beneath the shade nets?" He led me over and gestured grandly towards a low, rusted surface. "That's a type of drum fan, from the mining industry. And you see that flange? Ross Engineering machined it for me and dropped it in. The same for each object here. It's all artifice: a temple of artifice. Everything that's lost and cast aside in Central Australia comes back here for a second chance: whatever can be saved and given further life."

I pointed at the corrugated iron hulk beside us. "That shed, too?"

"It's not a shed: it's a World War II officers' mess. Very humble, simple, successful architecture. It was built here – but everything inside it has been brought to refuge. You see that heart, behind the wire – that red, inverted heart emblem, nearly as tall as you? That's a thickly coded symbol! It came from the old Ford Plaza in the heart of Alice Springs: but that place's design was copied from the Gold Coast, it was an exact copy of the Paradise Plaza, in fact – only on the Gold Coast version the hearts were green, and as the sole concession to the Red Centre the developers here changed them to red. When the ownership of the complex passed into different hands and they put up a new emblem, I felt it would be good to souvenir the heart. They had it hidden away in an underground car park somewhere. I sent an emissary out to get it."

"It wasn't a job for you?"

"I was pretty much on my last life by then with the authorities, on the civil-disobedience front."

"You were living dangerously!"

"Actually, I've been contemplating my last moments quite a lot recently. There are several scenarios: something mundane, like being crushed by the Blitz truck, which almost happened the other day. Or just jumping off a skyscraper, falling and flying..."

Something flashed by us.

"Look," said Gillam, with a surge of enthusiasm. "Is that a singing honeyeater? Aren't they lovely? Just look at the paradise we live in. There's more than a thousand species of plants within a hundred-kilometre radius of where we sit – and all the birds to go with them, too. And there – see? The babblers are back – over there, beside the corkwood: are they white-crowned? One of their more common names is 'happy families,' because they argue all the time."

I listened, rather swept away. The sky had cleared; light clouds were racing overhead. My heart beat fast.

"It's strong, isn't it, this coffee?" I said.

"Absolutely," Gillam nodded. "What was it you always used to quote?"

"'Black as the devil, hot as hell.'"

"The only way to have it; strong, like life. And who actually said that?"

"Talleyrand."

"A wise man."

"A survivor, anyway: and certainly a connoisseur."

"Of what?"

"Wine, women, food, ironies, espionage; architecture, perhaps most of all. I wonder what he would have made of these..."

I pointed at the two Silver Bullet cabins facing us. They shone and glistened, and the individual raindrops on their metal surfaces flashed and caught the glare.

"Do you actually like them?"

"They're your trademark. Naturally I like them – but now I think of it, I realise I have no idea what they were made for, or where they came from. You see them in the bush, of course, here and there, in out-of-the-way places."

"They're a very interesting response to a particular problem," said Gillam, professorially. "The earliest are early '60s. They were all built in Ballarat by Franklin Caravans, on special commission, after an education expert came back from a trip to the Apache home-lands in the States, quite convinced he'd found the answer to the schooling problems of remote Aboriginal settlements."

"And what was that?"

"It's been a recurring dream, hasn't it, it's true! There was a grand new idea: that we needed to build inspirational classrooms, and tow them out to remote places, where they could serve as beacons of civilisa-tion. Maybe that's why they were silver, to give a kind of lustre and allure. They built them on Bedford axles, 15 metres by 4.2. And they took them all out. The early truck drivers have great stories about tow-ing them, and young Aboriginal initiates walking down the tracks in front of them chopping down the trees so they could get through. They're classic desert ephemera. They were meant to last twenty years, at most. I think they're beautiful things. We realised they were being trashed, right across the Centre. I've seen them with multiple spear holes stabbed through them: they're just a thin, frail aluminium skin. Even in the late '80s, you could get them pretty cheaply. I have four of them: that one there was a schoolroom, at Murray Downs; the one over there came from Willora, out of Ti-Tree; that one was a health clinic: it was brought back into town from Amaroo..."

"And they're your emblem of vanished grace and elegance?"

"And the irony in their circulation and return is not lost on me, you can be sure."

"Perhaps," I said, "eventually you could even integrate them with the artworks in the garden, like the pavilions at Sanssouci or Nymphenburg."

"They're part of the ensemble already! There are rhymes and echoes everywhere. Look at this iron goanna here on the air-con fan. It's doubled by the live one that hangs out beneath the last Silver Bullet, at the far end beside the whitewood tree."

"The sculpture's not very lifelike," I said. "Who made it?"

"My bulldozer driver friend, Simon Holding. He's got real talent. You try making a lifelike lizard from wire, and scrap, and the expansion chamber from a motorbike exhaust. I think it's a special thing."

Gillam caressed the goanna's tail, then stroked the wire curvature of its jaw.

"In fact," he went on, "I think it's perfect, and beautiful. How could you not fall in love with it?"

"I know they're important to you," I said. "After all, you once almost laid down your life for one."

"Look, that's a bit of a bush legend, actually," said Gillam, becoming slightly flustered. "It wasn't like that at all."

"So tell me the real story."

"Isn't it you who should be telling stories? After where you've been, and all the things you've seen."

"Some things are best untold. Or the way to tell them best is not to tell them," I countered. "Go on."

"Well," said Gillam, with a fast-vanishing air of reluctance, his manner shifting by degrees as he spoke, until his second identity, as reptile lover, consumed by fine points of anatomical detail, in thrall to species listing and field collecting, had emerged in all its sharp and urgent splendour. "Let's be precise. In the first place, it wasn't a lizard, it was a monitor – a perentie. A very big one: *Varanus giganteus,* a female." He held up his hand and pointed: "You can still see the faintest scars, there, on my fingers, from the bite."

I looked: I could make out pale, straight marks, lightly indented, on the skin.

"It must have been a while ago."

"Oh, this was in ancient history! It all happened at the Arid Zone, the research centre, south of town. I used to work there, when I was still active in the mainstream scientific world. Here, of course, we very often have interrupted winters. The weather's fitful: it has no consistency. So you very often find large perenties in this country, at that point in the yearly cycle, starving; it's almost a matter of routine. A very big lizard, a heliotherm, which controls its body temperature, likes to emerge from its hiding place on a warm day, to lie in the sun. And that's when a perentie is most vulnerable. They'll come out and burn energy, but they're unlikely to succeed in eating, so they end up in poor condition, just like the one I'm talking about. It was about five kilos, and almost two metres long – I found it in the scrub around the research buildings and brought it in. I kept it in my office."

"So you were serving as a kind of wildlife sanctuary?"

"I was going to feed it up and then release it. We'd made a little progress; it was improving, I gave it a mouse, and then I went off to find it another – thawed out, but dead. Naturally, I had the smell of mice on my hands..."

"Never a good thing."

"No, indeed – it lunged and snatched at my fingers. Now, by chance, all this was happening on Christmas break-up day at the lab. There was a party on; in fact it had been on for a while. I was trying to get on top of this emergency rescue; but everybody else was outside, pissing on. I had the giant perentie hanging off my fingers: I was trapped. I couldn't even reach up to the telephone. Every time I tried to move, this thing would crunch its jaws and I'd feel a cold, bone-jarring sensation. There was blood pouring everywhere. I didn't know quite what to do. After a while, I decided I'd have to move the perentie, manoeuvre it with me, centimetre by centimetre."

Gillam dropped down to the surface of his veranda, at this point, and gave a demonstration.

"It was a slippery floor – it took me about half an hour to reach the doorway."

At this, despite my best intentions, I burst out laughing.

"It wasn't funny," said Gillam, laughing himself.

"No, it's a story of mythic grandeur – but it does have comic elements. And what then?"

"I made it to the lab's long corridor, perentie attached, and waited, lying on the floor: it seemed like hours. Eventually, one of the chemists came back in. I was able to call out. He saw me. Then my vet friend Taffy came down, and with him he brought the director, who was fairly charged. They produced a container of chloroform and put it underneath the animal. It had no effect on the perentie – but fairly soon I was starting to be overcome by the fumes. Then the director pulled out a huge butcher's knife with a yellow nylex handle."

"He wanted to cut its head off?"

"Naturally, being a science bureaucrat – but I refused. I shouted at him, or tried to – but I was almost fainting, from the chloroform and from the pain. Everyone was there by that stage, watching, cheering; it was one of those scenes that gets out of control. In the end, logic prevailed: Taffy found a knife-sharpening tool and levered the perentie's jaws apart. It took all his strength; the poor thing was terrified."

"And that's the end of the story?"

"Of that phase: my fingers were still locked into the top row of its teeth. I had to knock my hand out with a hammer blow. There was a trail of blood all the way down the corridor. Nerve repair took six months."

"That was quite a sacrifice. Do you think the perentie was grateful?"

"There's no reptile or snake – in fact no animal I wouldn't do that for," said Gillam.

"Because you love the world of animals more, in the end, than man?"

"Of course. They have truth, and simplicity: and what do we bring to the table? Murder, and scheming, and doubleness. That's always been clear to me: that awareness has shaped the way I live."

Nor, I knew, was Gillam exaggerating. I had heard tales of his exploits long ago, when he was a young nature photographer and had just come up from Victoria to Alice Springs. Early in his research career, he was put in charge of a wild-dog control experiment mounted by the pastoral industry with the help of scientists at Arid Zone: the campaign used new baits impregnated with 1080, a metabolic poison first identified by German military chemists in the course of World War II. But Gillam's commitment to the program was always in some doubt, and those doubts deepened in the hearts of his employers when they learned that he had a pet dingo on his block, a female of great poise and beauty, whom he doted on and took for long bush drives down the back tracks of the Centre and had even named "1080" – a choice that, it was eventually decided, might well be seen to mock the cause of wild-dog extermination in the country around Alice Springs. Gillam was moved on, to his true love, snakes, and snake portraiture, and many of his finest compositions can still be seen in a standard reference, the wall poster depicting the dangerous species of the North. The images were hard-won. There was one photo of a king brown, set on a dramatic red backdrop. Gillam had driven out to a distant claypan and was just attempting to pacify the snake, which was, like all king browns, nervous, unpredictable and highly strung. It struck at him through the canvas bag and deposited a near-lethal charge of venom into his hand – as did a western brown which he was photographing soon afterwards, during a fauna survey close to town.

"You can find it around here in seven patterns," he had told me, with great eagerness, at that point in his narration of these disasters. "Seven – within twenty-five kilometres. Now that's a high level of polymorphism! And the venom has a peculiar edge."

"Is there any significant species of Australian snake that hasn't turned on you?" I asked. "How many snake-bite recoveries do you think your organism has left?"

"To be truthful," said Gillam, "the last time I had anti-venene I developed a fairly severe allergic reaction. It may be that my snake-handling days are done. But that's not true for you, though. There's a world of possibilities."

At this, he brightened, as though lifted up on wings of grand surmise. "In fact," he said, "the moment is drawing near when you should have a snake."

At the time, I had brushed off this notion, but now I asked him about it again. What kind of snake had he been thinking of; what would he recommend? Gillam frowned, and adopted a sage expression. "There's really only one choice," he said at last. "For someone like you – with your mentality, and at your stage in life. An elapid would be a bad idea."

"A what? And what is my mentality, anyway?"

"Elapids are venomous: very self-contained, and full of grace. You'd be too fascinated by them, though, and too mesmerised. What you need is a snake with a certain inner tranquillity. I'd recommend a python: a carpet snake, for instance. They have the most magnificent markings, and an ease about them, and a charm, especially when they're young. Or maybe a Children's Python."

"But I'm not a child."

"They're not for children: they just carry the name of a Dr Children. They're gentle and good-natured, and they like to sit quietly on your lap, and all they do is hiss softly every three hours or so. They'd fit in with your lifestyle as well; they're completely nocturnal."

"I can't imagine how I've managed to survive without one until now. And what would be the best way to go about finding such a creature?"

"That's easy. They're all over the north Australian bush: anywhere from the Pilbara to the Gulf. They're particularly fond of eating microbats, and so you very often come across them lurking in caves, hanging from stalactites and waiting to snatch their prey out of the air. You could go on a python-hunting expedition into some country with good cave systems: the VRD, perhaps, or the stone plateaus of western Arnhem Land – although I suppose it might be advisable to stay within the law and buy one that's been raised in captivity from a pet shop instead. Under different circumstances, if I was still engaged in that world, I'm sure I could have come up with something – but my thoughts are elsewhere now."

"On environmental sculptures and landscape design?"

"On physical breakdown – and financial collapse: and caterpillars, too, of course. Caterpillars, more and more."

"In keeping with the spirit of place."

"It's true Alice Springs is very rich in caterpillar stories and ceremonial sites: old battlefields, egg and cocoon rock formations, even dance grounds created by their movements. That's the officially accepted, public side of things. But I find I'm very much in tune with them, and I see them in the country everywhere. These rock slabs, they remind me of the caterpillars in traditional Aranda storytelling, and that projecting rock there is leading them all back towards the sacred hill. And you see the winding markers I've put in along the boundaries of the pathways?"

"I was wondering about them."

"I always tell the children who come here that they're like the lines of processional caterpillars, those lovely creatures that writhe through every inch of the landscape."

"But what are they really?" I asked, bending down and touching one of them. "They feel like brushes. Did you have them specially made?"

"They *are* brushes, from the street-sweeping machines the town council runs."

"And at last they've finished their sad imprisonment in daily life, and come to the Silver Bullet and discovered their true totemic identity and purpose in the world?"

"Something like that. Like all of us. You too, maybe. What brought you back? I thought you'd slipped the leash and broken free." Gillam was speaking quietly, with focus, now. "Central Australia's not for everyone," he went on. "Nor the North. What do you think you have here, or need?"

I listened and let those words of his surround me. The question hung between us. He looked across.

"Somewhere to come back to," I said. "Unwritten country – but much more than that. I'm not sure that I have an easy answer."

"Of course you don't. There aren't the words. It's not an easy question. Do you think I'm not dancing on that knife edge? Do you think I haven't been, all through my life here? Chasing meaning. Pursuing shadows. Everyone who's alive here is. I gave up on words years ago: that's when I started making this garden. I was thirty-nine – I'd had a gutful of trying to communicate with people who wouldn't hear and had no time to see. It was time to articulate something physical, something that even the blind could get. I wanted to re-awaken people; to make them feel the life and pulse of where we are. I've made this my everything, now."

"Hele Crescent? I always thought of you as someone who was most alive in the deepest deserts."

"I spent years there, looking, making images – and I don't even know what I came back with. Have you ever been inside the gallery? In the officers' mess? No? Perhaps it's time."

He led the way across to the corrugated-iron building, running through the finer points of its façade as he went: the World War II shade netting; the wire-sculpted worm ouroboros; the vintage signs from the demolished newsagent in town.

"Take a look," he said, and held open the door.

Inside, in austere display, hung a selection of Gillam's most famous photographs: photographs that had been printed in books by the thousand, and exhibited in museums and galleries around the world. Photographs close-up and panoramic, ground-level and aerial: desert oaks in slant light; twisted white gums; Lake Amadeus salt pans; the red curve of the MacDonnells. One image above all drew my eye: it showed a dark, flayed shape, stretched out on the ground, before a landscape void.

"Where's that?" I asked him.

"It's gibber country, down near the South Australian border," said Gillam, almost whispering, standing close beside me.

"It's beautiful! And what's that shape?"

"The carcass of a dingo. Can't you tell? It's been shot through the hips and scalped. That's the reality of life, out in those rangelands." "That's what you were closing in on all the time?"

"That's why I lock this place up. It doesn't serve me well to open up the door. You always get a headache from the things you want to take pictures of. You bring back images – but they're faint ghosts of the things you see in your mind's eye. The world's full of photographs that mean nothing – that just show what there is."

"And that's why you don't go out into the bush any more?"

"It's not that simple. But I won't come with you – even though I want to, more than anything; even though travelling in that country is what I was always designing and shaping myself for."

"Because you've been there one too many times? Because there's a beauty and a grace in renunciation?"

"Because the way to pay tribute to a place is not always to go there and wear it down, and capture it, and make pictures of it, and describe it."

"Everything's the road to silence, you mean?"

"I thought you knew that! But there is someone who'll go out with you: in fact he's been expecting you. I saw him just the other day. The black cockatoo: your botanical friend, Peter Latz."

"Latz! I've rung him as well, hundreds of times, since I've been back – and left him messages. No reply."

"I think that's his way of saying that he's ready. You know he doesn't have a good telephone manner. If you go out to his block on Ilparpa, you'll find him waiting."

"Why didn't you say so before?"

"What's wrong?" said Gillam, half smiling. "Don't you think the conversation wound round the right way to its close?"

\*\*\*

I drove out along the curving highway, past the showgrounds and the Old-Timers' Home, hurtling by processions of town-camp dwellers on their trudges back and forth, and gazing through the windscreen at their faces as I went. Almost always, these men and women, desert people marooned in Alice Springs, pay no attention to the Landcruisers and triple road trains passing at speed so close by them, they walk on, oblivious to the wind shock and the diesel fumes, they maintain their stately progress as if they were promenading amidst the parterres of some eighteenth-century ornamental garden – but on rare occasions, one of them may pause and scrutinise the traffic, examining each oncoming driver with a piercing stare, absorbing the tableau before him as though its utter incongruity were becoming evident for the first time. And just as I was slowing and turning by the level crossing, an old man, whose face seemed familiar to me from some community in the deep western desert, cast a look in my direction: a measuring, assessing look, shot through with grief and dismay. For a split second, I returned it. He made a swift gesture with the palm of his hand, which was open, moving it from the wrist in a little arc as if to suggest the endless mutability of things – then he was lost from my sight, the flank of the range loomed ahead. With this welcome to country fresh in my mind, I sped on, westwards, past the swamps and motorbike trails, past the rural mansions and the hobby farms, until the last of the bush blocks, thick with ironwoods and stately ghost gums, came into view: the kingdom ruled over by the Linnaeus of Central Australia, the rangy, gauntfeatured, convention-disdaining Peter Latz.

It was a decade ago when we first met: a time of intense intellectual ferment and literary productivity in Latz's life, when he was just publishing his encyclopaedic monograph on Aboriginal plant use in the deserts, and refining his theories on the evolution of the landscape, the transformation of the inland from open forest into fire-raked plains, and the key role played in this upheaval by a single plant, the object of all his love and hate and urgent study – the carpet of the dune fields, the spiky, invasive *Triodia pungens:* spinifex. But even before our initial encounters, and my introduction to the wilder flights of his botanical enthusiasms, I had heard often of Latz and his exploits, so grand and so folkloric were the tales that clustered round him: the stories of his boyhood in the mission at Hermannsburg, where he had grown up among Aboriginal children, speaking Aranda and English as his joint mother tongues; the hard years he spent as a stock inspector in the Top End's scrubland cattle stations; his times of glory, too, as a field researcher in the Centre, when he was the sole scientist who could see the landscape as it looked to desert people's eyes. That vision had left its enduring trace, for Latz was a photographer, and exhibitions of his work were often held in Alice Springs – exhibitions that were admired, and widely seen, and even copied, although his pictures lacked entirely the candour and romantic sweep of his friend Gillam's work. Latz was chasing different quarry: he preferred the art of illusion, he loved the camera's capacity to trick the eye. His "desert abstracts" had the air of melting, panoramic vistas: broad, sluggish estuaries, mirages on the blue horizon, sand plains viewed from high altitude through hazy cloud. In fact they were all still lifes, riddling, deceptive closeups of minuscule, fragmentary things: paint flakes on rusted car bodies; wood filaments beside old campfires, the bark pattern on a she-oak tree – and this procedure seemed to illustrate a particular way of conceiving the world: a tendency, which I later came to recognise as highly Latzian, to see life's surface as fugitive, governed by hidden forces, concatenated at different levels, easy to misread. In those days he was still writing his short, elliptically structured masterpiece, *A Flaming Desert* – a work which mingles ecology and adventure narrative in the most intoxicating fashion: its detailed history of the desert in deep time is interspersed with puns and sharp one-liners and sweet memories of Aboriginal men of high degree. So disquieting were this manuscript's conclusions about the role of fire, and man's use of fire, in Australia's past that it failed, in its first form, to find a publisher – nor, for years, did any of the revisions Latz drafted, though its ideas have, by now, become well known in scientific quarters. They circulate in dilute, domesticated variants, stripped of all their tension and explanatory force: indeed, by a progression quite characteristic of the modern academy, they have been gradually dissociated from Latz's name and attached to new progenitors, and in that guise they form a part of the latest orthodoxy, a faint, disruptive murmur within the Solomonic temple of established desert science.

We spoke often of that book, and the ideas it set in mind are with me still: they became the foundation of a friendship which has much in common with the desert that lies, for Latz, at the heart of everything. It is austere, and close; reticent, yet undisguised; it is the antithesis of friendship in the modern, maintained and nurtured manner, just as the life cycle of an inland plant holds up a mocking mirror to the patterns of the coast. It lies hidden, dormant, seeming dead – until the slightest climatic signal: then it buds, blooms, seeds and dominates all round it in its lavish growth – and so things often seem with desert men like Latz. Months flow by, and I hear nothing of him, he is distant from my thoughts, and I am surely far from his, until the Centre, that stage where all must cross, begins to play its part, our paths draw together once more, and I find him, like a guardian being, standing at some inflection point in life, as that morning when I turned into his driveway – it was no more, in fact, than a faint track line, a suggestion in the soil – and saw him waiting, an expectant air about him. I jumped out. How like a familiar scarecrow he seemed then, in his drab, loose bush clothes, with his full beard and long grey hair blowing in the breeze! How angular, with his head tilted slightly to one side and a shoulder hunched: how like, in fact, his totemic bird, the black cockatoo of the inland, which pauses in just such fashion before it begins its stately flight.

I called out a greeting. He stared at me, appraisingly.

"You look like you haven't been handling life too well," he said. "In fact, you look half dead."

I let this go, and explained the circumstances of the visit: return; the Centre; Finlayson; the storm's enticement, the landscape's call.

"Of course," said Latz. "And I've been waiting for you. There's somewhere I've been meaning to take you."

"Docker River," I hazarded. "Mount Destruction. The Blood Range?"

"Don't get your hopes up," said Latz. "At least not too high. I've got the mutton curry ready – I'll just get my swag."

\*\*\*

An hour later, we were far down the dirt road that runs past Mount Ooraminna into the dunes and outcrops south-east of Alice Springs – a road that keeps, like many bush tracks, an undeviating setting, fixed in its progress to the horizon, so that passage through undulating country, with that red-dust arrow rising up and down before one, brings a kind of sand-sickness to the mind. I lay back: the corrugations jarred; there was the turn in to the rock carvings at Ewaninga; there was the Deep Well homestead entrance road.

"Where are we actually headed?" I asked. "Is it a mystery?"

Latz gave a saturnine nod. "Somewhere that's right," he said, after a few moments. "Right for talk, after so long. There's a waterhole, and peaks, and desert oaks to camp by. It's somewhere it's quite safe to take you."

"Safe for you?"

"For you. You'll see: it's close up, don't worry – just down this track."

"Your own country?"

"In a sense – it's soft, and peaceful: many conversations have unfolded there; the landscape's got used to that."

"And there are things on your mind?"

"On yours."

And Latz, of course, was right in everything he said. We set up camp, we walked, we went deep into the ravine that cuts through the sandstone of the range. Our memories came out, our thoughts fell into place; and I found it hard, after these first exchanges, which lasted through the hot time of the day, to be sure quite where my own experiences, which I had recounted to him in the most punctilious detail, stopped, and his began. It was as if we had been discussing dreams, instead of facts: the moment they had been sketched out and given depth, the episodes became diaphanous, and drifted, and began to vanish from my thoughts. We walked on, through the gorges, along the broken ridge line, down; he led the way, in steep, winding transects. We reached the desert-oak grove: there was the scatter of our camp. I was dazed: from speech, and from listening. My ideas would form, come to the very brink of words, then take on a weightless, transparent quality and dissolve upon my lips. Latz had dropped into a silence of his own. The sun sank in the sky; the range line glowed; the twilight fell.

"I know you think it's beautiful, don't you?" he said, rather heavily, into the void – then, before I could answer, swept on. "And it is: a beautiful landscape – beautiful, and destroyed. There's almost nothing left; it's a skeleton; it's been picked bare. No: don't say anything. I'll tell you."

In a soft, even voice, he then described to me a journey he had made some weeks before into remote corners of the desert: the Sir Frederick Range, the Ellis Range, the Wallace Hills. The names were still fresh in his mind, so closely had he traced their course upon the topographic maps. It was a belt of country I had always longed to see, around the community of Tjukurla, which lies at the western extremity of Lake Amadeus, surrounded by increase sites. For two weeks Latz had travelled through that landscape on foot, as a member of a scientific survey team, searching for signs of native fauna. They found nothing: the whole area was devastated. Rabbits, which were widely believed to be absent from the heartland of Australia, had survived, in this remote area, the onslaught of calicivirus. Indeed they were thriving, free from predators and isolated from infection's taint by the sheer distance separating them from others of their kind: their loneliness had become their guarantee of life. All through the dune fields and the plains, and even along the salt lake's barren shores, were vast, interlocking warren systems, deeply gouged, like subterranean castles, with wide, broad entrance tunnels, and radiating paths, and bastions looking out. Native animals, though, were less in evidence: there were no marsupials, large or small; nor did Latz see a single emu track on the wide salt-lake crust, where traces of a bird's passage can linger for many years. The country wore a forbidding aspect: it had been scourged, almost in its entirety, by savage wildfires, which had penetrated beneath the surface and carbonised the upper layers of the soil. Where once there had been groves of coolibah and bloodwood along creek channels, bare plains now reached away. Beside the wells and waterholes there was not a single surviving quandong tree to be seen, not even a lone charred stump, although in the early years of Latz's life these bush fruits had been common all through the ranges of the desert lands. From the air, on a more recent series of overflights, he had been able to take the measure not only of that stretch of country but of all the maze-like mountain chains, west to Warburton, east as far as Ernabella and Victory Downs. At that scale, and from that perspective, the Centre's fate was clear to him: the whole region was gradually turning into a single, unbroken grassland, a wilderness of spinifex, occupied almost solely by large, disconsolate, near-starving camel herds. Among these creatures, he said, there was an unusual preponderance of males, with predictable results: they were in a state of almost constant rut and tension, duelling, and skirmishing, and tearing each other apart.

"And that's your magic desert," finished Latz. "Your paradise! Still want to plunge back into it?"

"There's nothing else living there?"

"Donkeys – plenty of them – but nothing that belongs."

"No dingos?"

"Of course there are dingos. That goes without saying – there are always dingos. You'd need a nuclear explosion to get rid of them. Come to think of it, they tried that, didn't they, at Maralinga, and it didn't work at all. Apart from them, though, nothing: the devastated, biblical plain. Sodom and Gomorrah!"

"A bleak summation," I said, rather enjoying the emergence of this vengeful strain from Latz's Lutheran past.

"It's not bleak at all! That's what romantics like you never get. Biology is change: the dance goes on. There's no one correct, authorised way."

"And you don't mind what's happening? You don't miss the old desert: the dunes and parklands full of bloodwoods, and vines, and coolibahs; and the old Aboriginal men in their camps, singing, rainmaking and performing their ceremonies for months on end?"

Latz gave an operatic sigh, doctored the camp-oven on the fire before us and handed me a tin plate heaped with his mutton curry.

"Try some," he commanded. "It's got a kick. And you know very well there never was a golden age. There never was a past. If you look back into time in the desert, you run out of it right away. It was always newness. It's always life coming into being, changing, shifting: plants, animals, people too. Almost everything the old anthropologists used to think of as the essence of Aboriginality is new."

"Such as?"

"The skin-group system. It's just a cult, a fashion that was sweeping through the Centre when the colonisers came, and sowed their chaos, and froze it into place. You can see the appeal: it's complicated and provides the basis for a lot of argument. People, especially outsiders, think it's the heart of culture: it's become a kind of social resistance mechanism, now. And there's love magic, too. It's very clear that's a response to smallpox."

"It is?"

"Of course. When the epidemic came through, late in the nineteenth century, there were deaths everywhere. The whole society of the Centre was wrecked. It was impossible to find the right marriage partners, among the nomadic groups in deep, hard desert country. The women turned naturally to incantations and magic spells to lure and trap their mates. What's hidden, and absent, always seems to speak to desert people: concealed powers – uncaused causes. That's why you like them, after all. So: how does it taste?"

Latz peered at me in expectation by the campfire's glow. I had been toying cautiously at the curry with my spoon all the while this disquisition, so drastic in its implications for the standard history of desert Australia, was unfolding. With some reluctance, I lifted a small sample of the stew towards my lips: its acrid fumes assailed me. In it went. The shard of mutton, with fragments of onion, sweet potato and other obscure legumes attached, passed down my throat, twisting, writhing like a living thing. It had been coated in various burning chilli marinades: they produced a napalm effect. I swallowed, and half choked.

"Well?"

"It's wonderful," I said, after a few seconds gasping and gulping in the air. "Magnificent. A lovely, unfolding, articulated kind of flavour. However did you do it?"

"Look, I know it's not that flash," said Latz. "But when you're on those long-haul trips, you have to go for heavy seasoning."

"To mask the taste of cellular breakdown in the meat?"

"And combat any decay or bacterial activity triggered by all the thawings and refreezings along the way."

"That's very encouraging."

"Only joking. Anyway, I thought you'd appreciate some bush food from a real desert trek."

"You actually kept this all the time since that trip out to Tjuk urla?"

"Listen – this is luxury; this is the high life. We're close to town, we're camped beneath desert oaks, there's wind in the air and stars in the sky. What more could you want? And by bush standards, I'm a fastidious gourmet. I'll tell you how rugged things can get, food-wise. This is a true story."

He leaned forward, and had a last spoonful of curry, and rather over-demonstratively licked his lips.

"The best kind," I put in.

"Are you interested in hearing it, or what? About a famous old bush character, Bryan Bowman."

"You mean the man Finlayson knew: the manager at Tempe Downs? That's really time's long hand reaching out."

"The very man," said Latz. "In fact you could do worse than read him. He wrote a little memoir volume towards the end of his life: half of it's fantasy, and half pure gold. He was pretty brisk in what he said about desert people, at least in public, but for thirty years he lived with an Aboriginal woman he'd met on Tempe when he was still young. He contracted syphilis, like most of the old pioneers: eventually he died of it. I saw him in hospital, in town, just two days before the end. He was a fantastic horseman and he lived very rough: three months would go by before he changed into a new set of clothes. He stayed up at Coniston, in an earth-floored home. Once he had a visitor, from Alice Springs, who came in just when old Bowman was having his feed: sausages, straight from the can. Perhaps the tertiary symptoms were kicking in by then. Anyway, he was pretty sick. He threw up: out came the sausages, all over the floor, amidst the dog and chicken shit. And he just stuffed the whole lot back into the can. 'Waste not, want not,' he said, and ate them all again."

"The poetry of the outback," I murmured.

"I'm glad you're not too shocked, said Latz," in a rather disappointed way.

He fell quiet and glanced up. Above us, there was a faint, murmuring sound, like the echo from some impossibly distant shore. It strengthened.

"Look." He pointed: "See – there: bound for Jakarta, or Bangkok."

I craned my head back, in vain. Latz pointed once more overhead, and then I saw it: moving against the starfields, far beyond the point where its soundwave led the eye to search, an airliner's flashing wing lights.

"Qantas," he said, in an expert tone of voice.

"How do you know?"

"Who else would bother to fly here? Over this endless desert, just to link the world to Melbourne – or Sydney, even worse!"

"I've always found there's something beautiful about these nocturnal overflights," I said. "Watching the planes, lying in one's swag long after the fire's burned down, as they progress across the sky. I think of all the people sitting in that metal cylinder, staring at the movies, eating, drinking, trapped in their limbo, going over the triumphs and the failures in their lives – and maybe one in a hundred of them is gazing down through the window, at the blackness of the world below, and wondering what's out there. Or looking at the little screen that's supposed to show you where you are – and maybe there's even a place-marker, for Ooraminna or Deep Well, just the way there is for Durba Springs."

"For where?"

"Durba Springs, on the Canning Stock Route. If you fly from Perth to any Asian capital, you pass right over Lake Disappointment, and Durba Springs close by, and from the dot on the video map, at least, you'd think you were passing over Leinster or Kalgoorlie: some thriving inland town. But there's nothing, down at ground level, except a red range, and the sandy stock route, and a waterhole – and if you go at the wrong time of year, a campground full of four-wheel-drive expeditioners – until midnight or after, when the planes fly over, just like now. You look up and see them – and it's hard, then, not to picture yourself up above, staring down – hard not to have a twin perspective on your life, and see it in all its lovely futility: see its shape from the outside."

"A certain tone of melancholy there," said Latz.

"Of course," I laughed. "It's important to stay in character."

"But that's not the way you should be directing and stage managing yourself. Not at all: it doesn't have to be like that." He leaned over and pushed together the branches on the fire.

"I find, on the contrary, it does. And that's the best way, the only way, to cope with all the coldness of the world."

"And you think that's why you make your trips out here, and why you throw yourself against things: to have their measure, to feel the clash of swords, and the glamour of a landscape that can take your life?" I tried out the thought. I felt him looking intently at me.

"It may be there's something in that," I replied. "But the more I come out here, the more time I spend in the bush, the more it seems to me like a neutral space, and that's its real attraction – like one of those anechoic rooms, where you can hear the truth of things."

"And what do you hear? What does the bush tell you?"

"How beautiful life is – how precious, and how quickly withdrawn. We come into consciousness from nothing, for the briefest of spells, for no reason – and then, darkness once again."

"Let me tell you a story," said Latz, after a few moments. "One that might change your mind a little."

"What? You're not going to argue against that from your world view of total scientific rationalism?"

"Perhaps! Just listen. It's night time round a campfire in the desert: it's the time for tales and revelations, don't you think? Maybe the real reason why you came back, and why we're travelling together, is so you can hear this. It could be nothing to you: it could be something that you need."

At this, I settled back. He set the scene. The story came from several years before: a period of unease and transformations for him, when his thoughts about the landscape were shifting, he was travelling extensively, he felt himself lost and driven from his moorings by the tides of his own deductions and ideas – and this impression of drift and flux was only strengthened by the sequence of the account he then unfurled before me, which jumped from his usual laconic style into lofty, swirling passages of scientific theory-building, thought upon thought, idea upon idea, his speculations rising ever higher, as though impelled by their own momentum, until we reached the limits of some wholly abstract mental domain. I clung on: his voice shifted.

"It was then," he said, "that the experience I wanted to describe to you began. I'd been ill for several days; I fell asleep and slept heavily, for some hours, until the deepest point of night. Suddenly, I was wide awake, and in torment: pain had enveloped me; it pressed down on my skin; it was as though my body was being flayed. I struggled over to the house next door: you know how close it is. I barely made it there. They took one look at me and drove me straight into town, to Accident and Emergency."

"Alice Springs hospital – that was really taking your life in your hands!"

"Too right. I had a perforation of the oesophagus. I was bent over in a knot – I could barely speak. They assumed I'd had a heart attack. The doctors put me straight onto anti-coagulants, with a line of adrenalin poised. I had a severe allergic reaction: the effect was instant. I knew it; I was aware of it – I began to float away – there was a sense of peace: nirvana, a oneness inside the world, a being asleep and yet awake. Of course I'd read all about such events and internal states. People have quite different experiences, depending on their backgrounds, but it always seems to be fundamentally the same thing: pain, stress, then escape, and relief. The nurses were watching me: they saw me going; they pumped in the adrenalin. I came back – there was a slight tunnellike effect, and a tone, a mood, receding."

That sense of connection, and a high perspective, as though he was slightly above himself, remained throughout his stay in hospital. He was placed in a critical-care ward. In the room opposite, one of the most famous of the desert artists, Turkey Tolson Tjupurrula, his classificatory brother, was quietly fading away. Latz would wake at night time, and pace in the darkness down the corridors, and stand for hours at Tjupurrula's bedside, watching his laboured, heavy breathing. Then there would be some commotion: another patient would scream out, or have a fit; the nurses would respond in calm, efficient fashion, as though their acceptance of death's nearness had lent them all a beauty and a poise. Some days on, Latz was discharged and went back to his block, transfixed by what had happened to him. He turned it over and decided that the experience had much in common with the trancelike states induced by *ngangkaris* – the doctors of the western desert, who appear to slow the organisms of their patients before they work their healing spells. Perhaps, he thought, the proximity of death had triggered a sharp production of endorphins in his brain, and these were responsible for the floating sense that had lifted him away – just as, once, at Surveyor General's Corner, when he had scaled a high granitic boulder pile and felt himself stricken by heat, and vertigo, and half transported by a sense of union with all he saw. But even as he entertained these ideas, he knew he had been changed. He walked the boundaries of his block in slow reverie. He felt a deep love for each tree and plant. He was linked to them: the vines with their twisting flowers, the leaves of the bush passionfruit, the birds above him, singing. "Of course," he said, "I've always felt the landscape speaks to you – but it was speaking in especially pure form in those days. How intense it was, that new life! It was like being reborn. I came to feel that this was what the Buddha learned, when he was sitting beneath his tree."

"That death is just a screen, and what hides behind it is a full consciousness of life?"

"That only by being aware of death, and believing in death, do we truly die."

"And does the nature of the life one's had affect one's death?"

"This isn't a seminar," he sighed. "I don't know. All I know is that I felt awful before. I was sick, and in pain – and that's all gone. It changes your life forever, when you no longer fear death: when it's a completion, and not an end. Remember Mozart, and what he said."

I waited; he waited; the sentence remained between us, in the air.

"So?" I turned to him. "What did he say?"

"I thought that was your part of the world," Latz replied, in minor triumph. "Europe, Vienna, that kind of thing? Joy dissolving into sadness, and then back again? It was near the end for him, when he was pining away. I heard it on Radio National..."

"Practically first-hand testimony!"

"Do you want to know?" There was a slight, reproving pause; he went on. "This was in the winter months: he'd made his journey back from Prague, and the first performance of the *Clemenza di Tito* he was already writing the Requiem, which he was convinced he was writing for himself. I always picture him in those days crushed by the sheer weight of all the beauty he'd fashioned and passed through the filter of his mind. 'I used to fear the touch of death,' he said, 'as a fearful, lined old woman – but now I have seen her, I understand she is a beautiful young maiden, and I long for her final embrace.'"

Latz fell silent. The fire had burned down to its embers. I could barely see his face beside me.

"Why," I asked, "are you telling me this?"

"Isn't that what's on your mind, really – what lies there, at the end? Isn't that what you're trying to find out in this country; what you've always been trying to find out, in all your life's permutations – all your shifts and movements: how to die?"

\*\*\*

Still in the shadow of this conversation, the words of which seemed to reach back like a judgment deep into my past, I set off, some days later, on my long-planned trip out to the ranges, bound for Mantamaru and the Ngaanyatjarra lands. By mid-afternoon, I was nearing the low, symmetric line of Mount Conner, which rises sheer from the saltbush and red sand of its surrounds. On the far side of the narrow western highway, named, by some humorous soul in the Northern Territory roads department, for that unsuccessful tourist Lasseter, lies Curtin Springs – a bleak roadhouse, favoured by international backpackers, which I had avoided religiously for years. But I was low on fuel, and in a mood for experiment: I slowed and turned in, and I was almost blinded as I did so by the flash of light from chrome and steel. Perhaps a hundred Harley Davidsons, all gleaming in the low sunshine, were parked alongside each other, their front wheels turned in tandem and neatly aligned. In that harsh landscape, framed by a pair of stunted gum trees, with smoke plumes from distant bushfires hanging in the sky behind them, they looked like the elements of some fiercely ironising installation artwork, aimed at the wastes and vanities of modern life.

I went towards the seating area, which was mantled by a complex array of nets and shade-cloth canopies. The tables were full: leather-clad bikers, most of them ageing, grey-haired, with benign expressions on their faces, strolled about or lounged in the wooden chairs, drinking, smoking, eating, their exchanges drifting in the air. *Please assist in preserving the beauty,* entreated a sign at the entrance to this enclosure, alongside a large cage filled with listless, panting guinea pigs. I walked into the bar. Its atmospherics were unchanged since my last visit: it was cramped, and dark, and narrow. There was a clutch of backpackers at one end. A couple, in full leathers, both with long grey ponytails, stood just before me. Behind the bar, on a high stool, sat Peter Severin, the wiry, white-haired leaseholder of Curtin Springs, a founding member of the once-dominant political party of the Centre and a man with pronounced opinions on the proper order of the region and the world.

"You look familiar," he called out at once. "You've been here before, haven't you?"

"A while ago," I said, "but things seem much the same."

"Oh, we've been powering on," he said. "My wife passed away; my Holden FX is on its last legs; there are days when I can't remember my own dog's name."

"I'm sorry to hear that," I said.

I allowed my gaze to sweep across the wall; it was choked with the standard eccentric roadhouse touches: a military map of Iraq, a recipe for camel stew, a framed newspaper article, of faintly salacious tone, featuring Julie Andrews on 'My Favourite Things.'

"We've been updating," said Severin. "You can see. You're a valuer, aren't you? An insurance valuer – I remember now."

"I'm not a valuer," I said, "but I value things."

"Are you the ABC reporter for the convention?" asked the woman of the leather couple, who had been listening carefully to this elliptical exchange.

"Do I look like an ABC reporter?"

"No – come to think of it," she said. "On a second look, you don't have the kind of easy, open face one associates with a public broadcaster."

I searched for some reply to this coruscating remark.

"Oh, he doesn't look that rough," said Severin, emolliently. "In fact," he went on, "you get bushmen a lot less presentable than him all the time in here. We're almost friends, although I can't quite place him for the moment."

"What convention?" I asked.

"There's a Hogs' convention," said the woman. "It starts tomorrow at the Rock. I'm the event publicist. There are fifteen hundred Harley Davidsons converging on Yulara even as we speak."

"And doubtless a healthy police escort as well."

"Why?" said the woman, indignantly, putting her hand around her partner's leather-belted waist. "It's not as if we're Hells Angels, or gang members, or anything like that. Harleys don't always mean blood and violence. We're just motorcycle lovers, aesthetes of the road – people who like an edge of wildness and freedom in life. You should call in and see – you might be surprised. Are you headed that way?"

"Past," I said. I heard the low whisper of my voice, sounding as though it was giving a secret away. "Well past: Warakurna, Mantamaru, and then on – maybe to Wiluna."

"The beckoning west," broke in Severin. "That's mirage country out there: dream country, delusion country. You need to have your wits about you."

He repeated this last phrase and shook his head, as though to register his private alarm at my reckless enterprise.

"Stop in on the way," said the woman. "You might be quite surprised. We're going to circle the Rock: more than a thousand Harleys around Uluru – revving their engines at the nation's heart."

"That'll give the spirits there something to think about," said Severin. "Maybe I should go myself.

It's been fifty years since I started with the Rock. There was nothing there back then."

"You'd need a Harley if you wanted to drive round it with us," announced the woman, rather pityingly.

"There's an old 1935 Triumph out the back," said Severin. "I wonder how it would go."

We trooped out behind him to inspect this marvel. My eyes were drawn by a long line of meshed structures, set some distance away, at the far end of an open courtyard. More cages: aviary cages, I realised, as I went towards them. In each there was a pair, or family, of native parrots – scolding, chattering, whistling, calling, their voices mingled into a constant, modulating, chaotic blur, as though one drifted on a stream of sound and a whirlpool or waterfall was drawing near. I walked along the line, prompting flurries of attention from each enclosure in turn. There were superb parrots and red-wings, ring-necks and lorikeets. Some were perched morosely on the bare branches of acacias or eucalypts contained within their little prisons. Some were clinging to the wire mesh by their beaks and struggling along, with frantic, wholly pointless effort, keeping pace with me for a few steps as I went. Severin came up beside me as I reached the budgerigars.

"Marvellous creatures," he said in a proprietorial voice, at which the two birds chirped, and twittered, and darted from side to side of their cage with whirring wings – and with each gesture of Severin's in their direction, the speed of their movements mounted, until they became a haze of greenish light trails, impossible to follow except in the brief moments when they collided with the cage walls and beat vainly against them with their wings. I retreated, and Severin too. The birds came to rest, and flicked and shrugged their plumage; after a short pause they jumped alongside each other and began preening and gliding their beaks over their wing feathers.

"Strange," said Severin. "They're not usually that way."

"They look a bit mangy."

"Mangy – yes, it's hard out here, with all the lice and pests we get. And we've had the worst conditions: we've been in drought for years, it's been like those spells of unbroken heatwave they recorded in the '30s – and the fire."

"I can see." I nodded towards the distant smoke plumes blurring in the sky.

"That's nothing – you should have seen it in the bad times. We've had the most savage fires I can remember here. Two dreadful seasons. The whole of Curtin's been burned out. There's scarcely a stick of feed left on the place: it's like a wasteland. One fire burned for eight months – it's still smouldering, out on Lyndavale and Mulga Park."

"Perhaps it's not ideal cattle country."

"It's not ideal for any life form when you get a run of years like this. I've heard stories from the road-train drivers coming up from Kalgoorlie on the south road, through the Aboriginal reserves. There were flame fronts fifty metres high along the track, and palls of smoke hanging like layered veils above them; the fires burning on the ground were reflecting up at night to the dust clouds. There'd be a pink glow overhead, like some aurora effect across the sky – and when the trucks were passing through the desert-oak forests, they'd see the trunks bursting into flame around them: whole trees would go up like torches, sparks would blaze and catch, there were fiery leaf fronds and seed pods flying through the air."

In front of us, as though lulled by this alarming word-portrait, the budgerigars had composed themselves. They now turned to face each other and began nuzzling, with open beaks, their little stubby tongues emerged; they kissed, at first decorously, with quick bobbing motions, then more ardently, great, impassioned kisses, mouth on mouth, with locked beaks, tongue grinding upon tongue as though they were trying to excavate the deepest recesses of each other's throats. We watched.

"They're in love," said Severin, a touch disconcerted.

"Is that entirely normal avian behaviour?" I asked.

"There's nothing entirely normal left in this landscape, after so many nightmares, and such disruption," said a tall, striking blond-haired man in leather motorcycle leggings, who had just come up.

He stood appraisingly in front of an empty cage.

"What's in there?" he said.

"A night parrot," replied Severin.

"True story?" said the man, and looked with greater focus at the little enclosure. On its stone floor was a fully filled water bowl, surrounded by the white flecks of droppings.

"I thought they were extinct," I said, "except in the realms of imagination."

"Oh, they're common, really," said Severin. "Ornithologists just say that to give a bit of spice to their lives. They're all over the place – you often see them at dusk, poking through the spinifex."

"So where is it?"

"It's a night parrot," said Severin, in a wry voice. "Obviously it's not going to come out during the daytime; it's asleep, in its shade box. If you want to see it, you'll have to overnight here, won't you? There are rooms free. We've got new deluxe cabins. Ninety dollars a night. How does that sound?"

"You're headed for Wiluna?" said the tall man at this point, somewhat combatively, and brushed back his long hair from his shoulders.

"News travels fast: Warakurna, Mantamaru, then maybe on."

"Down the Gunbarrel? Past Carnegie homestead? Do you know that country?"

"Do you?" I parried.

"Why are you going out there, to those communities? Or do you have a taste for pulverisation and cultural collapse?"

"More for tranquillity and friendship," I said.

"A true believer," laughed Severin at this. "With all his dreams and ideals intact!"

This exchange, which had the quality of sparring, flowed on: the life today in Warburton, and the country round about; the desert river channels, the ranges and their undetected mineral reserves, the sites of ritual power scattered through the west. Severin broke in a few times more, but found no response, and, night parrot forgotten, he moved away.

"And how come you know so much about the landscape?" I asked my new companion. "Who are you exactly?"

"I didn't say. And I didn't ask you who you were, either. Sometimes conditions of anonymity favour true dialogue, don't you find?"

"Are you a scientist?"

"I was once an anthropologist," he replied, with a little emphasis upon the tense.

And he did indeed have something of the faintly used-up air that tends to mantle the members of this profession – that air of grievous knowledge, painfully acquired and nobly borne – but there was something else as well. I looked at him more carefully. His manner was resigned, irony-laden, yet easy, with a slight edge of energetic malice that peeped out when he made his thrusts and jabs. He told me something of the circumstances that had brought him to the deserts, going into minute detail at obscure link-points of the causal chain, then skating abruptly over crucial episodes. I tried to follow this strange self-presentation: it resembled nothing so much as a medieval world map, with vast inconsistencies in measurement and scale. Life and background had made him a student of man, he said in cryptic fashion. By this stage we were sitting amidst the convention-goers, who received him as one of their own and gathered round, with the result that our talk took on an almost dramatised quality, and his words and gestures became more fluent and expressive as his tale wound on.

"It's an inclination, anthropology," he said. "It always was: a kink of character. Some people like ideas and their interplay; some like power. I like the poignant attributes in life: the things you only encounter in the minds of human beings."

"Such as?"

"Hate. Deception. A sense of beauty. Love. Those were the things that fascinated me, once."

"This all has a nostalgic feel," I said.

"But isn't it obvious," he said, with a soft, expansive gesture to his listeners, as though the narrative unfolding could serve quite self-evidently as a portrait sketch for every one of them. "We're an army of the lost – all of us. We're gypsy riders, drowning in nostalgia – otherwise we wouldn't be riding these machines of sadness down the open road. When I was studying in Adelaide, I knew a woman who had a striking theory about the course of our journeys through life. She believed that the longer we live, the more damaged we become – and the more we inspire love – love being, as you know, a response to need and loss."

"In the giver, or the receiver?"

"Both, of course."

"And was she beautiful?"

"Naturally – why else would one pay attention? She influenced me. She'd spent time in the remote world; in fact she was brought up on the Ernabella mission – and she felt that in all our engagements with traditional Aboriginal people, no matter what the warmth and friendship, we're never doing any more than peering over the horizon of ourselves, and vainly trying to see what lies beyond."

Those thoughts, impetuously thrown off, led him further. His training; his days in the field; his commitment to the cause of land rights, which drew him, as the first outstations and homelands were established, ever further into the desert's deep redoubts. He came to rest in the southern Pitjantjatjara lands, and from there made remote-area field trips into the Victoria Desert's southmost reaches – country long since regarded as empty, silent waste, trackless save for a single red-sand access route.

"You mean the Anne Beadell Highway," I said.

"You think you're a real bush connoisseur, don't you! Even then, we'd dropped that name: we called it the Serpentine Lakes Road."

"It must be a little impractical for motorcycle touring."

"Impossible, it's true. It's the kingdom of the troop-carrier. There's a large biosphere reserve down that way, full of desert kurrajongs and marble gums – or it was back then: the Unnamed Conservation Park."

"That's its name?"

"Most things in Australia of real importance are unnamed – haven't you noticed? But in this case that's the gazetted name. I found I was travelling out there more and more, on field trips from Iltur and Wartaru, to escape from the chaos all around me. It was hard to believe in what you were doing when everything you were researching – everything – was dying and falling apart before your eyes. That was an implacable backdrop: I saw myself clearly when I lived in the outstations."

"How could one not?"

"And it was hard, out there, not to feel the beginnings of a contempt for myself and all my colleagues. Man studying man: what gave the right? What could you learn that wasn't theft? What could you give?"

He fell silent.

"And then?"

"Then there was a contact episode. Or a quasi-contact episode, it would be better to say. It's not well known. It wasn't written up."

The Harley riders sitting round him drew closer: they looked like the attendant figures leaning inwards at the edges of some carved nativity.

"You remember the last nomads – those ones who came in during the '80s, near Kiwirrkura? And you've heard of Warri and Yatungka, out in the Gibson? And the desert dwellers, down in the spinifex lands on the Nullarbor? Well – there are other stories like that. There are people out there in the deserts; old Aboriginal men living out their days."

"You're sure?"

"Outstation families see their fires. They come across their tracks. It's an open secret – and I could leave it at that."

"But you have experience of your own?"

"I do – and it was enough to change my tilt on many things."

Towards the end of a hot, rainless January, he had travelled out, alone as was his habit, deep into the reserve. He was driving beneath clear skies, when he saw, straight in front of him, a spinifex fire take hold. He stopped, in puzzlement; it turned to excitement, then to a kind of sharp and painful joy. He stepped down from the troop-carrier and went cautiously ahead, quite aware what was happening to him, exalted, almost dazed by his sense of anticipation: how closely he had studied the contact stories from decades gone by; how much they meant to him! It was as if he was himself now one of the characters in those heroic tales, or an actor in one of the grainy documentary films. There, ahead, was a lone, tall man, with spears, wearing a hair-string belt, standing, one hand raised up. They walked towards each other across the dune: they stopped; they said nothing. They looked at each other.

"And the look I saw there in those eyes stays with me still – it was such a look: it destroyed me!" He laughed, but bitterly. "There are so many stories about the desert and the secrets that it holds: the Dreamings – the ceremonial journey lines, the sacred places: so many stories being generated by outsiders. All the fantasies and projections we bring with us. And that's what's really there: what I saw then. He looked at me with the eyes of love so deep it made nothing of everything – every feeling I'd ever had in my life. For a minute, perhaps longer, he gazed at me, as if he was reading me – and then he turned, and with long, loping strides he ran away. I watched his figure receding over the dunes; he never looked back. He ran from me as though I was carrying some dreadful infection or annihilating plague."

"And when was this?"

"A while ago," he answered, with studied vagueness. "Before there was GPS equipment. I was tempted to go back, of course, and find that place again, and him – I decided not to. It was far away, where I'd seen him: it was the furthest I'd ever travelled into that landscape. The weeks went by. After that, you can imagine I found it hard to take my professional tasks too seriously: in fact impossible. I understood what the real deserts are: us: our death and taint. I'd look at all our frontier encampments, our little bush empires – the brick-block outstation houses, the metal roofs, the water tanks, the sick children, the scabies-ridden dogs, and just want it all to vanish away. That was what we made as desert life; that was our idea of tradition going on. I could see the world that we were building there, with ourselves as overlords: all the council clerks, and program managers, and executives; and the anthropologists, too, like gods of the outback, presiding, advising, being sensitive as they inquire and probe and wreck."

"That's a fairly apocalyptic vision," I said.

"And the desert people in the homelands, too," he swept on. "Those places are tombs for them: they go along, and answer all our questions, and paint the art we want, and surrender all the furthest details of their belief-systems, and stare back at us with their limpid, compliant eyes – and that's enough for us to keep our little fantasies of co-existence and cultural survival running on."

"And all that – that loss of faith – came from one meeting in the desert?"

"Perhaps it did. At any rate, I began to feel that I was living in a world of shadows on the outstations: a world where everyone was dying or fading or had suffered strokes so debilitating they couldn't think or speak. It was the palest echo of the world before. My dreams had dissolved. I chose, as you can see, a new course in life."

"And what do you do now?"

"I have a nomadic existence," he said. "I travel – and I consult, from time to time, on First Nations issues, for a multinational" – and this rejoinder, with its various glinting ironies, brought our conversation to an end.

I got up and went to find my deluxe accommodation, but ran straight into Peter Severin.

"Unusual man," he said. "I'm not sure I've seen him here before. Any revelations?"

"One or two."

"Believable ones?"

"Of course – and maybe even true."

"Almost time for the scenic sunset tour of Mount Conner," said Severin.

"Mount Conner: the home of the ancestral ice spirits? Too dangerous for me."

"But it's one of the three great tors of Central Australia – and the only one in private hands. Just a short trip down a station track."

He stepped out from the shadow of the accommodation block and pointed: the mountain's flank glowed and shimmered in the sunset light.

"It's the real thing," he said. "A genuine natural wonder. Better than staring at that panorama painting of it they used to have in Alice Springs."

"Used to have? You mean the Panorama Guth?"

"Didn't you hear? It burned down last night: down to the ground. It was on the TV news. The fire was so fierce they couldn't put it out – it burned almost until the morning came."

I left him. With deliberate steps, I walked back to my vehicle, started up and drove east, at speed, passing with metronomic regularity little fleets of bright-painted combi vans, swerving round the thin, exhausted herds of cattle as they loomed before me in the half-light. First Ebenzer roadhouse came, and then Erldunda. I joined the Stuart Highway and its procession of mining trucks, and livestock transporters, and caravans, weaving my way through them until, two hours later, the range line before Alice Springs and the mast lights on the peak of Mount Gillen showed. I reached the heart of town, and turned into Hartley Street, and looked: but there was nothing where the crenellated tower had once been. The enclosure was cordoned off. A fire truck was parked nearby, its red lights twirling. The front building of the Panorama had been saved: beyond was rubble, wreckage, black, twisted beams and disordered concrete slabs. I was taking in the scene and its surrounds – the car yard, the motel bedroom block next door, both quite unharmed, despite their proximity to the fire – when my gaze fell on a little plaque of polished bronze. I bent down, beneath the flowering shrubs that marked the edge of the Panorama's property, and, almost overpowered by their sickly scent, I made out, by the red flashing light, the words engraved on the metal. It was a message Guth had designed as his envoi: *I am proud since I came to the Centre. I have done this for this country and this nation with love and thanks. When I was gone, I left something special behind me for your children and grandchildren and the next generations.* And so are our best desires subverted, I murmured to myself. Alongside was another plaque, of similar style and shape, recording the opening of the Panorama, which had been presided over, on the first of November 1975, *by the Honourable E.G. Whitlam, Q.C., Prime Minister of Australia,* in one of the final public acts of that statesman's brief, eventful reign.

\*\*\*

Some days later, at Keller's Restaurant, a landmark of Alice Springs, which offers a strikingly divided menu of Swiss and Indian dishes and serves as the natural backdrop for conversations of any substance in the town, I heard more about the Panorama's fate from my friend Dick Kimber, the historian of the Centre in its many different faces, a historian whose work verges on artistry, so serene is its interweaving of the roles of chance and coincidence in life, so evenly does it present the beliefs and actions of each figure it plucks out from the mirage-like pattern of the past. I told him at once how eagerly I had gone back to the Panorama on my return from overseas, how much it had come to mean to me, despite its old-fashioned look and the rambling, inchoate nature of its exhibits, those objects in it which had remained resistant, almost invisible, even though they were spread out before one's gaze.

"Indeed," said Dick gently, with a smile of utmost tolerance, and, after several preliminary diversions, began his account. The fire, he said, had broken out in the small hours of the night, and had been caused, in all probability, by an inconsequential fault in the wiring of the structure. The emergency crews were quickly called, and had been able to reach the front galleries, but they were driven back from the main building by the smoke and by the heat of the blaze: and despite their best efforts, the panorama itself was wholly destroyed before their eyes – as was only natural, for its sloping, sand-strewn foreground was covered with dry, intensely flammable spinifex grass, which had served as fuel, while the skylight, so like a fan vault, designed to light the canvas in an even fashion, had become an air vent, an inadvertent chimney, drawing the flames upwards and creating a firestorm effect.

"And was anything saved?"

"The desert watercolours: the Namatjira works, and others of that school, but all the more perishable artefacts were burned up: the cockatoo-feather headdresses, the kadaitcha shoes, the decorated wooden boards. The flames burned for a day. When at last the fire teams could make their way into the main galleries, they found the sacred stones – incinerated, seared, but still intact: all the carved stones, you remember, with their fine patterns, circular and rippling, all the treasures of the old Aranda men who confided them so lovingly into Henk Guth's hands, and who saw the Panorama as a kind of sacred cave. There they were, seemingly preserved. The moment, though, that they were moved, or even touched, they all disintegrated, they turned to powder and to dust."

"Almost like the objects found in Egyptian tombs: you know all those stories about wooden spear hafts collapsing and their metal points clattering to the ground the moment the entrance seal was breached?"

"Perhaps. Afterwards, the fire and emergency services calculated that the temperatures had reached about a thousand degrees centigrade: enough to melt the thick steel girders. The crews had been pouring on the water: it evaporated even before it touched the flames."

Much of the glass in the Panorama had liquefied, Dick went on, after a pause, in which he seemed to struggle not so much to maintain his composure – invariably absolute – as to make his mind a space of contemplation broad enough to frame the phenomena he was seeking to describe. And that liquefaction could be seen in the form of glassy strands and fine stalagmites where the display cases had once stood – while the remainder, the glass in the skylight windows, for instance, had simply been vaporised by the flames and blown away – and on hearing of such things, he said, it was hard not to turn one's mind to the firestorms that devastated the great cities of Europe in the wartime years – those years, so far away from us, yet so close in the imagining, when Henk Guth's life was turned upside down and his long journey into exile, and towards Central Australia, began.

# Return

—

# I

In the last decade of the nineteenth century, a young, flamboyant financier named Albert Calvert made a series of expeditions through the north-west, into the coastal regions of the Pilbara, where life and death seem always to lie closely intertwined. Calvert was a speculator and investor, a share trader and company floater, but his shifting loves and interests ranged much wider than mere capital: he was a philatelist and racehorse trainer, an artist and a newspaper proprietor, a publicist and an obsessive author, indeed a graphomane, a figure wholly possessed by the desire to see his words in print.

This multiplicity and taste for self-invention reminded many observers of his prodigious grandfather, John Calvert, a man of vast wealth mysteriously amassed, who claimed to be the first discoverer of gold in New South Wales. And it was stories of this kind – stories akin to the foundation myths of his own lineage – that were uppermost in Calvert's thoughts in the days when he equipped and set out upon his little expeditions through the bush. He was cautious, though, to avoid the trap of casting himself in the old tradition and describing himself as some kind of "explorer." The frontier was almost closed when he began his journeys: gold rushes had scattered new towns across the North; there were only a few blank spaces left upon the continental map. No, Calvert viewed himself more as a traveller, a narrator, a watcher with a creative sensibility. He preferred to regard his ventures into the landscape as "tours," and he was also quick to stress his practical qualifications as a mining engineer. When a journalist from the *Western Mail* asked him if he objected to being called an explorer in his own right, Calvert had his ready answer: "I consider that I have far more claim to be called a pioneer, for my work in the colony as well as in the old country has been mainly directed into this channel."

In truth, he was tracing out his own version of a familiar trajectory, which had exerted its pull not only on his grandfather but on many of the outsiders drawn to the Pilbara in the years when the north-west was being opened up.

Even today, this austere landscape, with its basalt piles and dark peaks rising from bare red soil or yellowing spinifex, seems too much for the eye to bear. Men flinch from the country, they seek to master it, but not to know it: they gouge it up, as though its lunar splendour was offensive to them. They are there for minerals; for treasure: and both Calverts had heard that call. All through the first years of northern settlement, eccentrics and conspiratorial types loved to exchange tales about the secret riches of the country, or pass from hand to hand the coded topographic guides prepared by early prospectors, or whisper to each other of the secret Portuguese forays south from Javanese outposts to "Provincia Aurifera" – that region marked so tantalisingly on antique maps that seemed to sketch the Pilbara coast. Even Calvert's restrained, punctilious biographer, the geologist Geoff Blackburn, cannot resist the passing observation that Roebourne, the constant centre of the young man's expedition efforts, is the only gold-bearing coastal locality in the whole north-west.

Such was the gleaming lure that drew Calvert into the country, the same lure that he himself dangled to raise funds repeatedly from his syndicate of willing backers, incorporated in London as the General Exploration Company, and based conveniently close to Fleet Street's newspapers and printing presses. Four times between 1890 and 1896 Calvert made the long sea trip out from London to Australia, travelled north and engaged in his "tours," or mine-site inspection visits, each of which he recorded in his brisk prose style, accompanied by vivid line drawings in his own hand: sketches of a remarkable fluency, which convey the look and feel of a grand expedition, and show lithe, keen groups of men on horseback, escorting their supply wagon across flowing river channels or along dry, sandy creek beds. The tone of the Pilbara is precisely captured: the low, overlapping hills of the horizon, the white, wide-trunked gums with drooping branches – and this accuracy makes the fictive nature of these scenes more poignant, for even on his most ambitious journey, the second tour,

Calvert had only two companions, one of whom, after a fierce dispute, abandoned him in the bush and absconded with his best riding horse. From the scant surviving evidence, it is plain what Calvert was about: he was quietly quartering the latest prospects around Roebourne, omitting nothing. On one trip he even took care to travel to the new-found Nichol goldfield, which lay so low and so close to the shore that its quartz veins were submerged, at certain seasons, by the incoming tide.

But there was also a deeper motive alive within him: Calvert was seeking to test and take possession of a particular, somewhat confidential story, which had long been playing on his mind – and it was this that drove him to make his fitful stabs into the back country of the first explorers, and to sift and study all he saw.

As he writes in his account of his deepest inland voyage, the *Narrative of an Expedition into the Interior of North-West Australia,* he set out in discreet fashion from Roebourne on Thursday, 18 September 1891, in the footsteps of earlier travellers, and made his way past Whim Well and the gold workings at Mallina and Egina, through the broad, sparse catchments of the Shaw, the De Grey and the Oakover for several hundred miles, watching, making his neat line drawings, writing down his immediate impressions – until, abruptly, he reached dry terrain: he had struck the margin of the Great Sandy Desert. The high dunes barred his further passage.

Little of geological interest came from this substantial foray, which left the prospectors of the region quite baffled, but Calvert was marked by the experience. In those days, he was much possessed by questions of evidence and authenticity, of claim and fabrication, of rarity and loss. During his initial visit to the southern cities of Australia, in 1890, he had travelled with his grandfather, John, who was making his first return in forty years to the continent of his earliest prospecting triumphs. Their trip was wholly financed by the London syndicate. Their aim was to begin mining operations in the remote central deserts and in the new goldfields of the western colony. John Calvert soon sailed on, across the Pacific, to his long-established mines in Latin America, but before the two parted, he told his grandson the full, confidential tale of his youthful adventures in the far north-west. They involved, predictably, gold, danger, privation, Aborigines and death – and they were, like almost all the Calvert family's stories, so extreme and preposterous as to seem guaranteed by their sheer implausibility.

John Calvert, as his grandson well understood, was a man with a vexed relationship to conventional truth. His origins were unclear, and several different backgrounds have been proposed for him. One of the most attractive of these traces his descent from a father with pronounced artistic leanings, who knew both Samuel Palmer and William Blake. There is no strong reason to doubt Calvert's claim that he was born in

Cornwall, and was himself a mining engineer and geologist; nor that his expertise in gold-finding stemmed from his early wanderings in the Ural mountains and through Siberia and Transylvania with the mineral hunter Henry Heuland. An authorised biographical sketch, printed in his last years, records John Calvert's youthful efforts at scientific theorising, which have a hectic, imperious quality about them. He had already begun assembling his magnificent collection of rare crystals and mineral curios; he was on the way to perfecting a mysterious process, involving the element manganese, for extracting gold from its ores. He had devised an automatic radiometer and made studies of the tails of comets, which led him to ideas about condensed gases, and circular and elliptical systems, and thence to the nature of time itself: it was no more than "an accommodation for the registration of a few events," as he explained in *The Solvent of Matter and Motion in Life,* a work which so offended the clergy that they clamoured for its immediate suppression. But Calvert swiftly went beyond this pamphlet and its bold claim that water had been the key force in bringing all gold deposits to the surface of the earth. His next effort not only described the distribution of the metal in the earth's crust, but set out the laws governing its presence there – and soon after its appearance, Calvert made for the Atacama mountains and the mineral fields of Bolivia and Peru, where he found gold in great profusion, and made his first fortune, and dashed off another work of theory, predicting, on purely geological grounds, the location of the undiscovered gold provinces of the world. Chief among them was Western Australia: he decided to head south and prove his ideas.

All this, the young Albert Calvert – he was only twenty-one at the time of that first journey – knew well. What he did not fully know was the secret sequel, which he now learned, and which dazzled him. His grandfather had visited New South Wales, and made his gold finds there, and next moved on to New Zealand, and repeated the performance. Then, in 1847, he had quietly purchased the brig *Scout,* fitted her for gold exploration and sailed the Tasmanian coast, before making directly for the far north of Western Australia – at that time unsettled and unmapped terrain. In the first account of this episode, John Calvert claimed only to have made a landing near Shark Bay, and to have come upon the crater of an extinct volcano, containing diamonds, while in another formation close by he found "the richest outcrop of gold he ever met with." The story, whatever its initial degree of truth, was rather different and much more highly coloured when it made its appearance between hard covers, in Coningsby's *Discovery of Gold in Western Australia.* The tale now has a fierce, biblical aspect. John Calvert makes land close to Exmouth Gulf, near the northwest tip of the continent, and heads into the interior with seven men and horses, instructing his crew to head for Turtle Bay, far off at the mouth of the De Grey River, and wait for him there for a year. The party follows the winding creek line of the Ashburton; predictable disasters strike; water is scarce, the explorers, with the exception of Calvert, die; he is rescued by Aborigines, and escorted towards the coastline and the sheltered inlet where his vessel waits – the same inlet that was chosen as the site of Condon, now a ghost town, once the first port of the Pilbara coast.

The final version of the adventure adds grotesque details: "The story of that terrible journey will never be written: two of the men went raving mad after killing one of the baggage horses and drinking the feverish blood. They bolted into the bush during the night and were never seen again." The rest of the party succumb to thirst and hunger; emaciated, they die. Calvert struggles on, is revived by a tropical downpour and pursues his journey, until he is guided to the coast and reunited with his crew. The *Scout* sails to New Guinea and New Zealand, and is eventually wrecked, and sinks, with all her cargo of gold samples, off the New Caledonian coast. But Calvert's looping journeys continue, taking him repeatedly through the South Seas, plotting, prospecting and inventing ever more outlandish metallurgical processes, until he returns to England some years later, bearing with him, as the newspapers of the day dutifully reported, a ton of pure bright gold.

On the basis of this wealth and his freight of well-disseminated stories, Calvert was able to launch a range of syndicates and mining companies. He opened a museum of curios and established himself as the patron to many artists and writers; he secured an invitation to Buckingham Palace; he became friendly with the mineral-fancying Prince Consort.

Captured by the sweep and splendour of this narrative, and above all by his grandfather's tale of gold in the Australian desert – a tale which only became public knowledge in the year of Albert Calvert's own first journey, and which he may very well himself have had a hand in publicising – the young man promptly set about retracing the ancestral epic. Albert had also acquired, or been infected by, the family mania for publication. A year later, he dedicated his own first book to his grandfather; in the decade that followed he poured out a slew of further mineralogical titles, each of them revising and elaborating on his dream of the golden west.

At which point, the question arises: in fact it can no longer be hidden or decently suppressed. Did the younger Calvert, born as he was into this mythomaniac dynasty, and bearing its royal sponsor's Christian name like some heraldic letter patent, actually believe any of these stories? Was he himself a mountebank and fabricator? Did he devise them, and perfect them, and use them as the basis for the constant fundraising ventures which fed the family empire? Or was he, in his constant journeyings and his literary reworkings of the north-western landscape, simply making an attempt to come to terms with this legacy: assaying the evidence before him and seeking the veins of truth in his ambiguous inheritance? It is hard to resist the impression that Albert was drawn into the bush out of a desire to approach and know his grandfather; that he was always journeying towards him in his thoughts, that he admired him, and wished to believe in him, and was engaged, all through his life, in a bid to live up to the Calvert name.

But Albert was also a manipulator, an impresario. He adored the limelight, he staged constant dramas of his own; and they were always Calvertian in their grand ambition and the absurdity of their scale. At the outset of his third expedition, he took care to fill the Melbourne newspapers with reports of his plan to build a transcontinental railway, from Roebuck Bay near Broome across the desert; at the same time he was talking up his scheme of founding a national art gallery in Perth, with portraits, specially commissioned, of heroic explorers from Western Australia's early days. Soon, propelled by a gale of publicity, he was on the road to Marble Bar, and Bamboo Creek and Nullagine, buying up mine leases and claims – and all this activity was always being described, and magnified, in his racing, scurrying prose. There were talks, lectures, articles; on his journey back to Plymouth he launched a shipboard newspaper. In London he founded the weekly *West Australian Mining Register,* which he filled with breathless reports on the latest gold strikes and alluvial diggings throughout the colony. At his newly opened offices on Old Broad Street he displayed maps and charts and ore specimens for curious passers-by to examine. These props were sufficient to entice investors: the Mallina mining company, which Calvert helped launch, was the first Western Australian gold stock to be floated with British capital. In late 1894 he named himself managing director of two more grandly titled enterprises, Big Blow Gold Mines of Coolgardie and Consolidated Gold Mines of Coongan and Marble Bar. This paper empire continued its expansion, and eventually included stakes in thirteen equally impressively constituted companies.

Word of his triumphs spread before him. His next trip to the west was a hero's progress. He sailed for the Pilbara, the focus of his speculative energies, and when at last he reached Roebourne in the blazing heat of late December, he was feted at a banquet "attended by nearly fifty gentlemen" at the Jubilee Hall. The building had been tastefully decorated with "flowers and bunting" for the occasion – and one can almost see the pale mauve mulla mullas and heliotrope blossoms drooping from the pediment. The time soon came for Calvert to launch himself from the little town into a fresh tour of the goldfields, most of which, at that point, belonged to him. As he relates in a brief, poignant passage, oddly fictive in its accents, his young brother Lennard, who had accompanied him on the voyage, fell ill with typhoid on the morning of their departure, just as the four-horse dray was being loaded up before the front bar of the Victoria Hotel. Lennard came out, leaned weakly against the veran-

298

da's wooden post and waved goodbye. Calvert travelled out as far as Woodstock station, a stretch of flat spinifex country studded with sandstone platforms that bear rock art upon almost every surface. At the homestead there, he too fell gravely ill. He was brought back to Roebourne by stretcher: his party reached the Harding River just in time to hear the church bell tolling Lennard's requiem. Calvert's own recovery was slow. He went south, then back to London. It was his last visit to the Pilbara; it had been full of drama, like a novel: there was fortune, there was the shadow of fatality; he caught it in dark, emotive style in print.

Just after the appearance of *My Fourth Tour in Western Australia,* which proved to be by far his most successful publication, Calvert's life was again turned on its head. Early on 5 November 1897, at the family residence in Caversham Road, his grandfather, "that citizen of the world," died, most likely in his eighty-sixth year. Behind him the old man left a jigsaw of financial interests, and the remains of his fabled collection of curiosities, which he had begun to dismantle, displaying a grim determination in the task, much like a revolutionary who seeks to annul all trace of his conspiratorial designs. Already he had sold off to the government of New South Wales the set of zoological, botanical and mineral specimens amassed on Captain Cook's *Endeavour* by Sir Joseph Banks; only days before his death he received from J.C. Stevens Auction Rooms the proof catalogue for the sale of his "Savage Curiosities." Minerals, shells, coins, books, the giant eggs of cassowaries, auks and emus: he planned to sell them all. The detailed, admiring obituary printed in the *Mining Journal,* and written "by one who knew him," dwelled on old Calvert's 10,000 fossils, his portfolio of prints by Dürer, his diamonds, his "regiments of emerald, topaz, sapphire and other precious stones." Quite forgetting the sad context of the time, the author – almost certainly Albert Calvert at his most enthused and prolix – descends into long accounts of the collection's special "freaks of nature," the veined jaspers, or the mocha stones, elaborately patterned, in which imaginative eyes could trace the likenesses of the kings and queens of history: Marie Antoinette, for one, or Ramses II, the Pharaoh of the biblical Exodus. Another mocha stone seemed to show two lighthouses with the reflected gleam of light upon water between them; in another still, "nature's accidental markings depict a fleet of ships at anchor in the bay." The writer then, in a manoeuvre typical of the younger Calvert, turns to the old man's time in the bush, his survival in the desert, and that profound discretion, too, which left his books devoid of a single detail of personal adventure – so that "save in social moments or in congenial company his curious experiences were never referred to." How could one ever know, or be on level terms with such a man: with such a screen of silences? His agates and his rubies, his Siberian minerals and his cherry coppers – what was their secret: what did they mean?

And what, now, was Calvert, death-surrounded, deprived of his grandfather, and of all the stories? There is an acute portrait sketch of him from those days, drawn for the social pages of *Vanity Fair* by the well-known caricaturist "Spy." It shows a frail, uncertain individual, with a fragile, reclusive look lurking in the eyes. Calvert is in his full racing finery; indeed, the costume is somewhat overdone: morning coat, cane of bamboo, top hat, kidleather gloves, coral pink and iridescent greenish-black bow tie. Yet a mournful air hangs over him, and this tone is only heightened in the posed photograph he included in several of his early books. It portrays the author gazing out into infinite distance; a large, wilting rose-bloom flops from the lapel of his dress coat; a pearl-tipped tie pin stabs down towards his heart; his expression is soft and otherworldly. The old man had always radiated a very different manner. One sees no commonality between the two. John Calvert's face was little more than a disguise, a front, half masked by a tumble of thick white beard; a pair of defiant eyes, like burning coals, would stare out; while upon the rough, sackcloth material of his waistcoat, a Ruritanian medal, suspended from a golden chain, declared his wealth and grandeur to the world. Believe me, it said: believe in me – here is my gilded proof.

A year was sufficient for the Calvert financial empire to crack under the young man's sole guidance, and go under. But the ensuing bankruptcy was artful and allowed the investors who had trusted in the Calvert name a smooth retreat. The mines, so grandly advertised and laboriously acquired, proved largely empty. The grades were low in Coolgardie; there were scant returns from the Yellow Aster and from the Golden Hope leases close by Marble Bar. The Calverts had poured plant and capital into only one of their ventures, the workings at Lower Nichol on the Indian Ocean shore, which had seemed to them so like the site of *Provincia Aurifera* – but when it was visited by a government geologist some years later, the winding engine, pumps and boilers had stopped working, following a prolonged submersion in seawater floods. And Mallina, the Calvert Exploration Company's pride – Mallina, where the region's gold rush began, in 1888, when young Jimmy Withnell picked up a lump of quartz to hurl at a noisy crow and saw the rock was flecked with gold – even Mallina had failed. John Brockman, the acting warden of the regional goldfield, filed a succinct, bleak report from the site only a year after Calvert's last, triumphal "tour": "This place for the want of capital is almost deserted, and the deputy registrar's house, offices and effects unfortunately have been burnt down recently." A few months more, and all the mine workings in the neighbourhood were abandoned; the bush camps of the Pilbara had fallen quiet.

In London, Calvert quickly found a new channel for his literary energies. His attention turned to Spain: Spanish mines, Spanish art, history, architecture. He wrote no fewer than thirty-six books on Spanish themes over the next quarter-century. One of his publishers, the Bodley Head, even set up a special Spanish imprint for him: there were monographs on Spanish sculpture, appreciations of Goya and Velázquez, a life of Cervantes, a description of the Alhambra, Granada and Seville. Spain was everything, or almost – he did allow himself a hundred pages on questions of authenticity, and Sir Francis Bacon's secret authorship of Shakespeare's plays; he strayed once into the unlikely field of horticulture and penned an authoritative text on daffodils. At last the charms of Hispanic life and culture paled; he promptly made himself into an expert on the German colonies of Africa and their mineral resources. This gave way to a fascination with Freemasonry and its chain of secrets: his final volumes were devoted to Masonic themes. During the greater part of Calvert's eventful life, he was rich, and generous in the gifts and endowments he made – but at the end some financial reverse befell him. He died penniless, in 1946, and for all his Stakhanovite literary production, he would be wholly forgotten today were it not for one act, which he soon came to regret.

Determined to ensure the survival of his grandfather's name, he decided, in the mid-1890s, to equip an exploring expedition, which he hoped would fill in "the remaining blanks of Australia" and reveal the deepest mysteries of the continent to Western eyes. It was to be the final flourish of the great tradition.

He may even have half believed that some golden mountain would at last be found in the folds of the Outback, and give substance to the first and boldest of the family's claims.

The Calvert scientific expedition, overseen on his behalf by the South Australian branch of the Royal Geographical Society, had as its declared goal the mapping of the Great Sandy Desert between the Murchison and Fitzroy rivers. It was placed under the steady leadership of Lawrence Wells, a veteran of many surveys and explorations; with him travelled a full complement of scientists and cameleers. The story of the expedition is well enough known, and yet somehow it is routinely avoided, reduced to a brief footnote in the records of the exploration age. The tale is too tragic, too pointless, it unfolds in country too remote to imagine – it has been cloaked in that characteristic unreality which hovers over everything touched by the Calvert name. The great disasters and heroic failures of mid-nineteenth-century exploring have almost all preserved a degree of celebrity: Burke and Wills have the dig tree on Cooper Creek as a memorial; Sturt has his Depot Glen, and Stuart his highway, while all the Simpson Desert's dune fields serve as Leichhardt's extended monument and grave. The Calvert expedition's victims, though, perished quietly, nobly, at obscure Joanna Spring, where four-wheel-drive tourists never go. The country Wells and his team traversed is regarded now as an indigenous landscape, interrupted by the occasional mine and traversed by a bumpy, disused stock route. The seven explorers, for all the excellence of their equipment and the loftiness of their scientific aspirations, were engaged in a purely subsidiary venture; the likely pattern of their experiences was already known and set. By virtue of its place in the succession of events, the expedition was more an enactment of the idea of exploration than an exploration itself – and that odd, trickedout quality was clear even in the first exchanges between Calvert and the Geographical Society, when its officers, in their most wheedling, flattering manner, advised their patron of the scientific benefits that might accrue from a large-scale survey. The Great Sandy needed to be traversed and measured. There were salt-lake chains to be followed up; there might even be high ranges of hills to be found. "You yourself have traversed its north-west area," they wrote, "and, therefore, know what exists there." Albert Calvert, of course, had hardly penetrated further than the goldrush dray routes and the station tracks which still wind through the inland Pilbara, while it would be a brave soul who dared guess where John Calvert had been, or what he had done. But for all their fakeness, the Calverts, with the desert expedition, at last achieved something true: it was the grandest, most majestic of advances into unknown country, it was the final journey through the shimmer of the dune fields, beyond the contours of established maps. It was structured in the style of a narrative, with self-conscious actors, its outcome was all but predetermined by its ground conditions. It posed, in the stark, hard style of drama, the question that lay hidden in every explorer's heart: how to perish, how to face death – marooned, in silence, alone.

***

In keeping with its end, the first portents were ominous. Wells and his party were late into the field. It was mid-July before the expedition's camel string left the prospecting camp of Lake Way and began crossing a stretch of sand-ridge country, dotted with desert gums, and bloodwoods, and bush grasses so thick they seemed like fields of waving corn. After a month's fitful progress, with the weather already hot and menacing, Wells split the party and led a rapid reconnaissance into the ranges, bound north-east, in search of water – but as he pushed further, the landscape changed: there were dry, deceptive channels, and fields of conglomerate and rubble; the dunes stretched to the horizon line. At each crest, his camels struggled; they lost condition: they looked to his eyes like starved kangaroo dogs.

"I feel thoroughly disgusted with my trip so far," Wells lamented to his journal. "Everything seems against us – sand ridges, poison plant, sore eyes, and no water discoveries. On starting from Lake Way I had great hopes of finding some good country about this latitude, but now I am afraid those hopes are smouldering in the ashes of despair." His thoughts filled with the tales of earlier explorers in that landscape – Forrest, and Giles, and Warburton, and the privations they had each endured. Wells decided to turn back – but the very next day, walking in front of the string, he flushed a crested pigeon, gave pursuit over the next dune and found a belt of lush tea-tree and outcropping limestone. There were the remains of Aboriginal encampments. There was a serviceable waterhole. This, optimistically, he christened Midway Well; it would be his depot – the portal that would guarantee his passage through the desert. There was rejoicing; the men bathed; the camels drank their fill. Late in the afternoon, when the day cooled, and the birds flew in to drink, Wells, gave in to an impulse that seems near-universal at desert waterholes: he raised his gun and fired a shot at a pigeon, but succeeded only in breaking its legs – the intended victim escaped, blood-spattered, in torment, and fluttered away. "It afterwards appeared to me a cruel return to perhaps the identical bird that led us to this haven of rest," wrote Wells that evening – but then, as he consoled himself in philosophic fashion, "man's hand is ever slow to spare and ever ready to strike."

When daylight broke, conscious of his mandate to fill in the bare spaces on the charts, he set a new, south-west bearing for the route back to the main party, passing alongside a low, deep-red range system, to which he gave Calvert's name. To name was to discover. Increasingly, though, the landscape he was passing through seemed to him not empty, but full: full of signs and presences: the tracks of old explorers, the faded traces of geometric carvings, the remains of ceremonial sites abandoned by the Aboriginal groups whose smoke plumes were burning all around the camel string as it maintained its loping pace. At last he and his men reached the depot camp; there were the firm reunion handshakes, the silent, heartfelt greetings of the time. The party regrouped and headed for the line of waterholes ahead, sure now of their path through to the distant Fitzroy Valley. But even as they advanced, the atmospherics of the journey continued a gradual, almost imperceptible shift: plains of burnt grevillea and towering, desiccated spinifex surrounded them. Dust storms flashed across the country; at night, thunder echoed in the distance, and continuous bolts of lightning lit the sky. It was already 30 September when the full expedition reached Midway – a time of year when the sand is burning to the touch, when the blood throbs in one's veins, and mirages glare and dance before one's eyes. "We will continue our course," wrote Wells, "and I can see that there must be no delay, owing to the lateness of the season. In so terrible a country as this, where glaring red sand-ridges, all trending almost at right angles to our course, present themselves to the view at every quarter, it is extremely difficult to proceed."

Once more, after a further find of water in a native well, he replenished his supplies; once more he split his team. On a northward heading he dispatched his two keenest, most intrepid men: his own cousin and deputy, Charlie Wells, and the student scientist of the party, George Lindsay Jones, who was only eighteen years old, and a specialist in the new field of photography. The pair were given the three best camels and provisions for a month. They were to travel 180 miles to the sand-surrounded well at Joanna Spring, which had been rather imprecisely mapped by its discoverer, Colonel Warburton, during his arduous desert crossing more than two decades before. This was their point of rendezvous with the main expedition. But if contact failed, they were to push on, north, to the Fitzroy River, that shining lifeline that wound down into the pindan plains. In the prevailing conditions, and at that season, these instructions amounted to something very like a sentence of death. But if that thought occurred to the two men, they expressed nothing, and they set off into the blazing sands.

Almost at once they hit hard country. Their camels struggled. They reached a winding salt lake, dead across their path, its soft crust impassable – "one shining surface of spotless white." As they stood on its shore, hundreds of zebra finches, the birds of blood and sacrifice in desert ritual, began whirling and circling above them, twisting in a spiral of ever-closer flight. Abruptly, they felt the horror of the landscape: fear gripped them. They retreated, by slow, painful stages, to their starting point, nursed their camels back to health for five days, then set off in pursuit of the main party – and it is a cause of amazement to those who know the country that the two did indeed reach the vicinity of Joanna Spring, a week later, after a constant ordeal of climbing and descending high, loose, jumbled sand dunes, with the temperature burning by midday, and the last frosts of the year falling by night. The waterhole they found was empty. They lit signal fires and waited: no one came. Their supplies dwindled; they weakened; the end drew near. Jones wrote, in pencil, to his mother and father, a last note. It is in the archives of the State Library of South Australia today. It allows the young man to step for an instant from the shadows of the forgotten expedition into a strong, sharp light.

"To My Dearest Mother and Father G.W. and J.R. Jones, Edwin Street, Gilberton, Adelaide," it begins: the hand is neat, and upright, and precise. "Do not grieve over me darlings," he says, before telling, in the briefest of summaries, the story of his fate: how one camel had died, how the two others had vanished into the bush, and there was no catching them. He had tried to explore the surrounds, but could go no further than half a mile, and then returned exhausted. There is a terrifying sweetness in his closing words: "Somehow or other I do not fear death itself. I trust in the almighty God. We have been hoping for relief from the main party but I am afraid they will be too late." Reading that note, seeing those letters on the page in the musty library some years ago, I remember forming the idea that they embodied something; that Jones, and Wells beside him, knew some truth they had been travelling towards, and which their journey had helped them to reach. And I imagined, too, that the desert claims those of sweetness and kind temper, for they alone can soothe the clang of its stillness; that it needs them, and they belong there, and they rest in its arms at peace – and the temptation towards such thoughts seems fanned by desert country, as if the landscape seeks the touch of man, and longs for us; and travels in the bush still breed in me a kind of carelessness about what lies ahead, a readiness for anything: joy, annihilation, insight. From time to time, in the months that followed, when the Calvert expedition and its unravelling was fresh in my thoughts, I would often picture the two men stretched out beneath the shade of a bloodwood and a handful of spindly acacias, on a ridge line surrounded by dry soak holes, a few short miles west-south-west of Joanna Spring, and think myself into that silence – and just such pictures formed in the mind of Lawrence Wells too, on his journey through the fiery dunes, as he turned over the fate of his advance team, and it slowly dawned on him they must be lost.

His own passage had been scarcely less arduous. His party had moved off in good formation, rested and strong. Within a week the desert brought them to the very edge of life. Each day, Wells wrote up his observations. Each day, his words become more jagged. From cool scientific writing, he drifts towards a surreal, broken narrative: dreams, wanderings, reflections: how bleak the spinifex, yet how necessary, in that landscape, to stop the shifting of the sands; how tall the ant hills; how loud the chirping of the crickets round the camp at night. The heat mounts: the camels cannot tread the burning sand by day: they rush to stand in one another's shadows and topple off their finely balanced packs. The leader adopts the only strategy he can: "Our position has now become most serious owing to the intense heat, the sand ridges, and need of both food and water. I feel I must give up day-travelling and endeavour to push on by moonlight" – and so the string, in ghostly fashion, proceeds through the silver night time, trudging slowly, up dune and down, over the crests at right angles, their strength ebbing, fading. Wells tries every bushman's trick. In his quest for water, he follows up the tracks of emus across the sand. He even turns his thoughts to the Aboriginal groups whose presence in the landscape round him he has regarded, all through the journey, with a chill, seigneurial detachment. Seeking their help, signalling to them, chasing after them, he almost strands himself, together with Bejah, his trusty cameleer. "Staggering over hot sand, parched with thirst, I became exhausted, and only able to manage a quarter to a half a mile at a time, sinking down at the top of each sand ridge in a half stupor, and falling into a sleep each time, only to jump up again with a start and urge Bejah to rouse himself. The tops of the ridges becoming cooler as the night advanced, we repeatedly pulled our clothes off and poured the cool sand over our burning skins."

The plagues of the desert then descended: ants infested them; bees attacked them; loose sand defeated them; one by one, the best pack-camels weakened and died. Mournfully, methodically, Wells unloaded all the specimens his team had collected, all the expedition's tools and provision boxes, all their personal possessions, and abandoned them, stowed beneath a tarpaulin at a campsite within fifty miles of Joanna Spring. Two days on, and almost at the rendezvous point, Wells saw a smoke plume rising close by, due east: surely it was the advance team! He set off, with nothing more than a half-pint of cold tea in a bottle, to find his men – but as he went, and fired the country before him, he noticed other, answering smokes, ahead, around him: one, two, several. It was not his cousin's fire. "Retracing my steps as best I could, I hardly remember how I got back to camp. Many times, at the semblance of a shade, I sank to the ground with a singing sensation in the ears, going off into a stupid doze, only to jump up with a start and push on again. In the flats of dense porcupine and coarse acacia scrub the atmosphere was like the heat from an oven. On one occasion, when rising from the ground I noticed my own boot tracks and found I was going the wrong way. Pulling my shirt, hat and compass off, I carried them rolled up under my arm and, on reaching the last high sand ridge, at 7p.m., I saw the signal fire."

He clambered up. He saw the camp, and heard the voices of his party. He was too weak to call out. He lit the bush: the spinifex became his beacon – he crawled towards them, and was found. From death, and wilderness, across the threshold, to camp, the settled space, and life.

By this stage in the expedition's narrative, even the most transfixed of readers will be aware that certain conventions and tropes are active in the tale. It unfolds in almost formulaic fashion: each of the actions Wells takes, indeed each of his thoughts, seems predestined. The mood has long been set: the dark omens, the closeness of the air, the dry rivers and mocking salt pans. The various episodes as well – the meetings with indifferent natives, the lost comrades, the dying animals, the ditching of scientific specimens, even the lone, near-fatal march – all these are familiar, they come straight from the pages of the first explorers, whose long shadows loom over Wells and his party – Leichhardt and Stuart, Ernest Giles and Eyre. As if to confirm this suspicion, at this very point in his tale, the point of greatest tension, Wells breaks off, and he cites at length the journey narrative of none other than Colonel Warburton, who had travelled through the same landscape, whose track he was now seeking to follow, and whose experiences were hauntingly like his own – until one feels oneself inside some infinitely doubling mirror-chamber of sensations and experiences, a desert of dreadful repetition. How not, as one nears the end of the journey, to let one's thoughts run. How not to picture that constant reader, Albert Calvert, that man of stories, waiting, spellbound, in his Broad Street office, beside the telegraph machine – address "Spinifex, London" – waiting for news of the great adventure being written in his name. How was the plot progressing, what was the drift of the story – or, since there was only one fitting end to such a story, how was it reached?

Wells himself, caught in this dance of influences, could do no more than stay in character. Exhausted, he led his party on, past Joanna Spring or its supposed site; he rode through the dark, now barely conscious, his body being scourged as he went by the sharp, burnt branches of acacia scrub. The surviving camels could hardly find the strength to walk. They moaned, and their throats rattled constantly; gluey, urinary liquids oozed beneath their tails. The country was no more than vague, repeating patterns, it was an abstraction, it was nothing – and so it stayed, until the horizon broke at last. It became a line of low, notched peaks, they took on shape – and then Wells recognised them from the writings of his brother explorers. He knew those books by heart; their charts and illustrations hovered constantly before his eyes. Mount Fenton, the St George Range – he could read the landscape again: he was safe. After four months in the desert, and 500 miles, the expedition cleared the dune fields. Before them were lagoons, fish, wildfowl, paperbarks, the Fitzroy flowing in its wide, clean channel.

"My only anxiety now," wrote Wells, as he weighed up his escape and his passage through that iron country, "is for my cousin Charles and Mr Jones."

Anxiety became obsession; then conviction of responsibility; then motive for a further quest. Less than a week had passed when Wells plunged back into the Great Sandy Desert, bearing emergency water supplies, in the first attempt at a rescue for the missing men; an attempt that was followed, over the next half-year, by four more journeys, made with ever-mounting passion, sweeping across vast swathes of red dune landscape, as the last episode of nineteenth-century exploration turned from geographic survey into haunted search. Wells had spread word quickly through the Fitzroy Crossing telegraph station. Within days, the most famous bushmen and pioneers of northern Australia were in contact, pleading to be included: from Adelaide, David Lindsay, who had led the Elder scientific expedition, and was uncle to young George Jones; from Halls Creek, the swashbuckling David Carnegie, who had just crossed through the central deserts with a camel party of his own. On the Oakover River, the West Australian surveyor William Rudall at once began a set of probes into the dune fields, while the celebrated overlander Nat Buchanan, equipped with a fresh camel string, came through to Fitzroy and offered his help to Wells.

There was a sense of final curtain in the air. The cast of an age was gathering; one feels the mood of closure, of stories meshing, joining, that comes when a soap opera's last episode is shown. And much in the North was at an end during those days: Federation loomed, pastoral stations were fringing the frontier, the surviving wilderness would soon be tamed by stock routes and straight, sealed roads. Repeatedly, in a state of fixed, glassy resolve, Wells drove his camels southwards; from Gogo Station, where the river country gives way to the bleakest desert ranges; from Fitzroy itself; from Luluigui and then from Gregory homesteads. He narrowed down his search area; he reached nearer the resting-place of his companions with each failed bid. A kind of wildness overcame him; he fell under the shadow of his fellow searchers, hard bush cattlemen and police troopers. He sought out the desert people, those vague, exiguous family groups he had seen and crossed paths with, creatures who had appeared and disappeared before him like ghosts. Wells began interrogating them, enlisting them as guides; and at their campsites he discovered telltale clues: a geological sketch map, spans of hoop iron, blades of metal, made from bent packsaddle frames. A fury gripped the search. On the last trip out, Wells took with him Sub-Inspector Ord and Trooper Nicholson from the Fitzroy Police Station. The methods employed were simple: two desert men were captured; a degree of constraint and violence was administered; the searchers were led directly to the bare ridge line where the dead expedition members lay. From the back of his riding camel, Wells caught sight of a tent rope hanging from a desert gum tree on the ridge. "I could then see my cousin's iron-grey beard," he writes in his journal. "And we were at last at the scene of their terrible death."

What, though, had Wells found with the end of this quest, which had lasted far longer than his initial desert crossing? He describes the moment with a fascinated horror, and in extreme detail he replays the movements of the actors in the drama; with his whispering voice, he reminds one of an archaeologist, penetrating into the lost tomb-chamber of some king from an ancient realm. "Dismounting, Mr Ord and myself went to my cousin, whilst Nicholson and Bejah went where they saw some remnants of the camp equipment, and found the body of Mr G.L. Jones, which was partly covered with drift sand. Where Charles Wells lay, half-clothed and dried like a mummy, we found nothing but a rug, and some old straps hanging to some burnt bushes, which held the brass eyelets of a fly that had either been rifled by the natives or burnt by a fire which had been within a few feet of his body."

Like the dead George Jones, Sub-Inspector Ord was a photographer. He recorded the scene in a set of grainy, disquieting images, so glare-distorted they almost recompose themselves into abstract shapes. The eye makes out the ridge, the two chained Aboriginal guides, the body of Charles Wells, his hands stretched out above his torso, his head twisted to one side, his features tight. Tradition, at such moments, demanded certain thoughts, and a degree of retrospect. "Looking at my cousin," Wells wrote that day, "as he lay on the sand with features perfect and outstretched hand, I recalled the last time we parted when I felt his hard, strong grip. I little thought then that this would be our next meeting! I remember we spent a lively evening, our last together, at Separation Well, when both he and Mr Jones were joking freely, hopeful and full of life."

He went on to set down a handful of lines from the dead man's favourite poet, Adam Lindsay Gordon. They were lines known by every bushman. They had been composed a generation earlier, for the unveiling of the monument in Melbourne's Collins Street to Burke and Wills.

> *With the pistol clenched in his failing hand,*
> *With the death mist spread o'er his fading eyes,*
> *He saw the sun go down on the sand*
> *And he slept, and never saw it rise.*
> *God grant that whenever, soon or late,*
> *Our course is run and our goal is reach'd,*
> *We may meet our fate as steady and straight*
> *As he whose bones in yon desert bleach'd.*

Grave, hackneyed, outdated, the verses caught the essence of the journey. Lindsay Gordon was in the expedition leader's thoughts, and on his lips, all through the desert crossing: he named a waterhole Lindsay Gordon Lagoon "after Australia's poet," he filled his notebook with Lindsay Gordon quatrains; bush ballads by the author formed his constant mental music. For Wells, by this stage, was a being wholly spun from the romance of exploration, he was hollowed out, his own identity was lost – and the long record of nineteenth-century desert travel seems, at this point, at the very moment of its conclusion, to collapse, its myths overwhelm it, it becomes a collective journey towards evanescence, depersonalisation, the destruction of the conscious mind. It is a turning away from progress, a rejection of the modern, settled world, in favour of sufferings, and the insights of mirages, and mystic union with the face of death. More deeply than any of his brother explorers, Wells had stared into the lines of that face – but it is very striking that he never spoke of what he saw there. Discreet, silent, he continued to take part in expeditions, both as a surveyor and as a prospector, penetrating into the furthest reaches of the western deserts, surviving until his seventy-eighth year, when he was fatally injured by a rail car close to his home in the hills above Adelaide.

## II

For a long while after I first gained a taste for inland travel I yearned, in vain, to see those far reaches of the Great Sandy Desert, a part of Australia that remains remote and little known today, although mining and resources groups will doubtless claim it in good time, and roads and airstrips and neat, geometric towns will come to shelter in the lee of its ranges, or along its dry creekbed banks. They have put their promissory marks on it already: in the 1960s, during a phase of fast-paced expansion in the world economy, precisely mirrored by the first years of war in Indochina, a handful of mining and oil exploration multinationals scoured the region, attracted by the reports the early prospectors had made. In their wake, these companies – Hunt Oil and Shell Oil were prominent among them – left shot, or seismic lines: sets of straight grooves drawn across the face of the desert, which remain visible today, and confront the traveller down bush roads, and convey the impression of a vanished empire's fortified redoubts. Fitfully, over the years, the great Australian mining houses – before their absorption into global conglomerates – turned their eyes, too, on the deep desert. Western Mining, under the tutelage of the exploration geologist Roy Woodall, even developed a little copper mine near Warburton, and its survey teams found many of the ore bodies that lie along the south road through the Ngaanyatjarra lands, where the Blackstone and the Cavenagh Ranges run. There, one day soon, new mines, extracting nickel laterites and cobalts, will stretch across the spinifex, their open pits balanced by acid-leaching plants and bright blue tailings dams. But the most poignant traces of mid-century exploration in that remote region are those left behind by the geotechnical arm of Conzinc Rio Tinto, the Australian group. Often, when I was a child, I heard that soft, sweet-sounding company name spoken, or its even gentler set of initials, CRA – and I would try to follow all its doings. I would scan the business pages of the papers, though they were far beyond me, and lean over desert maps and search them for its prospects and its mines, which were always in the centre of the remotest, emptiest spaces. For months, I pursued this arbitrary fascination, and brought it up repeatedly, only to be assured by those who knew more than I that Conzinc Rio Tinto had no distinct essence – it was just a name, a name for shares and men. The dreadful disappointment this discovery bred in me lingered in my mind long after, and when I first came across the old tracks left behind by the firm's geologists, and a desert friend of mine beside me at the wheel of the troop-carrier leaned over and murmured the soft syllables "CRA," I felt once more a little pang of sadness, as though the memory of some lost love was stirring in my thoughts.

Conzinc Rio Tinto exploration parties mounted several expeditions deep into the Gibson Desert, in quest of seismic anomalies or suggestive rock formations, and in the course of those journeys they left behind them fuel dumps: great 44-gallon drums of diesel, which are still lying by the tracks today. They are remembered with precision: I have seen them used as navigation aids, and doubtless they are well on the way to incorporation in the fabric of the

Tjukurrpa stories, the narratives of desert people, which wash smoothly over all features, new or old, that mark and fill the landscape. It was further north, though, in Calvert country, that CRA pulled off its masterstroke. Close to the location of Joanna Spring, in country first surveyed by William Rudall – country of mauve peaks and high bloodwoods – lies the Kintyre uranium deposit, rich in ore, outcropping on the desert's surface. The Kintyre exploration lease was long held by CRA, which decided, in a moment of lateral thinking, to sink a well nearby and install a hand-pump, bearing an inscription of goodwill from the company to the desert world. It stands there still, with its fading legend emblazoned on an iron plaque around its base, and it never fails to arouse a sense of wonder: water – salty, sandy, but water – pouring, flowing amidst the red dunes and the burnt spinifex. "CRA," the travellers on outback trails murmur to each other at their rest stops. "CRA," the convoy parties of desert men from Punmu and Kunawarritji call out with habitual affection as they pass.

\*\*\*

Such were the sentinels of my first journeys through that landscape: bore pumps and discarded tyres, and the wrecked car bodies and fuel drums that lie scattered, like exotic sculptures, at strategic points all down the Gunbarrel Highway and the Talawana Track. I was travelling, in those days, with photographers and with prospectors, with anthropologists and health workers, and I soon came to think I had a fair acquaintance with that stretch of desert. But now I look back on those trips, I wonder if I knew it in the slightest before I drove out one dry season, bound for the shore of Lake Disappointment with my friend Charlie Firns.

He was a kangaroo shooter, and he had a way of driving on constant alert, scanning the country, hunched forward, silent for hours, his eyebrows rising just a fraction, maybe, if he glimpsed old dingo footprints on the road ahead. Then suddenly, in the thick of the corrugations, he would slow and pull up, both hands clutching the wheel tight. With a grin, he would turn towards me; his pale, piercing eyes would look into mine.

"Now," he would say in tones of triumph, over the soft throb of his decaying Mazda trayback. "Let's just see how good you are!"

And it was my turn then to look; to gaze in all directions across the mulga, or the scrub and half-burned spinifex, searching in the glare for movement, shadow, tell-tale patterns. Nothing. I would shrug, and Charlie would shake his head: "Call yourself a bushman? Don't you see? There!"

And he would point, and after much more prompting, I might begin to make out, hidden, in deep shade, the curved flank of a reclining animal: a young blue doe, perhaps, asleep beneath a corkwood, half a kilometre away in the curtain of the bush.

"There she is!" – and he would laugh, delightedly, and gun the engine; the kangaroo would wake in fright and leap up, and Charlie would stare after her with a kind of gentle pride for several seconds before he drove slowly on.

All through those days, during that long journey we made through the backlands, he was my instructor, as I realise now, and my interpreter, more than a mere companion on the road. It was he who brought me closest to the desert's logic, the system at its heart, which is no system, but renunciation: order destroyed, the better to be reborn. We argued constantly, we disagreed – but his contention was a form of closeness. He was one of those inlanders for whom the country was a kingdom to be loved, protected – but explained, if at all, through tone and bearing, not in some easy, transparent narrative. And yet he led me into the glare, and silence, and slowly spread its world before me. I told myself the light had shown him a hidden language, and he knew the desert's signs and words.

It was early, even by his standards; the dawn's pale gleam was just showing when we set off from our first campsite on the desert's edge, but as we drove out into the grey, a series of tales from the frontier – each one flowing smoothly into the next, each one more finely honed in its structure and its interweaving – began: his exploits while deep-sea fishing off the tip of Truant Island; his duels with killer sharks near Ningaloo; his excursions down the rig road south of Hedland, a road that lost itself progressively and ran out into salt lakes and a fine, suspended cloud of dust. And there were stranger stories still, which he delivered in his most hypnotic voice: experimental aircraft sightings in the deep country; the Min Min lights, and their underlying physics; the ghost towns and lost graves of the north.

"Are you always like this, at the start of your bush drives?" I asked him, a few hours into our journey, as we hurtled down a sidetrack towards the Canning Stock Route, and the dark peaks of the Carnarvon Range slid past. I peered at the topographic map, which was almost devoid of names or distinctive markers.

"Like what?" said Charlie.

"Endless stories, breaking off in all directions."

I leaned back and tried to get on terms with the Mazda's cramped seats. They were worn, their metal support frame was showing through the fabric; they jumped then slipped back into place as we took each curve.

"We can just ride in quiet," said Charlie, sounding hurt by this. "Words can be enemies: you'll find the instinct to talk soon burns away." He proceeded to put this policy into strict practice: for most of the next two days, we pushed in deep, calm silence through the dead country of the stock route, past mournful wells and emaciated cattle, exchanging no more than a stray sentence here and there, until we turned off into bare, scorched desert. We struggled up a high dune in first gear. From the crest, a plain of red sand reached to the horizon.

"That's a bleak view," said Charlie then, with relish. "Enough to make you feel the bones beneath the skin."

"So what makes you come out here?"

"I've always liked what's far," he said. "What's open, and can't confine you. In everything I do."

"But why here in particular? What gave you the idea?"

"You wouldn't believe me if I told you. It's an unusual story."

It unfolded, in broken episodes, in the days that followed, as we explored our way amidst the creek beds and the ranges. Almost by chance, once his working days were over, Charlie had fallen into a pattern of bush travels, together with Jim Bailey, his oldest kangaroo-shooter friend. On each trip, the two pushed further out: past Lake Auld, and Scorpion Well; out beyond the survey and seismic lines; beyond the peak of Cromer Cone.

"It was really the never-never, there," he said. "High dunes, soft sand. It was as harsh as you could like. I always thought I'd be happy, living out in that country, just by myself. There's rockdrip water in the ranges, I'd have a good tent and a gas bottle, a solar panel or two. It's all worked out!"

"An Elysian picture!"

For several summers, he explored the margins of that world, turning over his life as he went: and often, in the range country, he found Aboriginal traces from pre-contact times. This became a compulsion with him. He would search for old campfires, caves, half-silted wells. One afternoon, on return to Meekatharra, after a long trip out, he fell into conversation with the bushman Stan Gratte. Stan recalled, at one point, the voyage that he had made in August 1977 from the nearby township of Wiluna, deep into the sand-dune country: the famous rescue mission, mounted to find and bring in the last nomads of the Gibson Desert, Warri and Yatungka, who were on the point of death from starvation after a prolonged, unbroken spell of drought. During the journey, as Gratte recounted it, the guide and leader of the mission, Mudjon, a Mandildjara man from Wiluna, led them past the Calvert Range. Gratte spotted a crested pigeon and realised there was water close by. After elaborate searching, he found a hidden gorge behind the cliff face and a deep valley full of paperbarks.

"And that was it," said Charlie. "When Stan told me that, it was as if a key turned. I realised that the desert was full of secrets, if you knew how to find them – full of life."

He decided at that moment to make a journey of his own towards that country, across dunes and ridge lines, and he reached those ranges – although it was plain to me that the journey he was describing had found its fullest realisation in the realms of metaphor.

"I suppose all that surprises you," he said then, sadly, reproachfully. "In what way?"

"I can tell. I know – you didn't think I was like that." Charlie stopped, and switched off the engine. "You thought I was just a roo shooter, didn't you? – a redneck, without an idea in my head."

"I hadn't really got that far," I answered.

"I don't care, you know, any more, what people think."

"I imagine," I said, cautiously, "it's a profession that would give you a certain perspective on life and death."

Charlie began shooting in 1961, together with his older brother, in the Gascoyne, on the pastoral leases surrounding the Kennedy Range. They would drive out together and shoot kangaroos for seven or eight nights straight, the time it took to fill the freezer on the back of their Holden ute.

"Six hundred and fifty, we'd reckon on. We used to get eight pence a pound, and that was good money in those days."

"You must have had a talent for it."

"Not at all: I wasn't an exceptional range shooter. But my aim's true. If you hold a bottle up at a hundred yards, I'll shoot it clean out of your fingers without blinking an eye."

"I think I'll take your word for that," I said.

"Once," Charlie went on, meditatively, "I got 167 roos out of 167 bullets. Often, you'd get a 60 or 70 streak going, but that was the highest. Don't look like that! It was your work. You didn't think about it. But then sometimes you'd wound one, and you'd almost wreck your truck, trying to chase him and kill him because you didn't want him to suffer. I used to reckon a head shot wasn't as good as a heart shot. Now, though, they're all head shots, and a lot of poor bloody roos get their heads half blown away."

"At least you wouldn't have gone hungry."

"Oh, we never used to eat them while we were shooting. That took too long. You'd work all night, and have a huge breakfast; you were working eighteen hours on the run. I don't eat them that much now, they're just not for me. Camels, sometimes: the meat's a bit tough, but you couldn't tell it from beef. Donkey's alright, too, a different taste. I wouldn't go near horses, though: they stink."

And Charlie hurried on, in learned style: the best technique for donkey culling; the correct disposal of orphaned joeys; the way to dress a fresh roo carcass at top speed. I listened, rather swamped by this tide of carnage. He caught my expression.

"What's the matter? I thought you told me you were a foreign correspondent. You should be used to blood and death."

"Absolutely," I said. "I am. It's just that animals seem more defenceless. Anyway, we're in the right country for you. That's Skeleton Pass, there, dead ahead – maybe you should put in a native-title claim."

"Native title!" he said, in tones of outrage.

"It's not a form of land tenure that you favour?"

"Who could ever fence this country, or divide it up? Who would ever think of it? Just look: it's nothing; it's freedom. It belongs to everyone."

"As a matter of fact," I said, "title over the Sandy Desert was granted by the Native Title Tribunal earlier this month: exclusive possession. I checked before I left."

"Are you trying to tell me I'm committing a crime now by coming out here? And who called it Skeleton Pass? That doesn't sound like a very traditional name."

"Well, I may be able to shed some enlightenment on that front at least." I reached for my copy of the Calvert expedition journal, which I had been struggling to read in tandem with our progress.

"Not that expedition again!" said Charlie, in a voice of scorn. "What's so important about who's been here before anyway? We're not doing some re-enactment journey. I don't understand why you always want to see what they saw. They were then. We're in another time. I don't even like the idea of people having been here. I hate seeing my own tracks in the landscape: they're intrusive – I wish they'd vanish behind us the moment we drive past."

His words fell through me. I looked down, as if from some high point of vantage, on my younger self: on the days when I used to pore over the exploration journals and their charts and engravings; when those clipped, repeating entries seemed the peak of tension for me, and the abrupt, florid outbursts of landscape description reached into the realms of the sublime.

We made camp, in silence. Night fell. Along the horizon to the west, a bushfire was burning. Its flames jumped and danced, rising, vanishing, then leaping higher, like the prominences seen when the moon's disc conceals the sun.

"I used to think," I said after a while, carefully, "that the explorers were the first real writers of the landscape. They knew it, they loved it as much as they hated it – they studied it. They opened a kind of way for us to be here."

"Of course they studied it! They had to, or they would have died. I don't need anyone to open the way for me. I just decided to come out here, and I did – and found what suited me. They brought all their illusions with them."

"And you have none, about the desert? None at all?"

"The desert's just a screen for life and death," he said. "That's what you should be looking out for. You see everything here for what it is. The order's perfect. There's no mistakes. A hawk dies, the other hawks eat it. A crow dies, the other crows eat it."

"But that's not true," I protested. "I've seen them in mourning, when another crow's shot or run over. They all gather and stand around, and lift up their heads, and make the most heartfelt, unearthly cries."

"And where did you see that?"

"North Star – outside Moree, in New South Wales."

"They'd have different standards over east," said Charlie, with a note of victory in his voice. "Out here, the desert only has one lesson: life's the way it seems, and when you can't see the hills for the mirages, it's the mirages you have to steer by."

"A very philosophic take on things."

"What other kind would you expect? Isn't everyone who comes out here a philosopher? And isn't that what you're here for, really: not just the landscape – not what's here, but what's behind it."

Those words of his came back to me some days later. We were in deep desert. The strange sense of harmony that springs up when two travellers ride through empty country had emerged: long, mazy conversations would begin, then die away, only to resume, hours on, almost in mid-sentence. The drive was becoming dreamlike: I found myself lost in memory, and worlds I moved in long before. The most vivid, lifelike pictures took shape inside me: whole imagined narratives unfolded, vanished, then reappeared, advanced in their progress, as though I had missed a vital scene or two. Repeatedly I would close my eyes, and surrender to this drifting carousel – then open them, and be shocked by what I saw around me through the windscreen: red plains, the horizon ringed by dark mesas and red, crumbling cliffs. The sun beat down; the engine pulsed. Drowsily, from time to time, I heard Charlie's voice. His exposition came circling round: the bush world: its harshness; the need for precision in all one did.

"The precision of an accurate shot, you mean," I put in.

"Of course," he said.

"So you'd be fairly relaxed, then, about taking your own life, if it ever came to it?"

"Man's an animal, and he returns to earth. We come from earth, and return to earth. Of course I'd be relaxed about it. But I'd want to do the job properly. I might even use that rifle there, behind you."

I craned round and noticed a slender canvas bag protruding just beside my head.

"For sentimental reasons?"

"Of course: it's a .243, made by Carl Gustaf of Sweden. It's a beautiful rifle."

"Do you have many others?"

"A muzzle-loader shotgun, a single-shot Lithgow, two target rifles – oh, and there's a double-barrel Hammer shotgun too."

"And that would cover most eventualities?"

"Not really – it's a basic selection."

He broke off. We passed over a crest line. The country changed.

"Now look at that," said Charlie in a soft voice, his manner quite different. "Isn't that a sight? It reminds me of the hills of the south-west when I was growing up. I remember when I first came out here, with Jim, years ago. We both took a deep breath when we came over that ridge. I felt it was the promised land."

He pulled up. We were in a bowl of red, crenellated ranges; thin, grey-leaved grevilleas and twisted corkwoods filled the valley; grass, tall, pale green, waving in the breezes, stretched away.

"So, what do you think?" he asked – and at once I knew we were in his chosen corner of the desert: the place he most loved, and lived for, and saw in his imaginings. "I wouldn't think many outsiders have ever been here," he went on. "Aboriginal people, plenty, the old ones. There's a ravine back there with trap water, and a walking track, a back way through the range, with paintings all along it, and there are grinding stones, too, in the cave up there."

"You know it well."

"I've looked around," he said, almost blushing with pride. "It's different here from other places. I was talking, once, to an old botanist at the museum in Perth, and he told me there are parts of the desert, far out like this, where the country's unspoiled. No cattle have ever been there. The ground is still the way it was: soft and springy. And you can feel that here. There's nothing alien: no plant that doesn't belong. Nothing foreign in the landscape."

"Except us."

I walked away from him into the shadow of the headland, and leaned back there, in the sun – and after some moments, the light, the warmth and the sound of the soft wind in the grevilleas transported me. I was once more in the valleys I knew in child-hood, far away: the distant roofs and fir-clad hills seemed close enough to touch; the peaks beyond them were still and white against the sky. From the grounds of the hotel, it was the briefest of walks into the forest, where the wide paths led downhill to the Cauma Lake, and beyond to woodland clearings, where no one went. And there nothing could be heard but birdsong, and the clouds in their silent movements passed overhead. But there were days when I explored further, in the long, still afternoons when I was free – and once I even made my way down winding paths, half-overgrown, until I reached the cliffs above the Rhine, which, at that point in its journey from the glaciers, flows through a rift fringed by dark ramparts – and along the edge a pathway had been made, as much by goats as men. It was narrow: there were points where one had to cross thin ledges, above a sheer drop, and hold tight to the rock face, until the path broadened, and only then, after a last flurry of twists and rock-strewn turns, did I reach the pasture straight ahead. It was filled with flowers, and above them hovered clouds of looping, dancing butterflies: blues, and purples, pale yellows and swallowtails. I still see that sight in my mind's eye, with exact recall, though so much one loves in life goes rushing past and leaves no trace. I see myself running back to the park hotel, up the forest paths, and searching for someone to tell my news – but I found only my friend Vicky, the cartoonist, a man of kind and fragile bearing, who had that summer begun holidaying with us there. I told him, I described the scene to him with every detail I could muster, I poured out all my joy and agitation – and he, as was his habit when I came to find him, produced a blank pad of sketching paper, leaned back in his chair and began drawing. With a few curving, fluid motions, as I leaned over at his side, he conjured up that valley and its dancing, coloured cloud of butterflies – but they were transformed by his hand, they had become more perfect, the patterns on their wings were blurred, and smudged, and shimmered more brightly than in life. "Something like that?" he asked, and tore off the sheet of paper with his customary flamboyance, and placed it in my hands – and as he did so, I had a sense of darkness in the world: at that moment, I knew there would be no more summers with him there, in that wide valley – and I was calm and quiet, next year, on a cold February day, when I was told the news that Vicky, who saw the line of truth in everything, had taken his own life.

"You're far away," said Charlie. "Very far."

"Yes," I replied, "I am," – and I laughed a little at myself, at the strength of what I remembered, and what it was that came to mind. "That's true. I was looking back. Back to somewhere I was very happy, once – and sad, as well."

"They go together," said Charlie. "This place does that to you. It's nothing, and it gives you a universe – it fills you up with dreams and memories, if you stay here long enough."

"Time to keep moving?"

"Of course: next stop, Lake Disappointment."

"A logical progression!"

And he was as good as his word. Some hours later, after further duels, and silences, and brief snatches of soft discussion, the Mazda, just clicking over its quarter-millionth kilometre, lurched over a dune summit, and the great salt surface of the lake loomed.

"There she is," Charlie called out. "A world of emptiness. The country you were looking for – at least, if you really wanted the end of the line."

"And who gave it the name?"

"Don't you know anything? I thought you were the expert on all that history. It was Frank Hann, of course."

"The Queenslander? Who walked off Lawn Hill Station and overlanded all the way across to the Pilbara? The one who crossed the Leopolds and opened up the North Kimberley?"

"That's him. I'm not too good on the timing – he passed through some time in the 1890s. He was flat broke, finished, at the end of his tether. I think he was looking for new country, out of Nullagine."

"And so he came here?"

"He was out this way. I suppose, like everyone, he was hunting for salvation of some kind. It must have been a very good season: he saw all the creek beds, winding down towards the lake, and he had the hope there might be water somewhere on its bed – he looked and looked, but what he found was what you see."

All round us was red sand and bleached spinifex. On a promontory above the salt flats were old, gnarled desert oaks, trailing their windswept leaves. Bushfire smoke was rising and unfurling on the horizon; the sun came beating down. Ahead, the lake's white, dazzling surface glittered: it was too brilliant to look at; it caught and magnified the glare. On the far shore, where the red line of dunes merged with the distance, mirages – vast, troubling likenesses of ships, or breached, decaying castles – boiled away. In the view, there was that mingling of quiet and anguish that the far deserts hold. The compulsion, too; the urge to look. Come, the landscape seemed to say: come – come closer; dissolve; let the whole world slip and go. I dragged my gaze away. I shielded my eyes.

"He was picking up on something, though," I said, "wasn't he? Something real: a mood, a tone."

"It's just country, like anywhere," said Charlie.

"That's not what Aboriginal people used to think. They could feel things, here. They were afraid of it: in fact, it filled them with grief and torment, if you really want to know – this whole region of dry lakes and dead river systems. They avoided it at any cost: they thought there were malign spirits here, and dreadful water snakes beneath the surface of the salt."

"Whoever told you that?" asked Charlie.

I glided by this question and began, instead, to tell him the tale of Helmut Petri, the German anthropologist, whose greatest breakthroughs came in remote Australia, though his name is largely forgotten in this country today. Petri, a linguist of extreme gifts, arrived in the far north-west in 1938, at the head of a rockart expedition dispatched by the Frobenius Institute, and he was able to complete a single, rich season of field research, travelling from Broome to Munja, and across the Kimberley, before his return to Frankfurt the following May. Within three months, war broke out on the Polish front. It was only after enduring six years of military service that Petri was able to resume his tasks of science, but his research material had been largely destroyed. The Frobenius Institute itself had been annulled by bombing raids, and when Petri was at last able to publish his bleak ethnographic masterpiece, *The Dying World of Western Australia,* he regarded it as no more than the damaged torso of the work he once hoped to write.

It is, in fact, a piece of literature, drenched by Petri's experiences of war and Europe's fate. It discerns, in the world view of Kimberley Aboriginal people, a tone of deep pessimism, together with a conviction that the end of the world looms, and will surely come if their new cults are not perfectly maintained. Petri formed a keen interest in these rituals, which he was seeing during their first, devastating northward spread. Kimberley people knew them by the generic name *warmala* – that was their place of origin, *warmala,* mysterious country, far away. It was a word of power, spoken in fear – but Petri soon found that it held such terrifying associations only in the far north. Among the coastal peoples at Lagrange Mission, where he based himself on his first journey back to Australia, in the 1950s, the word was merely a directional term, pointing to the desert country beyond their reach. In western desert languages, though, *warmala* describes the revenge parties of marauding warriors, on their march across the landscape, armed with spears – and these spirit beings, which hover between the realms of myth and fact, often take the guise of young desert oaks – trees which, with their slender trunks and trailing, tresslike foliage, do, in certain light conditions, bear a sharp resemblance to the human form. Through the whole western desert, the *warmala* parties were feared; and one still enters at one's peril certain large stands of desert oaks, such as the avenues near Docker River, or the valley where several lines of *warmala* trees join up, close by the Patjarr waterhole. Beyond this, though, the *warmala* by their sheer presence set their seal upon the landscape, they give it a gravity, and a disquiet, which has seeped into the desert's religious tradition – and it was this strain that Petri caught, and that found an echo in his mind, torn as it was by his memories of war and his sense that civilisation would not hold. For the rest of his life he maintained his links to Lagrange and Beagle Bay; he wrote ethnographic papers of great intricacy and strange predictive force, as if the powers of foresight possessed by the Australian magic men he studied had somehow crept into his heart. He died in 1986, in Cologne, his native city, which had been quite pulverised by bombs and rebuilt in new form. But the cults he gave his life to had subsided: the darkness the desert landscape transmitted northwards now lives on solely in his words.

Such was Helmut Petri. I rounded off my tale, which I had stretched out and interspersed with other stories of the Frobenius expedition, and the role it played as end-point of a quest. Its completion marked the end of Europe's search for clues in the Australian mirror: clues to its own face and heart. Charlie smiled at this, and allowed the narration to sink in, as though it had been a message from vanished, far distant times.

"That was a story," he said in an approving way, and accelerated.

We were travelling across high sand ridges now, thick with turpentine bush and bloodwood; they were closely spaced. The track swung sharply round, then doubled back; we rode between the dunes, down deep, twisting corridors. After some while, I began to make out a set of gaunt peaks, dark-coloured, looming in the west.

"The country's changing," I said.

Charlie nodded.

"Strange you should say that," he said. "Just now, especially. Maybe we are in agreement on a few things, after all. I reckon," – this intimately, with great emphasis – "that here, right here, is one of the secret borders of Australia. You can't see anything much, but everything's different that side. This is where the desert ends, and the Pilbara begins. And ahead of us, you could even say, the boundary marker: Georgia Bore."

A sand whirlwind jumped across the track before us. The sun dazzled on the red plain; the scrub branches drooped with dead, burned leaves.

"My God," I murmured. "What a desolate place: it looks like the way down to the Inferno."

"Don't be like that," said Charlie, in an aggrieved voice. "It's a regular, top-grade Canning Stock Route well. This is a good belt of country. In fact the Capricornia Roadhouse fuel dump's just up ahead."

"But what if that's what hell really is?" I went on, swept up by the landscape's mood. We drove slowly in, over deep corrugations. "Some people think of it as a place of fire. And there's the model of hell as a small, dark room, with confining walls and cockroaches. But what if it's actually a bore-head on the stock route, with bare, stunted trees, and red sand all around, and willy-willys patrolling the perimeter like guards to stop any escape. What if that's the true, authentic, modern face of hell?"

"Wait up," said Charlie. "Did you see that – just there? What was it?"

He eased ahead. He reached behind me to the stowed canvas bag.

"What are you doing?" I asked, in some alarm.

"Look. Can't you see?"

He pointed. There: something, sandy-coloured – moving. We stopped. I jumped out. The scene resolved itself before my eyes. The wellhead stood at the centre of a low scrub patch; yellow growths of spinifex were dotted through the grit and sand. All round us were dead, splintered, burned acacia stumps. A rusting car body lay beside the track, and in its shade a scatter of decayed fuel drums. There were aluminium cans, swept up beside an old camp-fire. Strewn round on every side I noticed odd, ragged flecks of tissue paper: soiled, dirt-covered, each beside a loose, freshly excavated depression in the sand.

"There she is," said Charlie, in a low voice.

I followed his eyes. In the scrub, watching us, padding here and there, was a dingo – she came towards us, she retreated; she hid, she showed herself; she stared at us with bright, pleading eyes. Charlie raised his gun. The dingo looked at me.

"She's beautiful," I breathed.

The shot rang out: the dingo, gazing at me, staggered, stumbled forward, panted, and fell. I wheeled round.

"Why did you do that? How could you?"

"She *was* beautiful," said Charlie, in a quiet, correcting voice. "Now she's dead."

I went over to the dingo and knelt beside the body. It was stretched out – her eyes were open; her tongue drooped. Her ears were still cocked inquisitively; her legs were thin: they looked almost sculpted, like the legs of some marble hunting hound. Charlie came over.

"She'd just had pups," he said, appraisingly, and ran his Blundstone smoothly along her flank. "I wouldn't think they'd have survived."

"You'd been waiting, hadn't you?" I said – I was almost shouting at him: "Waiting: to show me how to take life. You were longing for it! But why?"

My fury flared up. The sun, the heat, the bleakness pressed down: they felt like a stone lying on my heart.

"We can give her a Christian burial if it makes you feel any better. I never take life unless I have to."

"And you had to?"

"Look around, bushman. Can't you tell? Do you really want to know what the country's telling you? Really want to know what's at its core? We are! Our hand made all this. There is no nowhere now." He gestured round – his voice dropped. "Listen: you've got your ideas, and all your love of nature, and your soft-heartedness. But you can't even see the world we're in."

He drew himself up, went to the trayback, produced a shovel and, in silence, with a few swift, fluid movements, dug a hole. With a quick heave, he pulled the dingo's body over, then covered it with sand. I watched, not moving, numb. I felt complicit: I saw nothing but the dingo's eyes. We drove on. In the succeeding hours, as the road broadened, and the long, geometric fault lines of

Rudall River park stretched off ahead, he laid out his argument: how the Stock Route had destroyed the desert's equilibrium; how travellers moved up and down it in the dry, cool months, and made their campsites at its wells, and left their scraps, and this lush feast was enough to lure in animals and birds from distant corners of the desert; until the hot weather came, and the supply of four-wheel-drive enthusiasts fell to a trickle, then stopped altogether.

"And there's no retreat for the animals trapped there? That's what you're trying to tell me? They're in a prison of our making: they all die?"

"Exactly. Your little dingo was the last survivor, and she was on her last legs. I've come across that scene a hundred times. Didn't you see what she'd been feeding herself on? Just think about it for a second. Just allow it to sink in. All that toilet paper. She'd been digging up everything those neat, well-trained, eco-friendly tourists had buried. She was living on human excrement."

I made my accusations, I answered him, I parried, I conceded – I let the symbolism of his picture brush through my mind. The deep desert, I then murmured, inside myself: revelations; the curtain drawn aside. The road smoothed out; the purple ranges and the mine sites of the Pilbara drew near. Above us, the grey clouds thickened. I felt, more with each passing minute, the trapping, anvil pressure of the sky.

# III

Time passed: a month; a year. That stretch of silent country, and the various expeditions through it, and their glamour and disaster, faded from me, they lost their definition – and it was only long afterwards, when I came back from the Middle East and began travelling again, that the desert and its landscape resurfaced in my thoughts. Those days, as I described at the outset of these chapters, were ones of grief and emptiness for me. I was still possessed by the routines of war; my old surrounds seemed at once too familiar and quite foreign; I could see no pattern or path ahead in life – and if I made frequent journeys then, it was only in the hope that movement, any movement, might help me find my way back into the country. After one of these trips, which had proved especially unavailing, I drove back in to Darwin, called at the sombre, low-slung post office in Cavenagh Street, and found in my mailbox there the briefest of notes, hand-written. It had the force of a summons, or a pledge. "The landscape awaits," it read. It was from my friend John Galvin, a lawyer well known in the west, a scholar of Pilbara history, a man with an air at once of poise and of dark, well-mastered depths. My tie with Galvin had always been close; it combined formality and a faint tone of brotherhood. I called him at once, and told him something of my mood and situation, and quickly learned that he was at a cusp-point of his own in life.

We arranged to meet and set off on one of the bush trips we used to make in the years before I went away – and so it was, a week later, in the company of a crowd of miners and oil-rig technicians, that I boarded a Qantas jet for Karratha airport, our customary starting point.

By chance, that morning, there was a cyclone system close offshore; the flight veered inland, above the desert and the Canning Stock Route. I looked down on my old track across the dunes; I gazed down on the country with longing eyes. How austere it was, how full of grace; how unending in its scale, how precise in the repetition of its finest details. There, below me, was the Calvert Range and Durba Springs; there were the fine curved wisps of salt lake, like pale feathers laid upon the sand. The descent began; we banked over the Burrup coastline. I saw the evaporation ponds, the turquoise ocean, the gas plant's columns glaring in the sun. The plane came racing in and touched down heavily, as if returning from far dimensions to the world of man. On the tarmac, I quickly made out the figure of John Galvin. He was standing at the far entrance to the terminal, tall, aloof, one hand cradling an elbow, the other resting appraisingly at his chin. He wore his usual expression: reserved, a touch quizzical. As I came up, he turned smoothly and fell in beside me.

"The voyager returns," he said, after a few more seconds of assessment. "'Crank her over once again!'"

"What?"

"Don't you remember anything? It hasn't been that long. Our old theme song: Gene Clark – 'Gypsy Rider.' *Put your face into the wind/Find another road where you've never been.*"

"That would be hard," I said, "up here, for you."

"So: any wishes? Where are we going?"

"I'm at a loss," I said, and recognised the familiar Galvin technique: first, wrong-foot your conversation partner, then swamp him with the relentless application of detail.

"Lucky, then," he said, "that I have a complete itinerary planned, and a fully loaded four-wheel-drive as well, complete with recovery equipment, provisions and a moderate supply of audiovisual distractions in case you find the company begins to pall."

We had reached an antiquated Thrifty troop-carrier. Its front half was almost wholly concealed by a set of rusting, heraldic bullbars. They swept forward threateningly, while their spurs and supports curved round the wings of the vehicle, much like the reliefs that clasp medieval altars in a sheltering, protecting frame. The back compartment had been stuffed full with swags, spare tyres and battered metal workboxes. The roof-rack was covered over by a bulging khaki  tarpaulin, from beneath which protruded the blades of two shovels, a grease-stained kangaroo jack and several loops of bright orange snatch-strap cord.

"This is the four-wheel-drive?"

"What's wrong with it?" said Galvin in indignation. "It's the only vehicle on the road intended both by its manufacturer and its owner for consistent and unyielding abuse."

"I notice you didn't drive your Mercedes up."

"Those town four-wheel-drives are good for nothing – certainly not for where we're going."

We set off, the troop-carrier vibrating passionately. The waystages of the road flicked by: Roebourne's old stone buildings, their fronts boarded up; the saltbush plain that leads to Cossack; the new veranda of the Whim Creek Hotel. Soon the power lines that run from Port Hedland began to shimmer on the horizon; they drew nearer, across the spinifex, then receded; vast cloud systems swept overhead. Galvin had always been a somewhat silent driver, for whom the choice of music, as a tonal adjunct to the road, was critical, and in those first hours of our journey, a swirl of sound enveloped us. The Moody Blues, Roy Orbison: it was a realm of nostalgia and regret.

"You don't have anything more up-to-date, maybe – or more in keeping with the country?" I said in mounting frustration, after several attempts at casual talk had died.

"It's hard, isn't it," he said, "picking up the threads of old associations. But, you know, there are some things you just have to put up with in any human friendship."

"Like Roy Orbison?"

"To some degree. And besides, I think you'll find the prevailing ethos of the music extremely well suited to our eventual destination."

Hedland loomed. We swept through its system of fringing roundabouts and railway crossings: road trains, mine trucks, Landcruisers with numbers and flashing lights.

"My God," said Galvin, "It's become imperial. I remember when it was just the stockpiles and the port hotel – and even that was a hit and miss affair."

"You see an improvement?"

"It always had a kind of poetry – that is, if you go in for industrial monomania – but now it has the desolation of an unfinished kingdom, don't you think?  All the portacabins, and the new street signs leading  off to nowhere."

His voice trailed off. In the rear-view mirror, I watched the BP truck stop receding into the distance.

"The end," I said, "for the next 600 kilometres, of settled life. Which raises an intriguing question: where, actually, are we going? Eighty-Mile Beach? Pardoo Roadhouse?"

"Almost!" said Galvin. "Geographically close; but emotionally far away – so no cigar. We're heading for the lost town of Condon – the end of the old telegraph line."

That name was familiar, in a distant fashion: it brought up associations from long ago.

"Is there some connection with the Calvert expedition? In fact, didn't John Calvert end his journey there?"

"Those fantasists! I wouldn't worry about them. Condon was a bit more real than that. In fact, it was the key to the Pilbara for many years – though nothing's left from the old days now. It's the kind of place that might speak to you. It helps to open up your thoughts. In fact, it strips everything away and leaves you with the bones of things. You'll see: here's the turn – at least I think that's it. The roads here wind about, but they all seem to end up at the same spot after a while. It was Quandong Inlet when they founded it – then just plain Condon: the first port on this coastline, for the wool trains from the station country. And it was a pearl-shell centre, too – plenty of grief and pain and loss of life. You would have seen old photos from its glory days. There's one famous image, showing the sailing barque *Arabella,* loading wool on Condon sands. She was a tall ship, well decked-out; there was a marble fireplace in her aft saloon. She used to anchor a kilo metre off the creek inlet, and sit on the mudflats at low tide. Then the bullock teams from De Grey station would trudge out and they'd load up in the emptiness  – and if the tides came in too fast, they'd just unyoke the bullocks and let them swim back ashore."

"Quite a practical arrangement."

"Those tides," said Galvin, in a low voice, paying no attention, "were well known for one thing. They came in at speed, of course, but they'd retreat very far, so far you couldn't even see the waterline. And then, when they turned, and the water started rushing in, you could almost feel it in the silence – and at last, as the waves came closer, you'd begin to hear a distant, elusive, gentle roar."

We turned again; the road narrowed. It was little more, by now, than a faint suggestion of a track.

"I used to come here often," he then said, "when I was working up here: in my dark past! I'd heard about the place. My friends told me all about its splendour. Of course I expected something smooth and sandy, like Cable Beach – but what I found was flat harshness – samphire, salt pans, rocks. At first I thought it was hideous: pretty soon I was transfixed. I'd drive out this way whenever I could, alone, and make camp, and read, and look about. Something in the landscape got to me: there was some pull. I paid attention. I began to feel that dreadful things had happened here – and, this being north Australia, of course I was spot-on. The more I read about the area and its background, and the more I learned and spoke to people who were bush historians, or travelled up the tracks and came to know the country, the more I understood that the intuition I'd had was right. The Aboriginal population isn't here: they're a loud absence."

"But there are communities all across the Pilbara: Strelley, Yandeyarra."

"Inland, yes, of course; but look around you. How lush the country here is, how rich. There's a river; there are fish and freshwater springs – it should be full of life. I went quite deep into the records of the pearling industry and the stations; it was hard not to notice that in the old histories there were never any pictures of local people working in Condon, or in the country round about. I soon found out their fate: they were wiped out by the great influenza epidemics that hit in the early years of the twentieth century – those who hadn't been killed or driven away before. And that's part of the feel of Condon – for me, at least. Now look!"

We had come out into coastal landscape. Before us, sheltered by a dark promontory, the grey shore, rock-strewn, stretched off. A spume of salt froth in the middle distance marked a vague boundary between sea and mudflat. Galvin stopped and rested his hands on the wheel.

"The ocean!" he said with a proprietorial air.

"It hardly looks like the edge of a continent."

"No. Just an infinite stillness; a stillness like a medium of sound. The silence was what always appealed to me. And the townsite itself: deserted, unmade, absent; the ruins of the wharf, a well, and nothing else. And the emptiness about it, that weighed so heavy; but emptiness is something you can turn around, after you've lived it, and occupied it."

He drove on, speaking softly, running through the stories of his first explorations in that landscape, which was becoming bleaker and more exiguous with each kilometre. Soon, in exact time with his narrative – so that the experience took on a strange, doubled stereophony – the eucalypts gave way to blue bush and twisted vine-thickets. They vanished too: we were on the beachfront now; the salt on the rocks sparkled; pale grasses and bindweeds ran down to the shore.

"I always liked the approach this way, across country. I remember one time, coming in, when the grass was very tall, with a friend of mine: a hunter. We were on the roof of his Toyota trayback, both of us, just coasting along, letting the vehicle find its way slowly in the landscape and looking out for kangaroos. Then, suddenly, looming out of nowhere we saw a headstone: *dearly loved, never forgotten.* And see – this was the main avenue: these sand ruts here."

A rock spit reached to the mudflats; the shoreline, marked by mangroves, curved away. He stopped. I jumped out.

"That's it – and this was the bonded store, where those foundations are. And the two trees marked the end of Mystery Street."

"A good name."

"A fitting one. I pulled up here once – and camped right on the point, next to the inlet, was an old-timer who'd been born at Condon. He walked me round. He showed me where the post office once stood, and the hotel, and the school. He was about ninety then. He used to come up for a few days at a time from his home in Bunbury. He said he'd never been happy since he left. The town was degazetted in 1909: they took it away to Hedland, piece by piece. In World War II engineers even came in and blew up the long jetty, for fear the Japanese might use it. But my interest in

Condon really stems, of course, from an earlier military episode."

"Of course!"

"I'm talking about the *Emden.* Do you know the story?"

*Emden* was a warship, a light cruiser of the German Imperial Navy, the last and finest of her kind. She was built a hundred years ago in the Royal Danzig shipworks, and was assigned to the Pacific Fleet. Once commissioned, she sailed for the naval base of Tsingtao, in the short-lived German Chinese colony, and soon became known there as "the Swan of the East." But it was not her grace and elegance that had captivated Galvin, or her Oriental home, so much as the exploits of her commander, Captain Karl von Mueller, on his raiding mission in the first days of World War I. Von Mueller, who was a keen, not to say an obsessive student of naval history, steamed away from Tsingtao, fearing encirclement, the moment he received news of the outbreak of war. He made for the Indian Ocean, with vague, optimistic instructions from his admiral and a lone collier for support. The tales of his exploits still have the power to startle. He disguised the *Emden* with a fake smokestack to make her resemble a British cruiser; he used rain squalls as cover to elude the searches of his enemies, he terrified Madras and Colombo by his mere proximity, he cut the shipping routes between Ceylon and Singapore. In the first month of his raiding mission alone, he captured fifteen British vessels, which he sank or destroyed – but he guaranteed the safety and wellbeing of every prisoner he took, while treating the officers, and vanquished captains, with an extreme and mannered gallantry – a pattern of conduct which was much admired, and which ensured his later fame. British warships swept the Indian Ocean for him; he haunted obscure archipelagos: the Maldives, the Chagos, the Laccadives. He escaped a dragnet; he reached the Malay coastline, where he staged his boldest assault – a daylight raid, brief, convulsive – the so-called battle of Penang. In early morning, at top speed, von Mueller steered into the warship-crowded harbour, hoisted his flag and fired a torpedo at the Russian cruiser *Zhemchug,* sinking her, before fleeing, pursued by a fleet of French destroyers, one of which, the *Mousquet,* he also fired on and sank. From Penang, he took the *Emden* south, undetected, through the Strait of Sunda, bound for the Cocos Islands, with the aim of levelling the radio tower and cutting the Eastern Telegraph Company's communication lines.

"But how," asked Galvin then, leaning towards me – we had set up camp by this stage across the inlet, on the wide, bare shore – "how did he get there?"

His eyes burned into me.

"I don't follow," I said.

"It's very simple. How did he get from Penang to the Cocos, to Direction Island and his appointment with destiny? Don't you see? He didn't have enough water to make that journey. He must have put in along the way, on the north Australian coastline – and I'm sure he did so here."

"Why?"

"It's obvious. Von Mueller knew what he was doing. The British and the Australians were scouring the seas for him, of course; they were watching everywhere across the north-west. At Hedland, they were on red alert. But there was Condon. It was on the charts; it was deserted – and it had a well: fresh water, ample supplies. I love to think of that sleek, low-slung warship, slipping in and anchoring offshore, in this horizontal landscape. Have you noticed how space is organised differently here? There are no verticals at all: time and height are in a special dialectic."

"And what happened?"

"It was quite an opera. The *Emden* steamed on. Von Mueller thought he'd be safe. He knew the main allied fleet was in Albany, waiting to take on its contingent of men for the Dardanelles campaign. He reached Direction Island in the Cocos on 9 November – he sent a landing party onshore, under the command of his first lieutenant, Hellmuth von Muecke, to destroy the radio tower and the base. It was all very amicable. The civilians at the telegraph station co-operated; the Germans agreed not to bring the tower down onto the tennis court. But the raider had been spotted; her luck had run out."

Galvin's voice had become shallow; he hurried on. HMAS *Sydney* was close at hand on a troop-convoy mission. She reached the Cocos in less than three hours and at once engaged the *Emden.* She was much more powerful: in ninety minutes the raider was struck by more than a hundred shells; it was the end for her – she began sinking. Von Mueller beached her on North Keeling Island. The *Sydney* pursued the German collier, then circled back. Von Mueller refused to lower his battle flag, despite repeated demands for his surrender. The *Sydney* opened fire again.

Now Galvin gave the story full atmospherics. I reeled under his assault: he put me there, I was on the *Emden*'s gun deck as the shells came blasting in. By chance, a detailed, rather triumphalist sketch of the disaster survives. It was transcribed by Banjo Paterson, who encountered the *Sydney*'s Captain Glossop in Colombo less than a week after the event, and records their talk in his *Happy Dispatches,* Chapter XII. Glossop had gone with the rescue boats to board the stricken cruiser. "My God," he said, or Banjo has him saying. "My God – what a sight! Everybody on board was demented – that's all you could call it, just fairly demented – by shock, and fumes, and the roar of shells bursting among them. She was a shambles. Blood, guts, flesh and uniforms were all scattered about. One of our shells had landed behind a gun shield and had blown the whole gun crew into one pulp. You couldn't even tell how many men there had been. They must have had forty minutes of hell on that ship, for out of 400 men, 140 were killed and 80 wounded, and the survivors were practically madmen. They crawled up to the beach and they had one doctor fit for action; but he had nothing to treat them with – they hadn't even got any water. A lot of them drank saltwater and killed themselves. They weren't ashore twenty-four hours, but their wounds were fly-blown, and the stench was awful – it's hanging about the *Sydney* yet."

So Glossop– but his victory was incomplete. On Direction Island, the members of the *Emden's* shore team were just cutting the underwater cables when the two warships engaged. Once the outcome was clear, Lieutenant von Muecke commandeered an old, half-rotten barquentine which was anchored in the lagoon. And in that frail three-masted craft, with all his men and weapons, he made for Padang in the Dutch East Indies, a neutral harbour, which he reached unscathed after more than a month at sea.

"The Captain?"

"He spent the rest of the war in captivity, in Malta, I believe. Of course he had become famous. He was the last shining prince of Prussian chivalry, and his record stood out against the darkness of the time. But he suffered gravely from malarial attacks, and that illness, combined with his natural reserve, led him to retreat from public life. I find it quite in keeping with his character that he wrote nothing about his experiences on the *Emden,* nothing at all, in the five years remaining to him after the war's end and Germany's collapse."

Galvin stopped. The chunks of burning driftwood hissed and sputtered on the fire between us. The ashes gleamed. The stars began to show.

"And you don't sometimes worry," I said, "that it might be wishful thinking?"

"The idea that von Mueller put in at Condon? All I can tell you is that when I was ill, while you were away, I would see this coastline quite clearly. I'd be lying at home, at night, awake, and in my mind's eye I'd glimpse this scene – as clearly as a photograph, in perfect resolution: the silhouette of the ship on the horizon, its grey hull merging with the mudflats in the dawn – its funnels, and its low gun deck, its twin masts, the curved raking of its prow."

"Heavy symbolism," I said.

"I knew what it was, of course, in that sense – a ship of fatality, gliding near – but it was also something else: an echo, an innuendo, a memory – one that stemmed from being here."

And Galvin, in a calm, even manner, proceeded to tell me something of the experiences he had gone through during my time away, when the majestic pattern of his life – a life that had seemed, in every detail, balanced, geometric – began to fray, then fell apart. It started in the clear, hot weeks of early summer: he noticed a slowing of his reflexes, he felt a touch of weakness in his limbs, and this was all the more noticeable because he had been careful, always, to preserve a high degree of fitness and strength. At once, he put himself on a regime of strict exercise;

he made full-pack climbs in the hills outside the city. Nothing worked. He had to begin rescheduling his cases and his court appearances. Eventually, he went to see a doctor friend and had a complete medical. The signs were obvious: he had liver cancer: his readings were sky-high. The discussion the two men had was brisk. It had a surfeit of reality about it. It was at once a caricature of what such scenes should be, and the perfect version. The doctor broke down, and sobbed, and told him he had between two weeks and a month to live. Grimly, Galvin went about putting his affairs in order: he left his chambers, he sold his most prized paintings, and embarked on a stringent, intensive course of cancer drugs. He was given syringes and a supply of chemicals, and sent away. It began: he fell into the pits of suffering; he could barely drag himself from room to room. His dreams left him first. They had been his mainstay. They went back into the wider world, they had no wish to be dreams of his any longer, they had no feeling for him: don't summon us, he heard them saying: we can't help you now. Soon, sleep went as well: he began writing – each night, he poured out shards of memory, shaped into linked episodes, and they became his therapy, his contact with the wider world. Often, he sent them to me, by email, and I would receive them, in the internet kiosks of the Green Zone, and read them hurriedly, and delete them. Then, on some patrol or military flight, their glinting accents would come back to me, and I would feel the vanity and artifice of every word I wrote. Months passed for Galvin in this way; the treatment bit. Slowly, a large, reddish-purple weal began to form directly above his liver – for one unpleasant effect of the chemotherapy was that every sore or wound he had ever suffered re-appeared and turned into a hideous lesion or boil. Eventually, in desperation, Galvin lanced the weal with one of his syringes in the shower. A stream of pus and rotten tissue came out, and there was a little metallic click on the tiling of the floor – it was a fleck of shrapnel.

"Shrapnel," I echoed.

"A few days later, I lanced it again; another piece came out. After that, the liver readings began to fall at once. My health slowly recovered."

"But what were you doing with shrapnel in your body?"

"Didn't you know," said Galvin, looking sideways, half at me and half at the fire, "that I'd had an Indochina experience?"

"No!"

"I suppose you didn't – and I suppose, in a way, this is the beginning of what I wanted to tell you."

He got up, walked over to the troop-carrier and flicked the music back on – it was a west-coast compilation CD that had been playing in the background for hours.

"Again!"

"Music was quite important," said Galvin, "over there: it helped you to cling on to something, to define yourself. I hated *Dark Side of the Moon,* for instance. That came out in the last years of the war, and it was everywhere – those trapped, cloying chords. But I still remember the first time I heard 'Layla,' in Luang Prabang – and it spoke to me, especially the slide guitar. That was part of the soundtrack when we spent that year being sent out on missions to places people never came back from alive."

I absorbed this sentence, and listened to my own breathing, and his. There was no movement round us: no wind; no wave. The night was still.

"So why go on them?"

Galvin moved his hands faintly, as though to suggest a domain of laws beyond my grasp.

"You wouldn't have gone ahead with a single one of them if you'd stopped to think about it for a moment – you were living constantly in a state of denial – but in the years since, I don't see the slightest change in the tenor of existence. I look round, and I see us all, navigating the stream of lies and fantasies we keep telling ourselves. We go with the flow – just the way we did then, when we heard the music, the hits of the day – 'Gimme Shelter,' 'A Whiter Shade of Pale' – and they were easy to fold into our lives. Sometimes I think we almost lived for music. Once, I remember, when we were in Vientiane, we heard that Gladys Knight and the Pips were giving a concert at Da Nang, and we desperately wanted to hear them play a long version of 'Midnight Train to Georgia.'"

"A top priority!"

"Indeed. We went round to see a young helicopter pilot we knew. He was a real cowboy: he
loved the Indianapolis 500, that kind of thing, he'd
always give commentaries on the mission as if they
were races – 'We're turning down the main drag
now...' He had a stripped-down machine, with only
a single door-gun – it was a real hot-rod. We forged
our ID passes for the trip. The idea was to take the
long way round from Laos – you couldn't fly over
jungle Vietnam: you'd just die, they had so many
anti-aircraft guns. We had to fly south instead, almost to Phnom Penh, then across. We headed off,
but just before we left I'd been given my first tab
of LSD. I'd assumed the door-gunner's job, and the
acid had begun to come on: strongly, in fact. I decided to fill the whole of the machine gun with tracer
rounds – usually you put in one round in four, so
you can see where your bullets are landing, but I
decided – you know how acid takes you to strange
places – to load the whole machine gun. We flew
over, avoiding all the danger points. I let off a few
bursts. The idea is just to give the trigger a couple
of blips, but I was firing constantly – I imagined that
would show the Vietnamese how strong we were,
and keep us safe. I got a pretty firm tap on the
shoulder."

"And did you get to see Gladys Knight?"

"Of course – we always got what we wanted in
those days."

Galvin looked at me, measuringly. I was leaning over, bent towards him. Beyond the fire's gleam, the night was moonless. Low smoke clouds were spreading from the burn-off round Ettrick homestead, far inland. I settled back. Galvin resumed, in his smooth monotone – a voice that, for all its calm and cadence, was coiled now, and full of force. It was a delivery that enticed the listener in; it joined my act of hearing and his of recall. The dry season of 1970 was just beginning when he arrived in Laos. He was seventeen years old, although he passed easily for a man of twenty-five, and this duplicity felt natural there. He found a stageset world, where every character and set of circumstances seemed designed for conspiracy, and intrigue was the chief pursuit.

In the plateaus of the interior, the battle for control of Laos was at its height, but at that time Vientiane was still a neutral city, a listening post, a place awash with embassies and spies. The centre of this quadrille was the Constellation Hotel, where the photographer Tim Page and the cameraman Neil Davis, both documenters of the conflict, both already celebrities, could be found, standing at the bar, silent, like choric presences, playing themselves, sunk in the flash and shimmer of their lives. Soon Galvin fell into the company of the charming, well-connected Inez de Castro, a French Eurasian who had been married to a Corsican smuggler from the drug ring "Grande Indochine." She knew the town; she knew its opium dens; like many residents of Vientiane, she was herself a creation of the city's palimpsest-like past. In her villa on the outskirts of town was a library, which preserved many gems from the literature of French colonial days. Galvin was entranced by these accounts and memoirs. He immersed himself in them: he read them through with dictionaries, or Inez would translate them for him in his arms. He had a great sense that history had unfolded close by, and was now quite lost. He wanted to see the battlefields, he wanted to explore the trails where ambushes had been sprung, or track down the hillforts where the French made their last stands. For months, he lingered in this realm, which had been so thoroughly, and so recently, forgotten, though it was vivid and alive in print and seemed to live more urgently because it had been captured in French and was being relayed to him in such lush circumstances, by a woman's lips.

He read through the narrative of Dien Bien Phu and its desperate reinforcement by volunteer paratroopers, just days before the last redoubts of the fortress fell. Most of all, though, he was caught by the stories of the Man Yang Pass, between An Khe and the high inland. It was here that the North Vietnamese army entrapped an elite French flying column – the Groupement Mobile 100, which was, at the time, already gravely weakened and worn down by its long campaigns. The GM special forces advanced with their armoured carriers, half conscious they were headed into a trap: a French aircraft overflew them.

The transmissions from the men below reported tell-tale noises in the "nak-nak" grass – the tall, waving ground cover that always gave away an ambush in those hills. The enemy – 6,000 strong – attacked. A series of exchanges followed; almost all the members of the GM were killed. Just three days later a ceasefire, long planned, came into force. The French army, with their southern Vietnamese allies, regained the ground at Man Yang; they buried the dead standing up, facing towards France. Years later, Galvin made a pilgrimage. The battlefield was still untouched: wrecked tanks, broken half-tracks, stray bones, regimental insignias lying about.

"And those stories had a strong effect on me," he said. "I realise now that it was literature, it was written testimony that drew me into my life – and into war."

"You were in the right place!"

"There's some truth to that," he laughed. "And maybe I found my way there by some attraction – but I don't believe anyone who says they know exactly what the chains of cause and circumstance are in life. I see, instead, a kind of nudge and push by fate – I can feel the margins and percentages of cause; things that lead you towards the future, and you can decline them, or accept."

He found work at Wattay airport, just outside Vientiane; there was a rifle range there, where the US special forces trained. Since childhood, Galvin had been a marksman: he could hit the centre of a target from 700 metres out. One afternoon, he rigged up a .50 calibre machine gun with telescopic sights and brought it to the range. With it, he could fire steady out to two kilometres – and immediately he caught the eye of the old Wehrmacht commander who was in charge.

"Is there anyone in this story," I broke in, at that point, "who hasn't stepped straight from central casting? It's not like life, it's like a movie, complete with every stereotype."

"The flow went the other way," said Galvin, rather sadly. "That's how things were: art was still imitating reality. Remember, they weren't post-modern times – although that's very much the way it was going. In fact, you could make a case that that was what we were fighting for: to initiate that era. At any rate – I came in; I joined in, with them."

"With who?"

And then he told me – in his most circling, elaborate manner, in ellipses, disclosures and feints, until the story was like a trail of smoke rings, each dissipating within the orbit of its predecessor and changing its contours, and a tone, a mood of confession and reassessment, had permeated that dry beachfront air. Coolly, punctiliously, he described his years with the Special Operations Group – the clandestine army that was active at that time in the jungle reaches of the border between Laos and Vietnam. They were vivid tales. They centred, always, on insight, fear and death. They had the quality of moral episodes. Each illustrated some key theme of that secret life: never give up before the end of the firefight; never look directly at your target when you spot him in the jungle; never walk the trails too long.

"What?"

"For a long time," he said, "I'd wanted to know my limit, to reach the frontier: where the mind and the body refuse; where you feel fear's presence in its purest form. And we were told, constantly, in Vientiane: if you walk the trails long enough, your time will come."

"And it did?"

He sighed, and in that sigh, together with regret, there was a certain scorn for linear ways of understanding life and time. He circled back, to the beginning of his Vientiane days and the beliefs of his Khmer friends in the special forces. When death was close, they always placed a tiny Buddha figurine between their teeth. They thought of death as a woman, young and beautiful, they had seen her – and once Galvin thought he had too, when he was sent out in pursuit of a female sniper near the firebases of Kontum. Most of all, though, his missions were case studies in control: control of body, control of instinct, control of thought. What use could thought be? Statistics made the rules. Everyone on the teams knew the figures: four bomb-damage assessment trips up the trail, and your time had come. Galvin had completed his third when the day came for him. He knew the jungle intimately by then – he could sense the presence of "the others" – his adversaries, those veiled, masked dwellers beneath the tree canopy, who had walked the trails so long their skins were lily white. And he could feel them near, that morning, near the end of a short, successful mission, at the wheel of a 1952 Citroën Avant, as he was driving his team back towards Vientiane. They were already on the edge of Pathet Lao territory, and close to home. They had avoided two roadblock ambushes. They hit a third. It was well designed – they were caught, the mortars opened up. An armoured half-track was blocking almost all the road's width – a river bridge lay straight ahead. Galvin drove for the gap at top speed – a shell landed to the right of them. It tore through the vehicle; it killed the other members of his team at once. Its shrapnel cut through the body of the man beside him, and into his – into his right side, his legs, hips, arms. The Citroën collided with the half-track, its front sheared off, it lost a wheel, it careered on: it struck the concrete of the bridge support. Galvin reached behind him, as best he could. He seized the morphine and survival kit; he took his AK-47; he ran, staggering, bleeding, through the jungle. He collapsed beneath a lush overarching banyan tree. He hid between its roots. The Pathet Lao hunted him for eighteen hours, stealthily, silently, combing the country, listening. He lay there, morphinated, quite distanced from himself. He could feel the wounds; he traced his hands over the blood coagulating, forming its mats upon his skin. He became aware of a file of green ants, moving up his body, onto his face. They walked across his eyeballs, gazing down. They seemed like giant dragons or monsters – but some instinct told him they were there for him. He picked off a few; he put them in his mouth; he felt them biting and stinging as they went down his throat. Long afterwards, he learned they had antiseptic properties. He came to feel they had saved his life, and in years to come he treated green ants in the Australian bush with tenderness and with respect.

He was still. The pain rose. After spells of drowsy sleep, and a time when, as it seemed to him, he was drifting freely between life and death, inspecting the margins of both worlds, he began to make out a set of shapes before him, above him. They were blurred, in silhouette; they became distinct. The light had taken on a rich, grainy texture, there was a rose-pink colour to the background sky. The figures came closer – he saw their faces: it was a cavalcade, a procession of mounted, armoured knights, with shields and weapons in their hands. They carried banners, too – each one rich with crosses, a mesh of crosses, red, white, interlinked. The tableau had a tension – the knights were still, but their limbs were taut, they clutched their swords and lances, their pause was momentary, they resembled the frozen knights in battle paintings from the Renaissance, and the colours had a startling, painted quality as well: there was a copper sheen about the silvered metal of the helmets; there were pale glinting yellows on the shield-rims, the trailing cloaks were indigo, the grey chainmail had a bluish tinge. Those figures gazed towards him with indifference, and quite without hostile intent – their eyes were cold, indeed they scarcely seemed to notice him at all, though he was stretched out beneath them, helpless – and he realised they must be staring across a battleground towards another heraldic army, before the onset of some deadly clash. The picture receded. The sounds from his pursuers had gone. He waited for darkness, then half-walked, half-crawled his way back into Vientiane. He was helicoptered out. They took him to a military base in Thailand. He lapsed into a coma. When, after two days, he came round, the doctors stared at him as if he were a ghost; the nurses padded gently past his bed. No one thought you'd pull through, one murmured to him: your heartbeat was like a constant whisper – that phrase stuck in his mind – there was a stumbling in your pulse.

"And that was the cue for me to come to Darwin," Galvin said.

"Pre-cyclone Darwin?"

"That's right: that dreamy place – before tall buildings and the lure of progress came. I already knew the town, in fact, quite well. We used it often, at the start of operations. We'd go through Customs then with cases full of automatics and high-powered weaponry, no questions asked. This time, though, I was jangled, and torn up, inside and out. Pretty soon, I gravitated towards Lameroo."

"The beach?"

Galvin gave a smile.

"In those days, it was an important place. I'm not sure it wasn't the most beautiful place I've ever come across, the happiest as well. It was an unusual scene. Darwin was still quite small, and full of alcoholic public servants wearing shorts and long white socks. On the slope beneath the Esplanade, though, the counterculture had taken hold. There was a hidden world of tree-houses and cliff-side shacks poised half in the air, and elaborate, interconnecting structures ran between them all: walkways, lookouts, overhangs – and each house was always being improved by the succeeding groups of occupants. One had been worked on by a pair of Swedish architecture students, and even there, in the filtered shadows from the mahoganies and raintrees, and with mangroves growing up around it, it had a very stripped-down, Scandinavian feel. Beach and town rarely mixed, though. There was a degree of hostility, and that was understandable: they were worlds apart. Town was for the drinkers, and in the beach houses, marijuana consumption was very much the order of the day. It was a lovely, carefree jungle."

"The opposite of where you'd been!"

"Listen – I don't know that you should read your patterns into everything. That's just where I ended up. But I stayed there for a while. I started working at the Darwin Hotel, as the supervisor in the gardens. I used to walk the cliffs, and gaze out at the harbour, and let that landscape settle in my mind; so Darwin, and the clouds of the build-up, and those liquid sunsets were the backdrop for my return as well – and everything that you were saying about your experiences hit home and brought those days back to me."

He gave me a quick glance; the fire was down by now – I could scarcely see his eyes.

"Most of all, though," he went on, "I remember the water, the turquoise of the water, and the trips I used to make each afternoon. I had a kayak, to build up my strength, and I used to head out across the harbour in it, to Mica Beach, straight opposite, eight kilometres, fighting the tide, then back over, through the lightning and the storms. There was an old World War II US rest camp there, with accommodation buildings and even a dance hall, overlooking the sand – I don't think they came through Tracy in too good a state. Shells used to wash up there – large, wind-scoured trochus shells, and corals that looked like X-ray photos of the sun. The waves rolled in, slowly, so slowly it was sometimes as if they were still, and fixed, and time had ceased at that very moment in its flow. Yet I often had the feeling, when I was on Mica Beach, looking back to town, that I could see a rhythm to life, and I could feel the seasons were advancing – that from disaster, light could come, and in sadness, in the heart of sadness you could find joy – and I thought I'd tell you that story – and it would be my gift to you, and it might help to bring you, somehow, home."

***

I climbed into my swag, slept, dreamed heavily, and woke before the dawn. There was a pale light on the horizon; the landscape's layers, blurry, like the bandings in a carpet, reached away. I made out the edge of the scrub; the mangrove line; the sands, the promontory and its cliff, the glowing sky. Nothing human; an emptiness. I walked over to the troop-carrier, and then, by some odd impulse, after sitting in its passenger seat for some minutes, watching the light's slow change, I switched on the radio – though the last thing I longed for at that moment was the world and all its woes. Silence: I turned the dial. Suddenly there was a hiss of interference, then a voice: a woman's voice, in a timbre of dark, deep passion, singing. It was a cantata's opening theme – it was vaguely familiar, I began to place it; the voice, too – and soon enough I realised that I was listening to a performance by Lorraine Hunt Lieberson, the Californian mezzo, whose artistry had always seemed bound up, for me, with the illness that served as a companion in her life. She sang, through the surge of interference, through the waves of ionospheric storms, her voice shook and hung, it fragmented and faded. An announcer came on. I had tuned to an American classical music station, its signal thrown, by some mystery of climatics, right around the world.

"The sublime Lorraine Hunt Lieberson," said the announcer's voice in heartfelt manner. "And we heard her famous rendition of Johann Sebastian Bach's Leipzig cantata, number 82 in the catalogue – first given in 1727: a fitting piece for today, with all its intimations of mortality – sung there on stage, in a concert at the international festival of music in Lucerne, by the Californian who began her career as a violist, and died, after a long and unavailing struggle with cancer, this Monday morning at her home in Santa Fe. And all those who loved her will doubtless remember where they were on hearing the news, much as a former generation remembered what they were doing when they learned that President Kennedy had been shot in Dallas, Texas, so many years ago."

I switched the radio off, shocked by the casual speed with which it dealt its blows, and walked on for a while up the beach. There was a faint humming inside the silence – so soft it seemed almost to reach me, like some whisper of the bloodstream, from within the curving chambers of the ear. I listened for it. My mind was full of wandering thoughts: the idea came to me that one day, soon, recorded music will be like an archive of shadows and memory, and there will be more dead voices than live ones to choose from, if this has not already happened; that the performers we most respond to are more than actors, much more: they give life to the artists they interpret, they bring them back – and a word is nothing without a mouth to speak it, or an eye to read – and what we love is constantly being taken from us, and returned in memory, and so our longings gain their final shape.

I reached the cliff's edge: it was a maze of sharp, eroded, twisted rocks. Beach curlews and terns flew before me. The sun was up. Its disc had touched the lowest layers of the cloud – and what was that, out on the mudflats, where the salt crystals gleamed, and the line of sandbars shook and quivered in the haze? There: halfway to the horizon – the low shape of a vessel, dark gun-metal grey, drifting inwards; drifting towards me on the tide.

# Back Cover Material

**A KEY TO UNLOCK THE HEART OF THE COUNTRY**

This is the story of a quest – a journey down the red highway.

On returning from a war zone, a writer begins to explore the deserts and towns, sleepy coastline and hidden worlds of Australia's north. As he travels, his journey gathers momentum and finds a shape. He has unforgettable, even mystical encounters: with a nun, an explorer, a collector and a hunter. It becomes a quest – for knowledge and a sense of home – that builds to a stunning culmination.

Nicolas Rothwell is among Australia's most gifted writers, and *The Red Highway* is a one-of-a-kind book. It explores death, friend ship, travel and art, and evokes a unique and mesmerising part of the country.

"ROTHWELL'S CALM WONDERING AT WHAT HE SEES AND HEARS ON HIS TRAVELS LEFT ME WITH A FEELING OF ENCHANTMENT." ROBERT DESSAIX

**Nicolas Rothwell** is the award-winning author of *Wings of the Kite-Hawk, Heaven and Earth, Another Country* and *Journeys to the Interior.* He is the northern correspondent for *The Australian.*

## Books For ALL Kinds of Readers

At ReadHowYouWant we understand that one size does not fit all types of readers. Our innovative, patent pending technology allows us to design new formats to make reading easier and more enjoyable for you. This helps improve your speed of reading and your comprehension. Our EasyRead printed books have been optimized to improve word recognition, ease eye tracking by adjusting word and line spacing as well as minimizing hyphenation. Our EasyRead SuperLarge editions have been developed to make reading easier and more accessible for vision-impaired readers. We offer Braille and DAISY formats of our books and all popular E-Book formats.

We are continually introducing new formats based upon research and reader preferences. Visit our web-site to see all of our formats and learn how you can Personalize our books for yourself or as gifts. Sign up to Become A RHYW Registered Reader.

www.readhowyouwant.com

Printed in Great Britain
by Amazon